On Death and Dying

Rev. Paul V. Beyerl

On Death and Dying

Rev. Paul V. Beyerl

First Edition

Other works by the author:

The Master Book of Herbalism
© 1984 Phoenix Publishing Co., Custer, WA

A Compendium of Herbal Magick
© 1998 Phoenix Publishing Co., Custer, WA

A Wiccan Bardo
© 1989 Prism Press, Bridport, England

A Wiccan Bardo, Revisited
Revised Edition © 1998 The Hermit's Grove, Kirkland, WA

Painless Astrology
Revised Edition © 1996 The Hermit's Grove, Kirkland, WA

The Holy Books of the Devas
Fourth Edition © 1998 The Hermit's Grove, Kirkland, WA

Gem and Mineral Lore
First Edition © 2005 The Hermit's Grove, Kirkland, WA

The Hatchling
First Edition © 2007 The Hermit's Grove, Kirkland, WA

Andrius' Colouring Book of Numbers
Third Edition © 2009 The Hermit's Grove, Kirkland, WA

On Death and Dying

"There's nothing wrong with being compost."

published by:

The Hermit's Grove
P O Box 0691
Kirkland, Washington, 98083-0691

Dedicated to the Four Pillars of Medicine:

Dedication to the Joy of Learning
A knowledge of the Psychology of Astrology
Skill in Herbal Medicine and Alchemy
Commitment to a Virtuous Life

Cover photo by Diane Tice

(Sister of the author)

Taken at the Colby Cemetery, Colby Wisconsin, after the author's parents had purchased their plot.

design and layout by the author

coeditor - Heather Bennett

Monument drawing by Dianne Lorden

proofreaders
    Merle Holdren
    Heather Bennett

Library of Congress Control Number:
    2014922581

ISBN 978-0-9863639-0-0

First Edition © 2014

Table of Contents

I	**The Roots of My Death:** My relationship and history with death	1
II.	**What is Death?** .... Complications of definition	15
III.	**Memento Mori:** .... If I should die before I wake	29
	Fears of Dying	37
	The Ten salutary consequences of death	38
IV.	**What is the Soul?** .... Let there be light	43
	Do we have souls?	43
	The Soul or Spirit	44
	Living with one's soul	46
	Dying with one's soul	49
	The pitcher of god	51
	Souls of the world	52
V.	**Burial and Cremation:** .... What do we do with the body?	57
	Letting go	57
	Grief and Sorrow	60
	Rock ... Paper ... Fire?	62
	Air	65
	Fire	66
	Water	67
	Earth	68
	Spirit	69
	The dead, they are always with you	70
	The rise of embalming	71
	Embalming: The Facts	74
	Cremation	77
	Burial services are for the living	79
	The Cremation of Sam McGee	81

i

Table of Contents

VI.	**An Evolution of Death - Part I**	**87**
	The Earliest Times [Before 300 BCE]	
	The background story	87
	Underworlds and Otherworlds	89
	Immortality: Existence beyond the body's death	94
	Early burial practices	100
	Monuments and Markers	111
	Ishtar	112
	The Eleusian Mysteries	113
	Orphism	116
	Ancient Group Believed Departed Souls Lived in Stone Monuments	118
VII.	**An Evolution of Death - Part II**	**125**
	The Classical Times [300 BCE - 450 CE]	
	The background story	125
	Death & burial in the Roman Empire	129
	Changing Values: Setting the Stage	131
	Changing Values: The Mysteries	134
	Changing Values: Emerging Christianity	136
	Monuments and Markers	139
	Christian Expansion	139
	The Druids left no artifacts	141
	The Celts	142
VIII.	**An Evolution of Death - Part III**	**149**
	The Middle Times [450 - 1500 CE]	
	The background story	149
	The European Church	152
	The Art of Dying	157
	Returning to the Earth	162
	Theological Transition: Courtroom & Purgatory	167
	Urbanization	169
	Monuments and Markers	171
	Burial	171
	Vikings	172

Table of Contents

        The ibn Fadlan Account 174
        The Norse Expansion 175

IX. **An Evolution of Death - Part IV** 181
        Enlightenment and Romance [1500 - 1850 CE]
        The background story 181
        Notable Religious Reformers 184
        The Renaissance 186
        The Age of Enlightenment 190
        The first Industrial Revolution 193
        Romanticism 195
        Monuments and Markers 197
            The Good Death in
                Seventeenth-Century England 197
            Dear Without Fear 198
            Adonais: An Elegy on the Death of John Keats 198

X. **An Evolution of Death - Part V** 203
        The Victorian and Modern Eras [1850 - 2000 CE]
        The background story 203
        The background in England 205
        The American Civil War 206
        The industrialization of funerals 207
        Professionalism and the Funeral industry 213
        Changing Christian Values 218
        The Cemetery: Gardens of the Dead 222
        Changing Social Values 227
        Monuments and Markers 232
            In Tibet 232
            Under Lock and key 233
            Who stole the body? 234
            Cremation has renewed appeal 235

XI. **Heaven and Hell:** 243
        Where does the soul go?
        The Soul's survival 243

	Crossing over: passage by water	245
	Passage to Yaru	248
	Death and the Underworld	249
	The Book of Him	252
	Destination: Heaven	253
	Or maybe just over the hill?	255
XII.	**The Past and the Future**	**261**
	Ancestors and Reincarnation	
	If at first you don't succeed	261
XIII.	**Eating with the Dead**	**273**
	Gone but not Forgotten	
	Oh, the poor pigs	275
	Conduits to the underworld	276
	And elsewhere?	277
	The Ghost Festival	280
XIV.	**How do I view death as a Wiccan Priest?**	**284**
	There's nothing wrong in being compost	
	Armed and dangerous	284
	Appendices	
I	Entering the Wiccan Bardo	295
II	A Commentary on the Ritual for the Dead	304
III	Excerpts from The Ritual for the Dead of Lothloriën	316
	Bibliography	324

The Prophet

Kahlil Gibran

You would know the secret of death.
But how shall you find it unless you seek it in the heart of life?
The owl whose night-bound eyes are blind unto the day cannot unveil the mystery of light.
If you would indeed behold the spirit of death, open your heart wide unto the body of life.
For life and death are one, even as the river and the sea are one.

In the depth of your hopes and desires lies your silent knowledge of the beyond;
And like seeds dreaming beneath the snow your heart dreams of spring.
Trust the dreams, for in them is hidden the gate to eternity.
Your fear of death is but the trembling of the shepherd when he stands before the king whose hand is to be laid upon him in hon4our.
Is the shepherd not joyful beneath his trembling, that he shall wear the mark of the king?
Yet is he not more mindful of his trembling?

For what is it to die but to stand naked in the wind and to melt into the sun?
And what is it to cease breathing, but to free the breath from its restless tides, that it may rise and expand and seek God unencumbered?

Only when you drink from the river of silence shall you indeed sing.
And when you have reached the mountain top, then you shall begin to climb.
And when the earth shall claim your limbs, then shall you truly dance.

[Kahlil Gibran, *The Prophet*, Alfred A. Knopf, © 1923]

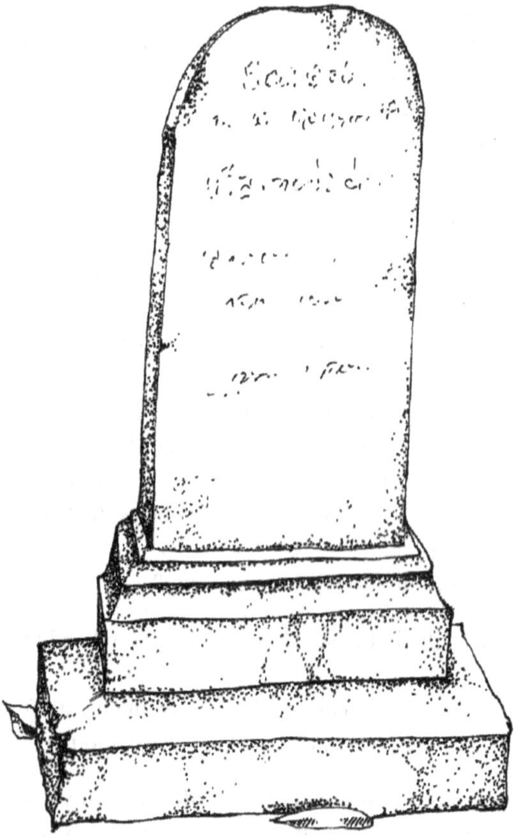

Chapter 1 - The Roots Of My Death:

My relationship and history with death

When I was young and reading voraciously (thanks to my late mother), I came across something in a book that described the elderly people of a culture in the far north of our continent. In that book it was written that when someone knew that death was coming, they climbed onto a small iceberg and floated out to sea. That seemed just *so right* to me then, and it does now. Even today I am a supporter of the Right to Die beliefs. One of the statements I am known to make frequently when teaching is that "there is nothing wrong with being compost."

All of my life is lived as preparation for my death, although that knowledge was not part of my consciousness when I was young. My parents lived on a small (failing) dairy farm in central Wisconsin when I was born. The farm had been built (literally, including the house, granary and barn) by my father's father. During those first ten years on the farm, death and birth were a part of life. I saw calves emerge from their mothers and livestock and poultry killed to become food. Wisconsin is also a state in which game hunting is a major activity. I did not do so well hunting with my father although I could bring down a squirrel, but I was far too interested in collecting live snakes while he hunted. Yet the sight of a dead deer hanging and skinned, was not unfamiliar.

My mother's father was a butcher, owning his own meat market. The slaughter house was a messy place. I remember the violently loud sound his pistol made when he would kill a beef cow, and how its body continued to thrash.

My brother and I caught, killed, and cleaned fish, although fishing was poor in the local streams.

Even after we had left the farm and lived in the small town of

Chapter 1 - The Roots Of My Death: My relationship and history with death

under 1,000 people, my dad would kill and clean snapping turtles. For that my mother would make home-made egg noodles and we would feast on a thick and tasty soup with their meat. The freezer nearly always had venison.

My father's family was very large (*very* large) and family funerals meant huge family reunions with many dozens of adults and dozens of children. There were tables of adults playing cards and laughing in every room and, in the warm months, outdoors as well. Huge meals were punctuated with the music of grandchildren romping everywhere. Funerals were great fun.

My parents were Roman Catholic and those years of my life brought me to be an 'altar boy.' When not assisting the priest I sang in the choir and, with a Catholic grade school adjacent the church, I participated in many funerals in varied capacities. My mother's father was a World War I Marine, and Veteran's Day meant heading back to the cemetery. I joined the high school band and was in the marching unit in my freshman year - now I played music as we *marched* to the cemetery.

Even within my family we grew up with a respect for cemeteries. My mother found them interesting and visits to other towns and cities would sometimes include a drive through a cemetery, where we'd note markers while looking for interesting or for familiar names, for dates and data often suggest stories.

All of this meant that a cemetery was a comfortable place for me, an appropriate and oftentimes attractive location where the dead were respected, usually buried (with chemical preservatives) in caskets. I remember that one time, ca. 1959-1960, my sister Jeanne and two others our ages all rode our bicycles out to the cemetery with picnic lunches. It was a wonderful day! The Colby Cemetery was perhaps 40 feet higher than much of the surrounding area of relatively flat but gently rolling farmland. Being surrounded by one's forebears always seemed an appropriate place to spend time although I didn't think much of embalming and caskets. That part of death and burial has never seemed the best way to remember someone nor was spending resources which would better serve the living.

Chapter 1 - The Roots Of My Death: My relationship and history with death

At this stage in my life, I no longer visit cemeteries as I once did. However, in a wonderful sense, the cemetery has come to visit us!

In the spring of 1977, Rev. gerry closed on the little house where we live now as I write this book. The cottage (today we call it the 'caretaker's cottage') sits on a one-third acre parcel of land. In the autumn of 1983, gerry was able to add a second, additional one acre parcel of land immediately behind the house and its lot. With a protected ravine at the far east end and the land holding the cottage and other structures, we hand-dug a garden which is now a 45,000 square foot private botanical and ritual garden. It took many years to bring these changes, and it has been a wonderful life for us, living so close to nature, our lives blessed by hundreds of species of plants and all of the creatures which inhabit such a space, from the miner bees to the Northwestern alligator lizards, with an abundance of birds and land which has become increasingly sacred.

Living with sacred land we had occasion for several individuals to bring some of the cremains of their loved ones to strew in the gardens. As is the lore of our religion, there were several ritual tools buried near the Stone Circle, along with cremains from some of those Rowan Tree Members, now passed over. All of this was informal. However, with my growing awareness of legalities as we signed over the back acre as a bequest to my Church in 1997 ce and the remaining land with its caretaker's cottage in 2008, I learned that we could legally, in this state, have cremains placed here.

When my dear student, Jason Hauser, passed over from complications having contracted Hanta virus in 2006 ce, a garden 'memorial' was planned. Looking about at the options at Barone Garden Decor, our favored source for statuary and more, I was taken with the idea of purchasing two granite benches. I chose the site for these in an open square at the entrance to the wooded area. Later Jason's mother flew out from Colorado and we consecrated the benches and placed some of his cremains there, as well as some about the gardens, unifying his memory and energy from the Otherworld with several other of his most sacred locations on this Earth.

The woodland has become the 'Memorial Grove,' and the square is the 'Memorial Square.' Other memorial benches have appeared since

Chapter 1 - The Roots Of My Death: My relationship and history with death

that time. These gardens will be able to accommodate a limited number of benches and, it is my hope, that my partner gerry and I will soon purchase one of those benches large enough for two (comfortably) and have time yet while alive to know where our cremains will be at rest at a later time (as well as those 'at work' strewn about the many gardens as well as the Stone Circle and Dancing Circle). [Update: We do have our own bench and it is comforting having waiting.]

Although we live in the midst of the very thriving suburbs, we have a quiet and tranquil agrarian lifestyle. When working the soil and tending the living things, I take comfort in knowing that some day my remains will be resting in this soil, some where one can sit quietly among the trees, and others where the plants are growing, the worms and beetles are busy, and I will be compost. How wonderful is that thought!

Over these recent centuries, we humans seem to have disconnected ourselves from the realities of death. Although I like to bring humor to a discussion of death by bringing up those who have aquariums, our great migration to urban life has removed us from many realities. So much of the world's population today has never experienced what growing one's own food requires. So few have ever seen a creature brought down with gunfire or an arrow, or watched it being hung by its legs as its death leaves its body as protein to enter our food chain. The aquarium folk? Well, fish seem to have *very* short life span and it seems that one is always removing dead fish (unless there are piscivores in the tank) and replacing them with new fish from the store.

Death is so much a part of life, every bit as much as birth. It is *normal* and we will all experience it, even if we are not prepared by experiencing the deaths of others. Few of you reading this book will have grown up with your elders dying in your home, where those of the larger family are born, live, and die together.

Earlier in time, learning to live with death and to be prepared for one's own death was part of our education, included in one's religion. In some cultures the knowledge of the cycle of birth, death and *re*birth is simply part of life. Although I did experience the deaths of animals, I was not present when any of my human relatives passed over. Family

Chapter 1 - The Roots Of My Death: My relationship and history with death

funerals, including my father's father, were more about the funeral and the family gathering. There was little if any discussion of what death actually was other than what my parents' church taught, which was much more about morality and judgement, punishment and reward. There were often deaths among the elder generation of relatives and, as an altar boy and choir member, I participated in numerous funerals. In the marching band, we were part of the Memorial Day observances, which included a procession with the Veterans of Foreign Wars, the American Legion and other local people from the downtown to the cemetery. I knew the sound of taps. I remembered visiting funeral homes, seeing the embalmed bodies in their satin-lined resting places. I had touched them.

But it wasn't until January 21, 1962, that death struck my heart. Juanita (Sybeldon) Schwab and her husband, Chuck, had been family friends longer than I had been alive. Juanita was a Registered Nurse and had been a childhood friend of my mother. She and Chuck were my godparents, and I thought them wonderful. In the summer of 1961 I had an amazing adventure. I went north to spend a week with them. That week was stretched on as I would plead my case to my mother. I had three weeks which were spent helping care for the three young Schwab children and golfing and sunning with my Aunt Juanita and being much an (almost) adult - having my earliest reciprocated male romance with Steve, the neighbor with whom I laid nightly beneath the stars, counting astounding numbers of shooting stars (not yet knowing about the Perseids).

It was not until Juanita's death that we learned the facts. This was the return of her cancer, and this time there were no longer options. She and Chuck had arranged for me to have that time with her even as she was marking the quick passage of her last months. Juanita chose to remain at home rather than be hospitalized so that she could be there for her husband and children every possible day, despite the physical agonies she endured. Her mother told us of Juanita's struggles, crawling on her hands and knees, yet refusing to face death while hospitalized and drugged. She faced her death while embracing every day, no matter how painful and agonizing.

My Aunt Juanita's death became a role model for me. No matter

Chapter 1 - The Roots Of My Death: My relationship and history with death

how difficult dying might be, I believed, and still do, that *advance knowledge* of one's death offered incredible advantage.

In 1963 I graduated from high school and was off to University in Stevens Point, about sixty miles from my childhood home in Colby. Although I was in school as a flute major, I'd had some experience playing brass when in high school, enough to land me a position in the Brass Choir and ... I was invited to play with them when they went on tour of various schools. I was so excited to learn that one of the concerts was to be at Abbotsford High School which was literally just a few blocks from my maternal grandmother's house. My Grandmother Bitter was that adult who most accepted me for who I was. Not only had I stayed with Grandma and Grandpa Bitter when quite young, but I worked in Abbotsford as a music teacher and then, my senior year, at the local drug store. I was privileged to have many, many days with my grandmother.

Pearl [Sante Onge] Bitter was another of my role models. During my elementary and early high school years it was not uncommon for her to be hospitalized. She lived with nitroglycerine tablets and suffered from heart attacks once or twice a year. She was a gentle, loving soul and never complained. I was able to have lunch with her the day of our concert and she was so proud of me. During our brief time together that day, I commented that it had been more than a year since her last heart attack. I was hopeful that something had changed.

On November 16th I received a phone call. My beloved Grandmother had died in her sleep. She was in Minneapolis, staying with friends, as my Grandfather was scheduled for yet another of his surgeries. The doctors determined that she died in her sleep, one final heart attack, and did not waken enough to even experience pain. I was emotionally devastated, already emotionally vulnerable at that stage of my development. She had been my rock and my strength for all of my eighteen years.

And yet, her intuitive knowledge of her own death became a role model for me. The mystical threads of my spiritual being had come down to me through her and her mother, although that is another story

Chapter 1 - The Roots Of My Death: My relationship and history with death

for another book. Prior to my grandmother's passing, all of her life concerns had been settled, other than that of wondering, as we had on several times, whether my grandfather would survive yet another very major surgery.

My grandparents had been of different Christian faiths and, in those days, a 'mixed marriage' was not so common and not so easy. They reconciled those difference by setting aside their religious activities, but Grandma had been attending her church again over the past two years. Saint Bernard's had outgrown the lovely, small church building of my childhood and now was a walkable distance from my grandparent's home.

My brother Joe had enlisted in the Navy shortly after his high school graduation in 1961 and was stationed on an aircraft carrier in the Atlantic and my sister Jeanne (his twin) enlisted the following year, also in the Navy. She was stationed in Bethesda, Maryland. Between my visit and her death, both Jeanne and Joe had been on leave and spent time with Grandma Bitter. All three of her adult grandchildren were doing well and she had seen all three of us.

After her death and funeral we learned that she had purchased our gifts, but enclosed notes which indicated that she expected to be gone. Numerous items throughout their home had been marked with small notes indicating to whom she wished that painting or this item to go. I know that it could have simply been Grandpa's intestinal surgeries and her cardiac history, yet somehow I could never remove the deep feeling that she *knew* that her time was arriving. This was my role model for having an *intuitive awareness* of one's death.

The difficulty I'd had with that wonderful, romantic allusion to the elders floating out to sea on an iceberg is that it always left me unable to grasp just *how* they would know. The final journey on a floe was a peaceful, if cold, and desirable option in my mind. But how would one ever know when it was time? My grandmother's death gave me the ability to believe that knowing intuitively was possible.

My older brother Joe's death provided me with another aspect to my relationship with death and dying October 30th, 1967. Prior to my

Chapter 1 - The Roots Of My Death: My relationship and history with death

parents adopting Jeanne and Joe in 1950 (I think it was), their life had been very difficult, coming from a family background which was very troubled. During his time in the Navy and after his discharge, Joe struggled to find his place in life. He worked hard, had a good job, but also enjoyed going out drinking with his friends, often driving home after the bar closed having had too much to drink. He totaled two cars and two motorcycles although he was never seriously injured. His final accident occurred when he drove into a ditch and overturned his car. This time he did not survive.

I was living in Stevens Point where I now taught English Literature and music at Pacelli High School. It had been years since my parents had been to see me in Stevens Point. I was now living in a wonderful house. My partner, Jerry Hild, and I rented the entire second floor of a marvelous, large house built during the development of the Prairie School style of architecture. The owner maintained that Frank Lloyd Wright designed the house. The style and detail were consistent with Lloyd of that period and he left his mark throughout that region. One night I did not sleep at all well. I wakened early and was at my desk in the guest bedroom when the doorbell rang at something like five in the morning, something completely unheard of.

I calmly went down the stairs to the front door, seeing my parents and my younger sister and brother, Diane and Dan, waiting for me. As I opened the door, I said something like, "it's either Joe or Grandpa (Bitter)."

My mother or father said, "it's Joe."

To which I responded, "come in. I have coffee waiting." And I did.

Knowing how my brother died brought home the hazards of *accidental death*. Even today, 45 years later, I live with no fear of death but I have apprehension over death arriving suddenly and from an accident, when one is deprived of that inner, spiritual strength derived from conscious and/or intuitive knowledge allowing one to be in a better state for Right Dying.

Ten years later I was living in Rochester, Minnesota, and my journey through life brought me to twice have my life threatened. Prior to the first of these events, one late night in Rochester, sitting around

Chapter 1 - The Roots Of My Death: My relationship and history with death

my living room with a coworker, Tom, and a mutual friend, Jim, Tom asked me what I believed in. I don't think I really knew, but as I began answering the question, thinking I didn't have much of a belief system, I found that, in fact, I did. I began by discussing Einstein's most commonly recognized Law of Thermodynamics, $E=mc^2$. Working from the layman's view of energy and matter, I used that as a foundation to explain the survival of one's energy when the body dies, the possibility that reincarnation might be a reality, and all manner of metaphysical principles. Discovering how profound the results of my life and exposure to concepts and religion had become, I found myself upon a path of endless study in the pursuit of wisdom. I was immersed in a variety of books: the *Tao Te Ching*, books on Buddhism, Confucianism, and reading (and rereading) *The Tibetan Book of the Dead* while striving to live without attachment and to be in the moment.

The first event was the result of road rage. I was driving for Yellow Cab at the time, having stepped away from teaching and management to have the time to discover, at last, who I really was. Rochester was a small city and I was easily identified, later stalked until it took police intervention. Although my life was threatened, it did not seem all that likely.

In 1974, however, a series of events led me to be in a most curious situation. A young woman I knew had spent time teaching on a reservation in the Dakotas and, during that time, became involved with a Native American man who had trouble with alcohol and, occasionally, violence. I knew only a little of that background until she told me that she learned that he had escaped from prison. She feared he might be on his way to her. By the time the FBI took him away, I discovered that I literally had no fear of death at that time.

Having to put my beliefs to the test, I did well and those experiences added real-life substance to the concepts and theory and ideas which I was embracing from my study of world religious and of mysticism.

Chapter 1 - The Roots Of My Death: My relationship and history with death

My first near-death experience was when I was perhaps three years old. I was with my parents in a small boat while my father was fishing. I toppled over into the water and nearly drowned. I no longer remember the event but for many years the experience was vivid and remained with me. What I remembered the most is that I had absolutely no fear, mesmerized by the color of the water as I sunk and bobbed to the surface a couple of times. A dairy farmer with the only local streams something you could step across or wade through, my father was not a strong swimmer, so it took some doing before I was retrieved. Dragged into the boat, my parents' fear and panic took over and replaced the total awe I'd had while almost drowning by water with fear.

I entered my maturity, my 30s, with my feet now firmly established on my spiritual and religious path, with teachers. During this time I also studied about reincarnation and learned how to conduct regressions, including those which allowed a person to explore their past and other lives. The work I did to explore spiritual reality within dreams and within regression brought me a number of experiences.

In Africa I was the equivalent of a village midwife. Something was going terribly wrong for the entire village and we were all fleeing into the jungle with great fear. I was a primitive villager, overweight yet running fast. The images from that single event of that life were so strong that the terror of feeling was the only view remaining. We were escaping what would otherwise be certain death.

In Nepal, I was an elderly man, bed-ridden in the upper level of my daughter's home. Once the local priest, I was now in my last weeks, waiting to be received by the gods.

More dramatic is the experience which happened during lucid dreaming one night ca. 1979. In an earlier time in what seemed European, I was found guilty of witchcraft and sentenced to death by hanging. I found good fortune in that the townsman who was to carry out the execution had a secret sympathy. Perhaps I had earlier tended his family? Thanks to him the rope which was used had been secretly delivered to him and was one which had belonged to me, a type of religious cord. At the end I was made to stand with my back to a post up on a platform. My cords were tied into a loop around my neck, draped over the post and caught over a large peg in the back of the post.

Chapter 1 - The Roots Of My Death: My relationship and history with death

When it was time, the executioner gave me a very subtle eye signal. I quickly dropped into a deep trance and pushed myself into an out-of-body momentum as the trap door beneath my feet swung down, my body dropping and neck to be snapped. I, however, soared free, as if out into the Universe.

This particular situation was so profound and so vivid, it was life changing for me. Four years later I went to see the 1983 movie "Brainstorm," in which the scientist Lillian Reynolds (portrayed by Louise Fletcher) dies of a heart attack. As that happens she puts on a device which she and her team of engineers are inventing, allowing her to record the mind's experience so that later, another could wear the device and experience that recording as reality. When Michael Brace, fellow scientist, puts on the head gear and plays the recording, he experiences her death, beginning with a vision of hell, but then being propelled away from the Earth and out, into the Universe.

This cinematic vision of death was so close to my experience in 1979 that I went back to see that movie again the following night and even today have a recording of it in our library.

Despite my best intentions, my desire to write this book was interrupted when I contracted HIV. Somehow, writing about death and dying in an era when my own death was in the foreseeable future felt too much a conflict of interest. I again took up my manuscript with all good intent in late 2008, having been brought through two major surgeries for kidney cancer which took place before and after my spleen ruptured a day after I'd come home from the first partial nephrectomy. I was nearly lost that time.

I have emerged, now, having had several flirtations with death. I have, at times, struggled with depression so severe that my longing for death nearly won out. To my complete astonishment, I am now on the verge of 70 and still doing quite well.

And I'd also like to add, with great delight, that through the internet I have learned that there are some who have expressed regret that the author Paul Beyerl should have died so early.[1]

Chapter 1 - The Roots Of My Death: My relationship and history with death

In many ways, death has been a companion in my life. I have long ago set aside any fear of death although I admit to an abhorrence at the thought of, for example, death by fire. Surely there are many who have danced a far more dramatic tango with death; there are many who see Death's many faces all about them on a near-daily basis. Death continues to fascinate me. I dearly wish to be consciously present and aware of that experience when the time comes.

> "'All that lives must die:' death is an inescapable fact of human existence whose essential nature does not alter in the course of time. But its causes and incidence, understanding of its physical aspects and beliefs about the after-life, the treatment of the dying and their comportment, the disposal of mortal remains and the ritual responses of survivors - all these have clearly changed, and the historian can study the process in a wealth of remaining evidence."[2]

As a student in the mid-1970s, I encountered a piece of Wiccan literature depicting what the Mother of Creation might say to us, and which contains the following:

> *I am the Gracious Goddess, Who gives the gift of joy unto the hearts of men and women. Upon Earth I give knowledge of the spirit eternal, and beyond death I give peace, freedom, and reunion with those who have gone before...*[3]

Within these words is much which describes my beliefs. Death is not described as fearful, but as an experience which opens the portal to that eternal spirit, which leads us to a restful time and to the potential of reunion. For the past twenty years I have lived with the gardens of my dreams. "There is nothing wrong with being compost."

I have so often been startled at the fear our culture has of death, of how pervasive that fear is. We do not have to accept the Western paradigm of death as a frightening experience to be avoided through medical traumatization and at any cost. If dreams are the little sleep, then death is but sleep across the Abyss. Is there no validation to the Aborigine belief which calls death the Dreaming?

Chapter 1 - The Roots Of My Death: My relationship and history with death

I believe, within my soul, that our ancestors were not so afraid of death. Well, to be certain, I doubt that they welcomed the attack of much larger and more ferocious creatures on the food chain; they would quickly flee a burning hut; they were fearful of falling from a precipice...: They would have been likely to have feared accidental death, but they also seemed to put great care into the burial of their loved ones. They erected great memorials which have endured longer than many human ages.

How have we come so far and yet, today, have such an inadequate relationship with death? Why are we afraid of living with death as a natural experience, one which is equally as sacred and essential as is birth?

◈

Something has spoken to me in the night, burning the tapers of the waning year; something has spoken in the night and told me I shall die, I know not where. Saying: "To lose the earth you know, for greater knowing; to lose the life you have, for greater life; to leave the friends you loved, for greater loving, to find a land more kind than home, more large than earth. Whereon the pillars of this earth are founded, toward which the conscience of the world is tending - a wind is rising, and the rivers flow."[4]

Chapter 1 - The Roots Of My Death: My relationship and history with death

Notes for Chapter One

---

[1] They have confused me with another gay author who also wrote a book on herbal magick and who was a noted Wiccan author, the late Scott Cunningham.

[2] Houlbrooke, Ralph, ed., *Death, Ritual, and Bereavement*, Routledge in association with the Social History Society of the United Kingdom, London, New York © 1989, page 1, quote from W. Shakespeare, Hamlet I ii 72

[3] From "The Charges of the Goddess," attributed to Doreen Valiente

[4] Wolf, Thomas, *You Can't Go Home Again*, Harper & Row, New York © 1934. I originally found this quotation in *The Adept* by Katherine Kurz and Deborah Turner.

Chapter 2 - What is Death?

Complications of definition

It would seem that if I am to write my work on death and dying that I ought attempt to provide some definition of death. I no longer recall when I wrote this sentence, but it has been in my notes for this manuscript for many years: *Death is when we no longer partake of life.* Rando writes that "Death erases us as experiencing and producing beings."[5]

From my perspective, death would be the separation (permanent) of the soul and the body. The presence of the soul or spirit is described by this line from our religious service, "A new star shines in the night."

At the risk of death by boredom, I hope to explore a variety of concepts in the process of trying to answer the question posed by this chapter.

Death is everywhere. To be born is to begin moving toward death, for only what we humans refer to as Deity seems to be eternal, and even that eternal nature may be open to question. Birth and death and rebirth are so universal in concept that the mythologies of our forebears seem to be a more accurate reflection of today's new physics than one might ever have imagined.

Even today, the 'big bang' is no longer considered the only option. It is quite likely that the infinite, eternal Universe, Herself, is endlessly dying and reborn. At one time humans experienced the deaths of others as naturally as they experienced life, perhaps with grieving, perhaps abandoning them to those other species who followed behind waiting to be fed. For much of our species' history, based upon artifacts and records, death is treated as a mystery.

At some point in time as our distant ancestors grew in knowledge, evolving religions and beliefs and emotional attachment, death became an event of greater import.

In an earlier rural lifestyle, an agrarian people, even in the cities of those eras, saw birth and death. They saw livestock born. They saw animals slaughtered for food. Their elders lived with them and died at home. Family members died of illnesses - at home. They knew when death occurred, for then the person (or creature) was no longer alive. The body no longer moved on its own, it no longer responded to external stimuli (calling to it, nudging it, administering pungent scents, slapping its face) and, eventually it no longer had warmth.

Unlike today, in those earlier times there was less urgency. If the cattle needed tending, if a storm was imminent, if the crops urgently needed to be harvested, life afforded waiting. Perhaps she will be awake when we come back in from the fields?

Death was indicated by the complete absence of signs of life.

At what stage in our development did we turn to others to determine if someone was truly dead? I can well imagine, very early on that a person in doubt, uncertain whether or not one of their kin was truly dead, would ask a parent or village elder if it were true.

As we continued our evolution and became more specialized, when some could provide services in exchange for goods or food or barter, then we would turn to our village midwives and priests and healers, for they would be seen as the wise ones.

At times, over the years as I've contemplated these definitions and topics, I wondered if some cultures might have defined death as the separation of the soul or spirit from the body. That, of course, implies a belief in there being a soul, something I wish to explore later.

To a person who has not given much thought to a definition of death, it might be expected that it should not be so complex. What is death? It's when a person is *dead*, isn't it?

Many define death as that time when there is a separation or loss of vital signs, of the person's energy, of their spirit. What one might expect to be a simple question has very complex answers.

> "Comprehension of death involves an intellectual understanding. That is, death must be meaningful in one's visual mind as a phenomenon of life. ... Moreover, there is no

specific way to comprehend death to the exclusion of other options or alternatives. Finally, the uniqueness and specific needs of each individual must be taken into consideration in order to deal with death in a healthy fashion. Hence, each person's reactions to a particular death may differ considerably from all others to the same death."[6]

Unlike my youthful behavior in which I considered them unnecessary, I now turn to a dictionary whenever wanting sound definition. When I graduated from Colby High School in 1963, I was given a Merriam Webster's dictionary. It had a blue cloth cover and that book lasted for twenty years. By then I was growing as an author, and now a dictionary lasts me only a few years before it begins to show excess signs of wear. A dictionary of mine gets *a lot* of use. My desk dictionary[7] provides the following:

> **death** (bef. 12c) **1 a** : a permanent cessation of all vital functions : the end of life - compare brain death **b** : an instance of dying <a disease causing many ~s> **2 a** : the cause or occasion of loss of life (drinking was the ~ of him) **b** : a cause of ruin <the slander that was ~ to my character - Wilkie Collins> **3** *cap* : the destroyer of life represented usu. as a skeleton with a scythe **4** : the state of being dead **5 a** : the passing or destruction of something inanimate (the ~ of vaudeville) **b** : extinction **6** : civil death **7** : slaughter **8** *Christian Science*: the lie of life in matter: that which is unreal and untrue - **at death's door** : close to death : critically ill - **to death** : beyond endurance, excessively <bored *to death*>

Frankly, that's not a helpful definition in some respects. The first option asks us to consider *brain death* which is a medical or scientific definition. The second, of it being 'an instance of dying' or number four, of it being 'the state of being dead?' That type of answer would not have allowed me to pass my exams. But O.K., I'll bite. What is it to "be dead?" Back to the dictionary[8] for another try:

¹die (12c) **1** : to pass from physical life : expire **2** : to pass out of existence : cease <their anger *died* at these words) **b** : to disappear or subside gradually - often used with *away, down,* or *out* <the storm *died* down> **3 a** : sink, languish <*dying* from fatigue> **b** : to long keenly or desperately <*dying* to go> **c** : to be overwhelmed by emotion <~ of embarrassment> **4 a** : to cease functioning : stop <the motor *died*> **b** : to end in failure <the bill *died* in committee> **5** : to become indifferent <~ die to worldly things>

²die (14c) **1** *pl dice* : a small cube marked on each face with from one to six spots and used usu. in pairs in various games and in gambling by being shaken and thrown to come to rest at random on a flat surface - often used figuratively in expressions concerning chance or the irrevocability of a course of action <the ~ was cast>

To be honest, my sense of humor (which is very word-oriented) finds the second entry the most fascinating. Images of Death shaking the dice to see whether or not it is one's time seems a fitting metaphor, but does not define the word.

I also tried Wikipedia, which is, for me, a convenient and useful resource for much information: In the midst of that entry is the following; "Historically, attempts to define the exact moment of a human's death have been problematic."[9] Seeing that statement was assuring, affirming what I'd found to be true based upon my looking in many other resources.

My view of Wikipedia as a reference for this type of definition is that it does quite well in reflecting where we, as a culture, are today:

"There are many scientific approaches to the concept. For example, brain death, as practiced in medical science, defines death as a point in time during which brain activity ceases. One of the challenges in defining death is in distinguishing it from life. As a point in time, death would seem to refer to the moment at which life ends. However, determining when death has occurred requires drawing precise conceptual boundaries between life and death. This is problematic because there is little consensus over how to define life. It is possible to define life in terms of consciousness. When consciousness ceases, a living organism can be said to have died. One of the notable flaws in this approach, however, is that there are many organisms which are alive but probably not conscious (for example, single-celled organisms). Another problem with this approach is in defining consciousness, which has many different definitions given by modern scientists, psychologists and philosophers. This general problem of defining death applies to the particular challenge of defining death in the context of medicine."[10]

Is death determined by the stopping of the body's vital functions? To accept that definition suggests that we defy the natural timing of death when we keep someone breathing by mechanical means, when we provide nutrition to the body through tubes and piping leading directly into the body. We provide mechanical means by which the body empties itself of waste. We can keep the body going for a long time, which raises all manner of questions for the field of medical ethics, some of which end up in the courts. Dying today has become morally and scientifically a complex issue. As Arthur Carr wrote, "... 'dying in *peace* has become difficult to achieve in this day of biological revolution.' ... consider these simple questions: When and by what means is it appropriate to disconnect someone from life support mechanisms? If an individual is disconnected and continues to live, what options remain?"[11]

Is death determined by the loss of brain function? How do we distinguish between a coma from which one will never return? Do we keep the body alive through what are called 'heroic means'? Just when I feel quite certain that this is questionable, there will be a news-making recovery of someone who had been comatose for a very long time who unexpectedly returns to awareness. Is, then, 'brain death' the appropriate marker?

> "Today, where a definition of the moment of death is required, doctors and coroners usually turn to 'brain death' or 'biological death' to define a person as being clinically dead;

people are considered dead when the electrical activity in their brain ceases. It is presumed that an end of electrical activity indicates the end of consciousness. However, suspension of consciousness must be permanent, and not transient, as occurs during certain sleep stages, and especially a coma. In the case of sleep, EEGs can easily tell the difference.

"However, the category of 'brain death' is seen by some scholars to be problematic. For instance, Dr. Franklin Miller, senior faculty member at the Department of Bioethics, National Institutes of Health, notes: 'By the late 1990s, however, the equation of brain death with death of the human being was increasingly challenged by scholars, based on evidence regarding the array of biological functioning displayed by patients correctly diagnosed as having this condition who were maintained on mechanical ventilation for substantial periods of time. These patients maintained the ability to sustain circulation and respiration, control temperature, excrete wastes, heal wounds, fight infections and, most dramatically, to gestate fetuses (in the case of pregnant 'brain-dead' women).'

"Those people maintaining that only the neo-cortex of the brain is necessary for consciousness sometimes argue that only electrical activity should be considered when defining death. Eventually it is possible that the criterion for death will be the permanent and irreversible loss of cognitive function, as evidenced by the death of the cerebral cortex. All hope of recovering human thought and personality is then gone given current and foreseeable medical technology. However, at present, in most places the more conservative definition of death – irreversible cessation of electrical activity in the whole brain, as opposed to just in the neo-cortex – has been adopted (for example the Uniform Determination Of Death Act in the United States). In 2005, the Terri Schiavo case brought the question of brain death and artificial sustenance to the front of American politics.

"Even by whole-brain criteria, the determination of brain

death can be complicated. EEGs can detect spurious electrical impulses, while certain drugs, hypoglycemia, hypoxia, or hypothermia can suppress or even stop brain activity on a temporary basis. Because of this, hospitals have protocols for determining brain death involving EEGs at widely separated intervals under defined conditions."[12]

But what of someone who is losing the struggle with Alzheimer's or a similar condition, whose personality has been absent, replaced by some being who is lost, angry, confused, who lashes out from a body which had never, ever thought to be physically aggressive toward another human? When the mind is no longer recognizable, the soul seems long departed, but the body lives on as a container of fears and anxieties, has not death already taken place at some level?

Clearly, there are many different causes for death, even when we read that someone died of 'natural causes.' That phrase, today, is different in meaning than it once was. Several centuries ago, it was not enough to die a *natural death*, as Lucinda McCray Beir writes: "A natural death, however, was not the same as a good death. Natural death relieved the dying person and the survivors of responsibility for an event interpreted as inevitable. Good death encompassed the duties of all present in the death chamber regarding the quality of the event itself."[13]

It was the role of religion and of society to prepare us for death. The concept of *Right Dying* which I first encountered in my studies of Buddhism in the 1970s resonated deeply with me and continues to shape my view of death and dying to this day. Today most humans live so removed from death as a reality yet immersed in the concept of death as, well, *entertainment* or as something removed from one's own life that it has become difficult for us to be prepared for our death. We have also turned over those roles which were once for family (the "all present" McCray Beir refers to) to the employees of a hospice or nursing home.

One aspect of my professional work is educator in the fields of healing and wellness, in treating illness. Well-versed in botanical medicine (I have been, at the time of this book, teaching this topic for nearly 40 years) and working with professionals in conventional medicine (both medical doctors and registered nurses), I do not know how we could ever call a halt to funding further research seeking ways to halt diseases, to combat cancer, to find ways to help those living in regions where malaria is rampant. Modern medicine has done much to extend the average life expectancy, although much of this numerical change comes from the difference in the loss of life which babies and young children experience.

Having a particularly terrifying experience with a tonsillectomy when only three or four years old, I spent most of my adult life certain that I would do everything possible to avoid invasive surgery. My younger idealism believed it noble that we should accept death when it was time.

I'm not a very good role model. In March of 1988 I learned that I had contracted HIV, quite likely in January, based upon my life at the time. In 1990, living in Dallas for a short time, I ended up with a fairly strong case of seasonal influenza, enough to pull my immune system down, leaving me with thrush and a low T-cell count. My doctor recommended I begin taking azidothymidine (AZT). Was I as ready to accept the possibility of death as I had thought I might? No, I steeled myself, examined my belief system as a Master Herbalist, and began a regimen of pharmaceuticals.

I often encounter the theory that there is some botanical medicine to be found which could 'cure' or treat every disease known to humans. I don't accept that, personally, for I believe that our bodies are transient, and that it is more natural for us to die than it is to escape death. And yet I take my pharmaceutical medicine daily.

On May 30, 2008, preparing for an appendectomy, the surgeon at Evergreen Hospital made me promise her that I would go and have some exploratory exams. Two and a half months later, I was sitting in the office of Dr. Tom Takyama at the University of Washington Medical Center's Prostate Oncology Center, hearing from him that the results of the tests and imaging from earlier that month came back and it was fact: I had malignant tumors on both kidneys.

Did I accept my timing? When he told me that he had scheduled my surgery for the following week, I simply said 'yes' and made plans. It did not occur to me to go home, plan to die, and make reservations on the next outgoing iceberg.

I'm working on this book on death and dying as someone who has escaped a 'natural' death more than once. In my defense, I tell myself that my work - The Rowan Tree Church and The Hermit's Grove which I've founded and which are still dependent upon me - means that I am still needed. My work is not done.

I do not pretend that I will continue to put death off forever, nor do I wish to. I am grateful to conventional medicine - *very* grateful - but I've been in many nursing homes and have known too many whose days are spent without any real quality of life. Their lives are gone, and their days are spent going from bed to meals, watching a lot of television, and waiting... Waiting... Many of them, including my father, in his upper 80s, would have preferred to be dead and yet, like my father, are terrified of death. [My father did pass over at age 89, avoiding being moved out of assisted living to a nursing home.] I could not even mention to my father in a telephone conversation that someone I know has passed away. Living in his tiny room, having lost his home, his wife, two of his children, all of the activities he loved ... No, I cannot wish for that.

We have moved so far as a species from those days when we lived our lives far more aware of and in tune with the natural world - a world which included death as a normal and expected function of life. In today's western culture the phraseology which has emerged during my lifetime leaves me deeply unsettled.

The amount of financial resources which are devoted to pursuing a dream of living longer and longer - of defying the natural role of death in our lives - is astounding, and I have no idea what the actual costs might be.

Over the past few years we hear more and more about people being concerned about their 'legacy.' I am of an age that one's legacy had to do with what we left behind when our bodies died. But no, now that we cannot think about ourselves dying, when we push that reality further and further from daily life, the concept of one's *legacy* is used for a politician, for an athlete and, in newspaper stories I read within the past year, even for a *college athlete*. Is this young football player going to die? No, it's just about whatever statistics and reputation might be left behind when he moves on with his life.

Far worse, to me, is another phrase which has been insinuated into our culture. Politicians and military strategists use this phrase more and more. Searching the internet, I found several sources which suggest that this phrase may have emerged during the Vietnam War. Today we hear this phrase far too readily, slipping from the tongues of the glib. '*Collateral damage*' is used so that the killing of innocent people can be acknowledged, but the fact that people are dead who should not be, killed by 'friendly fire' (meaning we killed them ourselves by accident?) or just because they were in the wrong place at the wrong time and our weapons and those who put them into play are unable to avoid killing them. Whether this is to provide a subtle misleading of the public mind, lest they withdraw support for wars being fought by the powerful at the expense of the populace on both sides, I cannot say. But that is about politics. Obviously I have some soapboxes to drag out regarding these topics, but this is neither the place nor the time for those rants, so I'll set them aside.

We live in a culture of mayhem in the entertainment industry in which humans die of violence at the flick of a button during a computer game or the young watch humans being shot, maimed, blown up or all manner of violent special effects until we are numbed to the reality. Modern civilization fills its entertainment and media with references to death, but other than the obituary pages, it's all somehow removed from reality by way of phraseology.

Although we are, more and more, providing hospice environments for those whose time is nearing, we do live in an era in which we are removed from the reality of death. "The United States today is often cited as an example of a more or less death-denying culture."[14] I contrast this with Houlbrooke's comments, written more than thirty years ago:

> "The basic premises we make about the nature of humankind also influence and help us form our theories of

death. For example, acceptance of the premise that death is inevitable generally facilitates a more realistic attitude toward one's own death. A belief in immortality may lead to a different perception of death. Recently, many of our premises and hypotheses concerning death have become inappropriate and obsolete. The high technology, prolongevity, and artificial life that we see and hear almost every day through the media or firsthand experience have rendered our past views of death outdated. Today, many people feel that death is appropriate only at a certain time in life and only for certain people. For instance, some may feel that death is 'appropriate' for a ninety year old whereas the death of a teenager is viewed by many as inappropriate."[15]

Although we may spend much time during life thinking about our own death, death is not a solitary experience for most. We think about death in the context of those who have died and, despite our plans, when we die those left behind will tend to our earthly remains for their own comfort:

"The desire of survivors to help their dead is a deep rooted one. Keeping their memory alive, and showing that they are not forgotten, does something to satisfy this desire, even in people who rationally accept that the dead are beyond help."[16]

So much of our human history is not about where the deceased has gone but more about how those who are left behind attempt to cope.

⁕

Death's signifying the ending of futurity presents us with an incomprehensible conception. We are future-oriented creatures, a capacity that distinguishes us from other animals. It makes death an ultimate threat, since it colors the anticipation that guides the majority of our actions and dampens the expectation that serves as a principal mediator of goal-directed and purposeful behavior... [17]

Notes for Chapter Two

[5] "Death and Dying Are Not and Should Not be Taboo Topics" by Therese A. Rando, *Principles of Thanatology*, ed. Kutscher, Carr and Kutscher, Columbia University Press © 1987 page 35

[6] "Prologue: Principles of Thanatology" by Arthur C. Carr, *Principles of Thanatology*, ed. Kutscher, Carr and Kutscher, Columbia University Press © 1987, page 27

[7] *Merriam-Webster's Collegiate Dictionary*, 11th edition, page 319

[8] *Merriam-Webster's Collegiate Dictionary*, 11th edition, page 347

[9] http://en.wikipedia.org/wiki/Death#Signs_of_Death February 24, 2011 ce

[10] http://en.wikipedia.org/wiki/Death#Signs_of_Death February 24, 2011 ce

[11] "Prologue: Principles of Thanatology" by Arthur C. Carr, *Principles of Thanatology*, ed. Kutscher, Carr and Kutscher, Columbia University Press © 1987, pages 22-23

[12] http://en.wikipedia.org/wiki/Death#Signs_of_Death February 24, 2011 ce

[13] "The Good Death in Seventeenth-Century England" by Lucinda McCray Beir in *Death, Ritual, and Bereavement*, Routledge in association with the Social History Society of the United Kingdom, London, New York © 1989, page 45

[14] "Death and Dying Are Not and Should Not be Taboo Topics" by Therese A. Rando, *Principles of Thanatology*, ed. Kutscher, Carr and Kutscher, Columbia University Press © 1987 page 41

[15] "Prologue: Principles of Thanatology" by Arthur C. Carr, *Principles of Thanatology*, ed. Kutscher, Carr and Kutscher, Columbia University Press © 1987, page 17

[16] Houlbrooke, Ralph, ed., *Death, Ritual, and Bereavement*, Routledge in association with the Social History Society of the United Kingdom, London, New York © 1989, page 36

[17] "Death and Dying Are Not and Should Not be Taboo Topics" by Therese A. Rando, *Principles of Thanatology*, ed. Kutscher, Carr and Kutscher, Columbia University Press © 1987 page 34

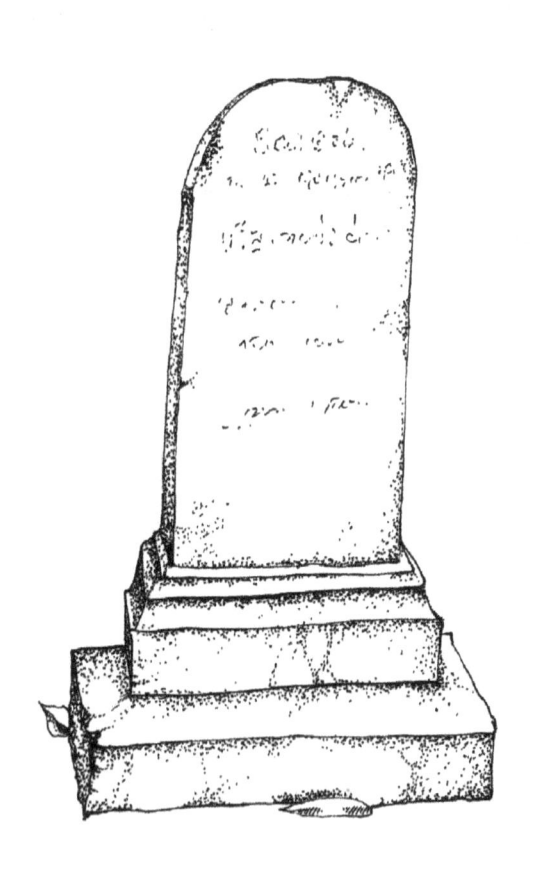

Chapter 3 - Memento Mori:

If I should die before I wake ...

Growing into my adult awareness, my only understanding of the historical evolution of our beliefs regarding death was initially limited to the brief human moments encompassing the cemeteries I'd visited with occasional awareness of ancient burials, such as the pyramids, burial mounds, and other sites which attract photographers and tourists. Although I had spent so much of my life thinking about death, thinking about *my own death*, it was not until I began studying *The Tibetan Book of the Dead* that I grasped the importance of death and of dying as a spiritual process, one given great regard by entire cultures.

"The exploration of Man the Unknown in a manner truly scientific and yogic such as [*The Tibetan Book of the Dead*] suggests is incomparably more important than the exploration of outer space. To stand in the physical body on the Moon, or on Venus, or on any of the celestial spheres, will add to human knowledge, but only to knowledge of things transitory. Man's ultimate goal is, as the Sages herein teach, transcendence over the transitory."[18]

Books on death and dying attracted my attention and I began compiling a small section in our research library devoted to that topic. Meanwhile, my world began quickly changing. Men that I knew, men I had loved, men who were my friends were falling ill and soon the dreaded AIDS diagnosis became part of our vocabulary. My work as a Priest grew to include and embrace my gay brethren who were in need of healing, who were afraid of dying, and who were dying. For several years I conducted weekly meditation and visualization sessions for AIDS-afflicted men both in private homes and in a center for those affected by catastrophic illnesses, including cancer.

As the founder of a religious tradition, I knew that Lothloriën must embrace 'right dying' and provide a ritual form which would encompass all of death's potential for spiritual growth as well as comfort those who were still living. It was in the spring of 1986 that our *Ritual for the Dead of Lothloriën* was completed. That accomplishment was of monumental importance to me. Two years later I found myself briefly hospitalized in Hennepin County Medical Center in Minneapolis, with a fever and dehydration as my body responded to the invasion of the human immunodeficiency virus. In 1988, that meant that I was clearly brought face to face with my own death. My desire to write a book on death and dying was evolving and it was a book which kept at me, wanting to be written.

By the summer of 1993 a circuitous route, originally meant to be a brief sojourn of two years in Dallas, found me living in Los Angeles, newly partnered with gerry, the life partner I had long dreamt of. For a time I had a student, Angelique, who was in the graduate department of UCLA and, through her, I was able to gain access to quite a few books which would otherwise have been beyond my grasp. In fact, the bibliography for this very book reflects those books from her graduate school, specifically Addison, Houlbrooke, Kutscher and MacDonald, authors and editors whose material gave me information which provided me with great insight.

The busy activities of my life kept me from actively focusing on this book, but my collection of research notes was never far removed. As my other written works and my teaching expanded, so too was our physical work growing and the land that gerry had acquired prior to our meeting became the physical home for The Tradition of Lothloriën. The 1.3 tract of former field and woodland evolved into a 45,000 square foot (private) botanical garden which includes two sacred spaces for ritual and is also where we now have sites where granite benches mark placement and memorials for some of our Church who have passed into the Otherworld, their physical bodies cremated. Preparing for death is not just a spiritual goal but also an intrinsic part of our lives as we turn the soil, as we weed the paths which meander among the memories of our loved ones.

I wondered how have we, as a species, have come to this place? I see our approach to death and dying not so far removed from that of our ancestors, for we frequently give thanks to all of our ancestors, not simply those of familial lineage, but all of the 'Ancient Ones':

"I am the offspring of my ancestors. It was they who learned to harness fire, to till the fields.

"It was my ancestors who first learned how to communicate with speech and it was the Ancient Ones who migrated past glacial fields, across deserts, moving from one continent to another in search of their future.

"I honor the Ancient Ones who were first to drum the tribe's heartbeat upon a stretched hide. I honor the Ancients Ones who found not only joy in the blossoms and fruits but also healing medicines. I honor the Ancient Ones who were first to heal with gemstones. I honor the Ancients Ones who first brought an animal into the tribe to live amongst them. I honor the Ancient Ones who first recognized that the life stirring within the womb was to be a baby.

"I honor the Ancient Ones who first found a relationship between the Moon and Sun and stars and what was happening in their lives.

"I honor the Wise Woman and the Shaman and those who lived their lives different from their peoples so as to be one with their dreams.

"I honor the Ancient Ones who cast the first Circle. I honor the Ancient Ones who struggled against weather, emigrating from one place upon the Mother to another, for it is through their many journeys that I have been brought to..."[19]

... this point in my life. This is text we read formally each year as life in the gardens seems to die, when the Mother of Nature appeared to our ancestor to descend into the Underworld. This is that time of year when many cultures remember their dead. My quest for more knowledge regarding this evolution and the integration of that knowledge into my daily life has occupied more than twenty years as I've worked to complete this manuscript. Over these years, I have spoken publicly on death and dying when traveling as an educator and I live with a daily awareness of death and a never-ending sense of wonder regarding the evolution of our human awareness of death.

I am known to refer to my passing with frequency. Finding myself to be HIV+ in March of 1988 ce, I accepted the mindset of the day. At worst, if my health were to fail, I would have five years. That seemed to be a common lifespan once one reached the tipping point, when the virus began to rule the body. I was but 42 years old and had invested nearly 12 years into what was emerging as a solid organization. From that Spring onward, I would remind the Board of Directors to avoid the expectation that I would be around forever, urge them to do some planning and hope for a few individuals to step forward and embrace greater responsibilities.

The years passed. My conversion to HIV put me at the cusp of medical changes. Ongoing pharmaceutical developments, along with my own knowledge of health and wellness as a professional instructor of botanical medicine, carried me through the decades and through some life changes. In June of 1994, I arrived in Kirkland, Washington, with my life partner of one year (spent in Los Angeles laying the groundwork in publishing and in preparing the organization for this transition). Life was good. Life was very good.

I continued to nag at the Board of Directors about being prepared should I pass over. It was very difficult for them to take this seriously, for I was a very healthy and fit man, HIV notwithstanding. I would periodically raise the topic in a Board Agenda and discussions would meander about. As an herbalist with a huge, organic garden, I came to recognize that my ideal passing would be if I could go out, lay down upon the soil, and have my body simply merge with the Earth. I knew that my cremated remains would end up there, for the gardens began to hold a stone bench here and there, put in place sometimes with a small stone box containing the cremains of a former student or family member. I found that reminding people that "there is nothing wrong in being compost" was a humorous but mindful way to put my views of death and dying before them in a simply but succinct manner. That statement would usually gently close the discussion in which someone would try to change my mind. I continue to be surprised at how much people feel uncomfortable with my own comfort at the expectation of meeting death some day.

Some years back I tried another tactic when speaking with one or more of the Directors. Urging them to put together some contingency plan to keep The Rowan Tree Church functional at my passing, I responded with the potential that gerry and I might, after all, be struck by a large meteorite at any time. Out of that comment, over the years, the phrase "after the meteorite" has become a reference point, and in fact great progress has been made so that, when it is my time to be compost, The Rowan Tree Church will continue to function quite well.

Allow me to once again meander with my memories of death's presence. In 2011 for reasons too complex to explain here, I proposed relocating the Stone Circle which was originally established in our gardens by gerry in the early 1980s. Over the years it has become a very sacred site for our Church. In October of that year, over a period of four days, the entire installation was moved. With the new site prepared, gerry and I moved the largest stones using some dollies and carts. With help from a joyful woman and former Member and volunteer, the three of us completed the final work Monday afternoon. As the provider of 60-75% of all garden labor here (my life is structured in this way) I literally moved over a ton of rock myself.

Less than an hour later, in the early evening, I received a phone call from my very alarmed neurologist. Now, a little more background, for this *is* relevant.

Earlier in the year, perhaps in June or July, while working in the Yarrow Bed in the gardens, I stood up to go and retrieve a tool and was caught with a wave of dizziness. This was so out of character but I thought little of it, assuming it would quickly pass, so I got back down on my hands and knees to continue working in the soil. Then, I woke up. It was so luxurious. I was laying there on the comfortable, warm soil in the late morning sun. It was so embracing that I had to decide whether to try to doze off again. Practical by nature, I got up as it was nearly time for gerry to be home and we'd be having lunch.

What a wonderful discovery. It was true! Laying in the gardens and sinking into the soil? There could be no better way to pass into the Otherworld. When I went into the house I checked the information on the new medicine I was taking for neurological difficulties with my legs and, sure enough, dizziness and fainting were possible. Months later, when I met with Dr. Weiss, I thought I was sharing a humorous story and that it was simply side-effects from adjusting to the new prescriptions but ...

Very alarmed and chastising me, Dr. Weiss wrote the order and I left the University Medical Center wearing a 24-hour monitor. Having received the device and having cardiology analyze the data, it turned out that my heart had electrical difficulties and I was diagnosed with complete heart block! I not only gained a Pacemaker, but I also learned that returning to the Earth, that 'being compost' is a beautiful and comforting feeling. Caution, this story will be told once more late in this book. Aging men forget.

Over and again in my life I have been reminded of my mortality, and given no option but to remember at all times that I am mortal: "Memento mori is a Latin phrase that may be translated as 'Remember that your mortality,' 'Remember you will die' or 'Remember you will die' - literally '[in the future] remember to die' since *memento* is a future imperative of the 2nd person and *mori* is a deponent infinitive. It names a genre of artistic creations that vary widely from one another, but which all share the same purpose, which is to remind people of their own mortality. The phrase has a tradition in art that dates back to antiquity."[20]

The images that are offered us in this reference are quite visual:

"In ancient Rome, the words are believed to have been used on the occasions when a Roman general was parading through the streets of Rome during a victory triumph. Standing behind the victorious general was his slave, who was tasked to remind the general that, though his highness was at his peak today, tomorrow he could fall or be more likely brought down. The servant conveyed this by telling the general that he should remember 'Memento mori.'"[21]

How many of us, as children, heard this prayer:

> "Now I lay me down to sleep
> I pray the Lord my soul to keep
> If I should die before I wake
> I pray the Lord my soul to take."

I don't know how old this child's prayer is. It was printed in the *New England Primer*, a textbook used in colonial schools, and perhaps the earliest standard for learning reading and writing before the 1790s. Young children of that era grew up and had children of their own and taught them this prayer, and they grew up to repeat the cycle. This is a version of 'memento mori' which reflects the norms of Christian thought which permeated many homes in the early United States.

Unlike the brave Roman general who was reminded by his servant, we have generations and generations of children (who become adults) who nightly had to remind themselves that death could arrive at any time. There are many adults who relate stories of that simple prayer causing them fear. The following reflects a further view of the medieval version of *Memento Mori*:

> "The thought came into its own with Christianity, whose strong emphasis on Divine Judgment, Heaven, Hell, and the salvation of the soul brought death to the forefront of consciousness. Most *memento mori* works are products of Christian art, although there are equivalents in Buddhist art. In the Christian context, the *memento mori* acquires a moralizing purpose quite opposed to the *Nunc est bibendum* theme of Classical antiquity. To the Christian, the prospect of death serves to emphasize the emptiness and fleetingness of earthly pleasures, luxuries, and achievements, and thus also as an invitation to focus one's thoughts on the prospect of the afterlife."[22]

We who grow up in agrarian environments are, I believe, far more accustomed to death. I occasionally add (humorously) that those who have aquariums, notorious for fish with short lives, are also accustomed to creatures dying. Did our primitive ancestors have such a difficult time when one of their tribe died? It is so far removed in evolution from where we are that, without remnants of burial customs, we have no way of knowing. By the time languages and the ability to record them evolved, there were death and burial rituals evolving, many of which became extraordinarily elaborate.

Today we observe the elephant species with their own death rituals and we observe the grieving and behavior of many, many species. They have some concept of loss, of the absence of a loved one, of the absence, even, of life from the dead body. Creatures seem aware of the change in scent. They will push and nudge and, if they are capable, hold the dying or dead corpse and vocalize grief and loss.

But are they fearful of death? Anyone who has worked with animals and who has had to put one down would, I believe, agree with me that they are. I've seen it in their eyes just before it happens, *and they know...*

I don't know that most other higher mammal species have the capacity of memory as we have so that they would *worry* about death, that they would have thoughts of it plague them and interfere with their daily activities, that they dream about it (for surely, a great many mammal species dream). But we humans do. So many of us, from our early knowledge of death - and particularly of the manner in which our adults handled death, spend our lives worrying... What "if I should die before I wake"? It could be argued that the above children's prayer is, in fact, to be comforting. 'There, there, sleep well. It doesn't matter if you die during the night. God will take care of your soul.' As a child, I was lost there. I could imagine my soul more easily than I could grasp infinity ... or the god of my parents' religion.

I am not, at this stage of my life, at all fearful of dying nor have I been for forty years, since beginning my conversion to a religion both pragmatic yet mystical. During those last two years in Rochester, Minnesota, my life was seriously threatened twice: once by a road-rage stalker which required serious police intervention over a period of time; and once by a convicted murderer, escaped from federal prison to pursue the love of his life (as he thought her to be) who just happened to be a coworker of mine. It was a remarkable opportunity for me to realize that I no longer had a fear of dying. Some concerns about the timing? Some wishes that maybe not by fire, may not with excessive, slow violence? But not at all what I think of as *fears*.

Therese A. Rando is a Clinical Psychologist and Thanatologist. She is highly regarded as an author of books on death and dying and has an essay in the book *Principles of Thanatology*. In her essay, which I first read twenty years ago, she writes about the fears of dying:

> **"Fears of Dying**
> "Leaving unfinished, with things undone and secrets poorly concealed; dying alone; facing the unknown; loneliness; impairment and loss of functions, roles, objects, body parts, and people; loss of control; loss of consciousness; altered body-image; shame; dependency; loss of integrity; becoming a burden; indignity; disability; suffering and pain; loss of identity; sorrow; and regression.
> **"Fears of Death**
> "Losing time; irreversibility; facing the unknown; loss of self and cessation of thought; loss of pleasure; loss of mastery; incompleteness and failure; separation; loss of identity; loss of control; extinction, 'ceasing to be,' or annihilation; mutilation; decomposition; and premature burial.
> **"Fears of the Results or Consequences of Death**
> "Fate of the body; judgement; punishment or rejection from God; facing the unknown; fate of loved ones left behind; what will happen to one's property, plans, and projects; and loss of control.
> **"Fears of the Dying or Death of Others**
> "Separation from and loss of others and the relationships with them; repetition of an unpleasantly experienced dying of another; vicarious suffering and disintegration; retaliation by the deceased; being haunted by spirits of the dead; abandonment; and vulnerability."[23]

I suspect that nearly everyone who reads the above will automatically do some type of self-evaluation. I'm caught right with her first words, although it is not so much a ... well, maybe it *has been* a fear of not getting things done. Having The Rowan Tree Church able to survive well and to continue the work I began has been important to me. Having even admitted the concerns about death making of my life a metaphorical incomplete sentence, I think back over many years. My diagnosis of HIV nearly 30 years ago? At the time there were real concerns about my dying 'too soon,' as it were. As I study this paragraph it may be the appropriate time to mention that sometimes I have wondered if it might not have been some odd concern about my own death which kept me from finishing this book.

A more objective perspective reminds me that I have often said - and with complete and genuine conviction, that many of my books which will be unwritten at my passing may well be penned (typed?) by my students after my body has passed. The research is done and their education includes many aspects of writing skills.

During one of my major research endeavors in 1993-94, I came across the following. From Koestenbaum's first four words - *we cannot escape death* - this is a wonderful list of concepts for reflection, for thought, and for changing one's attitudes:

"The ten salutary consequences of death are summarized below:

"1. We cannot escape death real or symbolic. We must construct our lives - daily actions as well as major plans - with the full and clear realization of this fact. We must accept, once and for all, without any reservations, misgivings, false hopes, repressions, or bitterness, the fact that we have been condemned to death. Then we can start living. By accepting this death we will neutralize an otherwise completely demoralizing and paralyzing fear.

"2. Once we have recognized and admitted the inevitability of death, we are on the way to becoming courageous, fearless, and decisive. Whenever indecision or lack of courage is felt, we must remind ourselves that life will end for us and that the symbolic threat of death, often the cause of our indecision, will disappear because its basic fraudulence will have been made manifest.

"3. By remembering the certainty and the finality of life, we immediately see the urgency of concentrating on essentials. We cut red tape, abandon excuses and procrastinations, and do not indulge in the luxury of wasting time.

"4. Only through the constant awareness of death will we achieve integrity and consistency with our principles. Basically there is no threat other than real or symbolic death. Once we have accepted this threat we will be well beyond fraudulent bribes and threats alike.

"5. Those who know they will die waste no time in attacking the problem of finding meaning and fulfillment in life. The pressure of the thought of death is a persistent, nagging, and most effective reminder that we are coerced to make some sense of life, and that we must do it now. Those who have faced death adopt a no-nonsense approach to the business of living successfully.

"6. Death makes it almost impossible to repress unpleasant but important realities. Death makes us honest and unable to accept excuses to postpone dealing with basic problems or to hide from ourselves and the reality of life.

"7. The realization of death-of-ourselves leads to strength. To be strong means not to be intimidated by real or symbolic death.

"8. To accept death means to take charge of our lives. Those who do are no fatalists; we do not feel strictured; we are the freest of anyone, with nothing holding us back but our own decisions. We have nothing to fear, nothing to be timid about, nothing to make us feel dependent, inadequate, or inferior, since we have conquered the ultimate threat.

"9. The thought of death urges us to assume a total plan for life. Through the vitality of death we are able to see all events in life from the perspective of total existence. This enables us to perform tasks that otherwise might be boring, discouraging, or senseless.

"10. The thought of death enables us to laugh off vicissitudes, pain, defeat, and disappointments. To take these too seriously suggests that we still harbor the hope that death may not be real after all and that perhaps we were meant to be immortal but have somehow missed our chance."[24]

There has been in the world around me, at least in our western societies, throughout most my of my life, a disconnect with dying. In an earlier era, rare would have been the young adult who had not already spent time in a family parlor where a family member was laid out for the duration of the mourning period, visitation, and all the various things and rituals one might do in letting go and being respectful.

Prior to the 20th century, when Houlbrooke wrote, "death was much more obviously the companion of life than it is today, because infections and working conditions killed so many more people before they reached old age."[25]

It may be that, during those centuries when a wake (literally, a *watch*) was held for the deceased in the family home, that daily life, even sharing the rug or cleaning the windows in this same room, part of the family home, means that we no longer needed that servant, reminding us of death.

Life, itself, did that for us.

⊙⊙

"In Egypt, death could only be greeted as a friend."[26]

Chapter 3 - Memento Mori: If I should die before I wake

Notes for Chapter Three

[18] *The Tibetan Book of the Dead*, compiled and edited by W.Y. Evans-Wentz Oxford University Press © 1960; preface to the paperback edition, W.Y. Evans-Wentz, page v

[19] *A Hallowmas Eve Journey*, from the sacred texts of The Tradition of Lothloriën, Rev. Paul V. Beyerl, © 2005

[20] http://en.wikipedia.org/wiki/Memento_mori - 1 i 2010 ce

[21] http://en.wikipedia.org/wiki/Memento_mori - 1 i 2010 ce

[22] http://en.wikipedia.org/wiki/Memento_mori - 1 i 2010 ce

[23] "Death and Dying Are Not and Should Not be Taboo Topics" by Therese A. Rando, *Principles of Thanatology*, ed. Kutscher, Carr and Kutscher, Columbia University Press © 1987 page 37

[24] *Principles of Thanatology*, ed. Kutscher, Carr and Kutscher, Columbia University Press © 1987; from Koestenbaum 1971: 269-271; in *Principles of Thanatology*, pages 59-60

[25] Houlbrooke, Ralph, ed., *Death, Ritual, and Bereavement*, Routledge in association with the Social History Society of the United Kingdom, London, New York © 1989, page 1

[26] Rev. Norman MacDonald, *The After-Life in Celtic and Oriental Folklore*, pub. 1970 by the author in Cachan Locheport, page 13

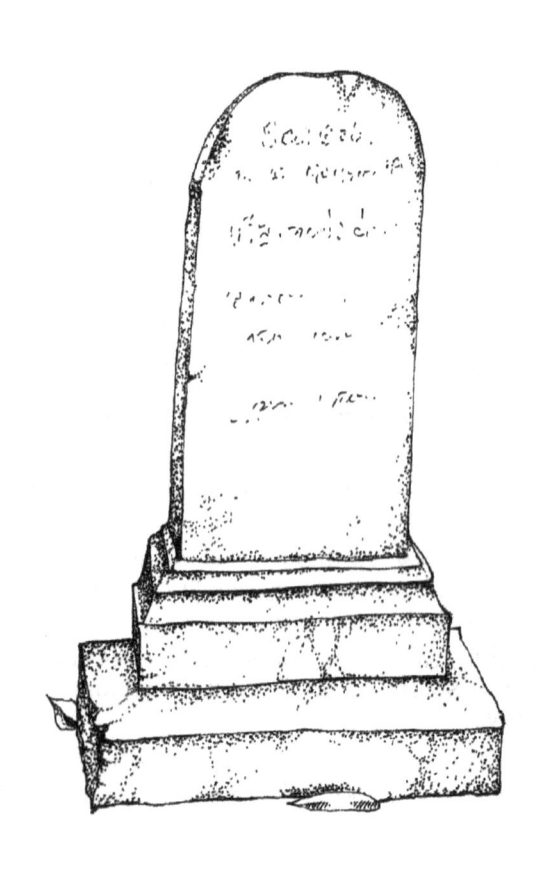

Chapter 4 - What is the Soul?

Let there be light.

Do we have souls?

When I wondered if some cultures might have defined death as the separation of the soul or spirit from the body that question, of course, implies there being a belief in a soul. When did our species begin to believe that there was a soul or a spirit, something which was connected with the body but was yet separate from the body, an essence which might endure the body's death?

> "French philosopher René Descartes offered the viewpoint that is dominant in the Western world today. He felt that the body was a machine composed of bones, blood, muscles, nerves, and skin and controlled by the brain. The soul, according to Descartes, was something only found in human beings and not in animals. It couldn't be divided into parts the way Plato said it could. It was unique, immaterial, and immortal. this theory was called dualism."[27]

While Descartes' theories may have influenced a great many schools of thought, I take issue with his statement of it not applying to animals. When I think about other species, there are some which clearly seem to seek the essence of that being, who have an understanding that the personality of being is separate from the body which dies. I am thinking of elephants, as I write this, but I would believe that whales and other higher order mammals also have a sense of these differences. I have seen cats and dogs interact with the dead body of one of their kin or pack and the dead body does not console them. They exhibit a sense of loss, and often call out for their lost loved one, not all that different from humans.

> "We cannot survey the whole range of after-life beliefs without noting that animals, too, have souls, and even plants.

They are of just the same sort as those of human kind and there is thought to be just as much reason to assume them."[28]

The belief in our having souls or there being spirit in addition to flesh dates back to times earlier than human records. Do I believe that there is this spiritual aspect and life to our being? How can I believe otherwise? During the years of my most intense disciplinary studies, which included a requirement to achieve an out-of-body projection at will, the experiences showed me that we do exist in conjunction with yet separate from our bodies. What is a visual perception through the physical organs of our bodies is, when purely sprit, the perception of light.

During those same years I also experienced what are often called *past* lives. But wait... out of body experiences, past lives, reincarnation, going toward the light, reunion with one's loved ones? Even ascending to heaven or descending into hell and despair ... all of these are ideas dependent upon the belief, the *experience*, that there is something which exists beyond the body's demise. If everything came to a complete halt at the body's demise, I do not believe that the belief in a soul, or after-life, could have existed for all of these millenia.

The Soul or Spirit

From a completely pragmatic point of view, all of these discussions regarding death are completely unnecessary if, at the corporeal body's demise there is ... nothing. Nothing at all. So much of a complete termination of everything that those who experience near death would experience only ... nothing ... and there would be no experiences, whether spiritual or real or mystical which would lead anyone to suggest otherwise. For me to write about 'death and dying' I must address the topic of the *soul*.

One of the teachings of my childhood religion was that I had a *soul*. I no longer remember what I was taught about this soul, save for one image which I will refer to later. I have a very faint recollection, filtered through decades of adulthood and vast research into other religions (all of which means this recollection is not to be trusted) of it being, metaphorically, a piece of god. I had been taught that god was *everywhere*, and that meant god was within *me* as well. This was pretty heady stuff for a boy only five or six years old. The 'god is everywhere' part made great sense to me, perhaps even more than it seemed to mean to those Roman Catholics who guided me through the memorization of the questions and rote answers from the *Baltimore Catechism*.

I believe it was when I was in the upper grades of elementary school at Saint Mary's in Colby, Wisconsin, that I was introduced to a complex concept. This is another of those which I think the typical Roman Catholic lay person does not often grasp. This concept has to do with *hell*. As a statement, it was grammatically very simple: 'hell is the absence of god.' Now *this* is a profound and challenging concept, one far beyond my intellectual abilities, for I was far more concerned about my milk bottle.

My *what* you ask? In my early years our instruction book had a visual representation of one's soul using a metaphor. Yes, the milk bottle. When we were obedient and followed all of the rules one's soul was like a bottle of milk, pure and white. When one was sinful (woe is me for I could not keep my hands away from my erogenous tissue at that age) that pristine clear bottle full of white purity now had dark spots: visible evil! Alas, my milk bottle was not one I'd want others to see. This, however, is about the existence and nature of the soul and not about this author's adherence to some religion's morality.

Back in 1973 I think it was, in a late-night discussion with a young coworker and a friend of his, one of them asked me what I believed in. I had no idea that my years as a *profound agnostic* meant that my separation from orthodox Christianity had been liberating and, in fact, my growth had included significant gestation of concepts of which I had not yet been fully aware. Speaking of one of Einstein's lawa of thermodynamics, $E = mc^2$, I took the concept of our physical and conscious self having a counterpart which was energy. The body was the *matter* and the energy would be the soul or spirit. I posited that Einstein's theory could be applied to having a spirit, and was able to extrapolate all manner of theory, from reincarnation to god being everywhere and ghosts, apparitions, psychic abilities such as I had experienced since birth, and nearly all paranormal phenomena.

I had stumbled through the doors of awareness and taken the first micro-movement toward enlightenment. It was also near this time that Kirlian photography was being co-opted by the publication of various books on the paranormal which were motivated by the coming out of astronaut Edgar D. Mitchell[29] and reports of the Soviet Union exploring the paranormal to see if these occult abilities might be somehow used to tip the scales in their favor against their arch-enemy, the United States, whose puritanical Christian beliefs left the populace far too uncomfortable with any aspect of the metaphysical realm.

Now that I could reconcile the existence of the soul with my paranormal past and accept the Christian paradigm as just that, not as what was a required essential truth for *me*, all manner of spiritual belief became possible. I could believe and acknowledge my energy self and accept the reality of a soul or spirit, but I no longer had to face a milk bottle.

Working from my personal paradigm of the soul representing the *energy field* of the body, there is then a measurable field, one which can be detected and measured with contemporary scientific and medical equipment. Having had near-death and out-of-body experiences, I am unable to *not* believe that the soul is energy which also represents awareness. It can feel a type of ecstasy at how ... how incredible one's experience of reality is when we are no longer connected to the physical body, It is able to feel remorse, to feel anticipation, to learn and to grow and to experience. Those states of being I have experienced when I am unencumbered with a corporeal body are, to me, the very philosophical substance of which I had read over years of studying religions, particularly those which accept mysticism, from Western (often within Roman Catholicism) to many Eastern religions.

Living with one's soul

While it seems appropriate, if not essential, to address some of the issues we face in living *with* a soul, I have reflected upon this concept and there does not seem (to me) to be all that much time and literature devoted to this topic. So much of what comes to mind has to do with the consequences of our obedience to a particular system of morality. In Christianity, for example, sinning imperils the soul.

Chapter 4 - What is the Soul? Let there be light.

I recall many discussions which were about adherence to the beliefs and codes of ethics. There were numerous admonishments to avoid stepping off the paths of temptation and indulging in pleasures of the flesh which were proscribed, or violating the social order with behavior that would also be criminal: murder, rape, theft, assault, and the like. There were many references to one's *conscience*. Is that part of one's soul? Does the soul evaluate our behavior or is it a reflection of one's self, for good or for bad (milk bottles aside).

I am writing about death and dying. One of the books which most influenced me and set me upon my path was *The Tibetan Book of the Dead*. When I read that Aldous Huxley had read this book and was profoundly affected by it, I brought it home for my library and began reading. I have read the book, the Evans-Wentz edition, numerous times, and studied the text in detail on several occasions.

Walter Yeeling Evans-Wentz (Feb, 2, 1878 - July 17, 1965), was a pioneer in bringing Tibetan Buddhism to the West. In his introduction to this book he writes that "... the Art of Dying is quite as important as the Art of Living..."[30] Discussions of one's soul seem far more connected with what happens to the soul upon the body's death. To paraphrase Evans-Wentz, we can also remind ourselves that the art of *living* is also of equal import. Today one face of this belief is found in the folk maxim about living each day as if it is your last.

Is the soul, then, an intangible counterpart to one's real-world self? "The soul has been widely defined throughout history. Some societies have believed that the soul represents the highest of human thought, and therefore, it is most abstract and difficult to define. Others have believed that the soul represents the source of life itself, while others have considered the soul only to be the source of afterlife."[31]

In my own vocabulary, I would describe the soul as one's astral self. Within the context of my personal religious belief, I hold little difference between the two, and yet there is no clear and finite definition. The soul is widely perceived as nebulous and other-worldly. Addison writes that "Everywhere we find the soul regarded as a kind of airy, filmy double of the body."[32] Addison also writes that, "For mankind at large, then, the soul is a breath-like image of the man himself - a duplicate, thin and vaporous. (His footnote: Usually it is life-size, but in most of Bantu Africa and in parts of Malaya and elsewhere it is only a tiny miniature.)"[33]

Going back to my theological roots, if 'god is everywhere,' then my soul is permeated with god. If I think of my soul as being my *astral* self, then I see threads woven from the same fabric, and it is about light. The word astral means star-like. Addison notes "...the widespread belief that associates meteors or falling stars with the souls of the dead."[34] With humility I read Carl Jung's statement that "the soul [or, as here, one's own consciousness] is assuredly not small, but the radiant Godhead itself. The West finds this statement either very dangerous, if not downright blasphemous, or else accepts it unthinkingly and then suffers from a theosophical inflation."[35]

Living with one's soul, then, becomes a matter of studying those techniques and disciplines which further one's daily life, mindful that we are at one with divinity. We discover the truth that living up to one's Highest Ideals - through the pursuit of the light of wisdom - kindles internal joy. We discover that cherishing one's inner light and providing it with safe and sacred space, no matter where we take our bodies, brings us a religious, spiritual life while being able to fully embrace the world in which we are incarnate. In other words, we will find greater joy and fulfillment if we live each day, not only as if it is our last chance to enjoy life and make it count, but for many of us every day is an opportunity to be mindful that we **are**, to varying degrees, at one with divinity. It is simply a matter of remembering throughout the day that we are filled with divinity (if it were that simple!).

My view of the Evans-Wentz version of *The Tibetan Book of the Dead* is of a stunning ritual, overlaid with the deities and symbols within the archaeology of their cosmology. It was deeply meaningful for me and, having spent a number of years studying Wicca and learning how to live as a Wiccan Priest, upon returning to again reread the text I was stunned to now realize that the ritual form had many similarities to contemporary Wicca. One aspect of this Buddhist belief which was far different than my own world view is that the, well, *liturgy* reads as ritual phrases to aid someone who wishes attain liberation and to avoid reincarnation. It is reflective of this quotation: "The body can be only a burden to the heaven-born spirit; life in the body is therefore a living death; and death is 'the door of freedom' for the soul."[36]

On one of the many times I returned to this text I found a gem in this text which indicated that one would read and practice this ritual throughout their life, thus at their death they would know it and the reading of it by the living would quite readily guide them forward. For years I believed this true and made frequent reference to this for I thought it a key element in preparing for one's death. In the past few years, however, I've scanned the book (*not* reading it line-by-line I ought note) and can not find this reference. I am not done looking but will not have time to reread my worn Evans-Wentz until this book is in print.

Dying with one's soul

Returning for a moment to my earlier Einstein reference, if the soul is energy, then it should be (very) long-lasting. However, if I thought I had a novel idea, or was an intelligent being referencing Einstein for my late night dissertation, some 2500 years earlier, "Democritus, a fifth-century BC Greek philosopher, felt that life was sustained by 'psychic atoms' that were spread throughout the body but were controlled by the brain, which contained 'the bonds of the soul."[37] Democritus, I didn't know you, but you were a stellar student of Leucippus, one of the first to postulate an atomic theory for the existence of the Universe.

The Laws of Thermodynamics indicate, however, that some energy would conceivably be lost each time it is transformed, but then perhaps we have ways to recharge and empower ourselves during an incarnation. Without some ability of that nature, reincarnation would be a process of diminishing returns. Whether or not the soul is immortal seems open to a wild diversity of opinion. Those of us who believe in reincarnation tend toward at least some degree of immortality, at least surviving for a very long period of time and many incarnations before being assimilated into the most Divine state of being.

Chapter 4 - What is the Soul? Let there be light.

If one's soul is part of a universal fabric of divinity, would it not then have qualities of immortality? I remember being taught that 'god is immortal.' God always was and always will be. Really now, a child cannot even grasp the nature of waiting a *year* for something or the nature of time passing between now and one's next birthday. How ever would we begin to comprehend the nature of immortality, or of infinity?

A different perspective on these topics comes from McDonald, who wrote that "both god and man had something to do with inculcating a belief in immortality. God gave a revelation of the afterlife to almost every race, a revelation which suited that particular race's circumstances, light and progress in culture and knowledge."[38] It seems to suit humans well if their gods are immortal and if they, the gods, can exist for all time (infinity).

I cannot prove, using the scientific method, that there is coherent and cohesive energy which survives the body's death. My casual review of my mental files suggests that all religions believe that something of us lasts beyond the body's death. And there are many who have experienced one form of near death or another and perhaps even more who have found themselves separated from their body during surgery or some intense life experience, each of whom seems to come away firmly believing that the death of the body is *not* the end of everything.

When completely separated from my body, what I am and what I have is ... is something I do not wish to sacrifice through a death which is traumatic, which has terror, which has intolerable pain or fear. Is it asking too much to wish to die, to have my *body* die, on my own terms?

There are many reports suggesting that, indeed, the soul does rise up from the dying body. I do not recall (I wonder why not?) any stories of the soul or spirit leaving a dying body and sinking downward. Perhaps it's just not visible if the dead body is blocking the view?

The religions and myths of most people do not have all souls and spirits ascending upward after death. The soul is rarely thought of as being stuck with the body, slowly disappearing as the body decays:

"Seldom are the souls of the dead regarded as confined to their place of burial."[39] Most desirable is the option that one's *own* soul would ascend, ultimately entering the realms of the gods.[40]

The average person, in particularly those of the modern Christian persuasions, wish to believe that their loved one would, at the death of her body, ascend heavenward.

The pitcher of god

Breath and divinity are very connected, just as breath and soul are divinity and soul. During the years of my transition from profound agnostic to acquiring a deep and life-changing understanding of the spiritual nature of existence, one of the books which moved and informed me was by B.K.S. Iyengar, an extraordinary man who is credited as one of the primary teachers who brought yoga into global consciousness. I was deeply moved as I studied the word prāna.

Learning to play the flute in late elementary school, I had much to learn about breathing, about taking long, deep breaths to utilize the full capacity of my lungs. This proved to be a solid foundation when I attempted to learn yoga from a book. I did well with the intellectual growth but failed miserably attempting to use this book as a role model for actual yoga.

In yoga, prāna "means breath, respiration, life, vitality, wind, energy, or strength. It also connotes the soul as opposed to the body."[41] The very thought that breathing offered me the potential of unification with deity and that it would be central both to living and dying, that one aspect of my goal, then, of working toward enlightenment was to live as a *kumbha*, or pitcher.

"What is obviously lacking, what plainly went forth at the moment of death, is the *breath*."[42] Many believe the soul or spirit has a deep connection with deity.

Was it simply a matter of the cessation of breathing being the most obvious to early humans? Breath, even speech, is often closely woven into the concept of soul. Certainly spirit is also connected with speech. Place your hand in front of your mouth as you read these sentences. To emit sound is to emit air. When your body is no longer able to emit air, it would seem that breath or spirit or soul has gone elsewhere.

As John the follower of Jesus wrote, "In the beginning was the Word, and the Word was with God, and the Word was God."[43] For most of my adult life I've associated this word with the force which brings the Universe (as we know it) into being.

Souls of the world

In researching different ways in which people have thought of the soul, I found some fascinating perspectives. Western thought can be traced back to the early Greek thinkers. They are often described as very independent and unlikely to accept another's beliefs. This changed with Plato. His concepts were so profound that concepts of the soul in the West were never again the same. Plato is a name known to nearly all, and yet his actual written works seem to be of interest only to classicists and those in graduate schools. Plato was born in 423 (or 424?) in Greece. The archetype of the Greek philosopher, Plato was a student of Socrates and founded the Academy in Athens. Many learned people consider Plato one of the most senior and important figures in Western thought. "Plato theorized that the soul had three parts - intellectual, irascible, and sexual - but only the first aspect had the virtue of immortality."[44] Certainly the latter two are more of the animal nature rather than the transcendent. "Plato was the first to achieve in philosophy the conception of the soul as pure immaterial essence, invisible and eternal. According to him the soul does not come into existence with the body. It has always existed. When a human life begins the soul is drawn down from its high spiritual state and enclosed in the body. There it remains an exile in captivity. 'The soul,' he says, 'is enshrined in that living tomb which we carry about, now that we are imprisoned in the body, like an oyster in his shell.' As he tells us elsewhere, 'The soul is in the very likeness of the divine and immortal and intellectual and uniform and indissoluble and unchangeable; and... the body is in the very likeness of the human and mortal and unintellectual and multiform and dissoluble and changeable.'"[45]

Plato's concept of the soul was prominent in Greek thought for several centurie until Galen (129-200), prominent Roman (by citizenship, Greek by birth) further evolved this concept. "Galen - the first-century Greek physician, agreed with Plato, but went further. he divided the soul into several functions. All of our motor and sensory abilities were attributed to the soul as were 'rational' functions such as imagination, reason, and memory"[46] In Galen's view, we can see that the souls ability to hold power and be a determining factor in the individual's life became the foundation for Western thought.

As the pre-eminent Western religion for a very long time and, until after the Reformation and subsequent splintering of Christianity into beliefs which could not be fit into the same room (and often do not wish to be in the same country), the following underscores my statement regarding Galen's views:

"The Catholic Church appropriated and developed Galen's concept of the soul, even offering opinions as to where the various functions were located in the brain. There the issue rested for almost fifteen hundred years, researchers and philosophers keeping their opinions to themselves regarding the soul lest they offend the doctrines of the church."[47]

The concept of *soul* is not limited to the west, however. And, as Dr. Melvin Morse writes in his stunning book based upon what he had experienced in his work with children who had near-death experiences, "Again and again in human speech the soul and the shadow are connected."[48]

"The Hurons thought that there were two souls... The early Chinese belief was in two souls, a light one which went on high and a dark one which lived in the grave; ... The Dakota Indians had four souls."[49] Perhaps, as a lad, had I multiple souls, one could have remained spotless and angelic while the others could have wallowed in my pleasures! I apologize to these Peoples, however, meaning no disrespect. It was a Sioux tribal elder who conducted our Handfasting Ceremony and I and the Lakota man have been in ceremony together on a number of occasions.

Those who check the bibliography would see James Thayer Addison (1887-1931). I cannot find much information on Mr. Addison. He was a scholar, on the faculty of the Episcopal Theological School in Cambridge, Massachusetts. His work, *Chinese Ancestor Worship*, indicates that he was living in Tokyo when that work was published in 1925. I have only that paper (found online as I made my 2012-2013 progress with this manuscript) and his book, *Life Beyond Death in The Beliefs of Mankind*. His bibliography for this work is huge: fifteen pages ordered by country.

Addison's vast research of the day led him to make this statement: "The belief that the soul of man survives his death is so nearly universal that we have no reliable record of a tribe or nation or religion in which it does not prevail."[50]

> "The natives of West Australia and of Java have the same word for breath and soul, and in most of the languages of our North American Indians, the word for soul is allied to those for air or wind or breath. In Sanskrit *atman* means both soul and breath. A like history lies behind the Hebrew word for soul - *nephesh*. The *nephesh* was the vital breath residing in the blood or in the heart, and contrasted with the body or 'the flesh.' Of similar meaning is the Arabic *nafs*, the breath or principle of life which escapes at death. More familiar to us is the Latin word *anima*. Whenever we say 'animate' or 'inanimate,' we are using the Roman word for soul, but it never lost its first meaning of breath or wind, like the Greek words *pneuma* and *psyche*."[51]

These concepts, that of the soul being *light* and that of the soul having this strong connection with *breath* and as well with speech, with one's word. When the body is no more, speech cannot be formed for speech requires vocal chords. And yet, when I am not with my body, I do have words, and I have light. And my light is not unconnected with all about me, which also radiates light.

❦

> "... An important lesson from these teachings, or at least in appreciating the greatness of the *Bardo*

Chapter 4 - What is the Soul? Let there be light.

Thödol, which vouchsafes to the dead man the ultimate and highest truth, that even the gods are the radiance and reflection of our own souls."[52]

Notes for Chapter Four

[27] Morse, Melvin M.D., *Closer To The Light*, Ivy Books, New York, © 1990, pages 109-110

[28] James Thayer Addison, *Life Beyond Death In the Beliefs of Mankind*, Houghton Mifflin Co., © 1932, page 7

[29] Mitchell's book *Psychic Exploration*, G., page Putnam's Sons, New York © 1974 was published right at this time and provided me with validation of my field of interest and believe in psychic possibilities.

[30] *The Tibetan Book of the Dead*, compiled and edited by W.Y. Evans-Wentz Oxford University Press © 1960; preface to the second edition, W.Y. Evans-Wentz, page xiii

[31] Morse, Melvin M.D., *Closer To The Light*, Ivy Books, New York, © 1990, page 109

[32] James Thayer Addison, *Life Beyond Death In the Beliefs of Mankind*, Houghton Mifflin Co., © 1932, page 3

[33] James Thayer Addison, *Life Beyond Death In the Beliefs of Mankind*, Houghton Mifflin Co., © 1932, page 6

[34] James Thayer Addison, *Life Beyond Death In the Beliefs of Mankind*, Houghton Mifflin Co., © 1932, page 70

[35] Psychological Commentary by Dr. D. G. Jung, *The Tibetan Book of the Dead*, compiled and edited by W.Y. Evans-Wentz Oxford University Press © 1960; page xxxix

[36] James Thayer Addison, *Life Beyond Death In the Beliefs of Mankind*, Houghton Mifflin Co., © 1932, page 109

[37] Morse, Melvin M.D., *Closer To The Light*, Ivy Books, New York, © 1990, page 109

Chapter 4 - What is the Soul? Let there be light.

[38] Rev. Norman MacDonald, *The After-Life in Celtic and Oriental Folklore*, pub. 1970 by the author in Cachan Locheport, page 6

[39] James Thayer Addison, *Life Beyond Death In the Beliefs of Mankind*, Houghton Mifflin Co., © 1932, page 12

[40] This would be an appropriate place to acknowledge that there are many pantheons which have "realms of the gods" found in the underworld as well, and that it is not always a location one might wish for an eternal habitat!

[41] *Light on Yoga*, B.K.S. Iyengar, Schocken Books, New York sixth printing 1974

[42] James Thayer Addison, *Life Beyond Death In the Beliefs of Mankind*, Houghton Mifflin Co., © 1932, page 4

[43] The Gospel According to John, *Holy Bible: Revised Standard Version*, second edition 1971, Collins World, Cleveland

[44] Morse, Melvin M.D., *Closer To The Light*, Ivy Books, New York, © 1990, page 109

[45] James Thayer Addison, *Life Beyond Death In the Beliefs of Mankind*, Houghton Mifflin Co., © 1932, page 111

[46] Morse, Melvin M.D., *Closer To The Light*, Ivy Books, New York, © 1990, page 109

[47] Morse, Melvin M.D., *Closer To The Light*, Ivy Books, New York, © 1990, page 109

[48] James Thayer Addison, *Life Beyond Death In the Beliefs of Mankind*, Houghton Mifflin Co., © 1932, page 4

[49] James Thayer Addison, *Life Beyond Death In the Beliefs of Mankind*, Houghton Mifflin Co., © 1932, pages 8-9

[50] James Thayer Addison, *Life Beyond Death In the Beliefs of Mankind*, Houghton Mifflin Co., © 1932, page 3

[51] James Thayer Addison, *Life Beyond Death In the Beliefs of Mankind*, Houghton Mifflin Co., © 1932, page 4

[52] Psychological Commentary by Dr. D. G. Jung, *The Tibetan Book of the Dead*, compiled and edited by W.Y. Evans-Wentz Oxford University Press © 1960; page xxxix

Chapter 5 - Burial and Cremation:

What do we do with the body?

Letting Go

I am appreciative to have been reared in a family which had a healthy interest in cemeteries. For many years one of my first explorations in a new city would be of its cemeteries. I found a couple of early settler-era, abandoned rural cemeteries in the farmlands of the upper midwest, overgrown with grasses and weeds. Those touched me the most, the graves ignored, forgotten, unkempt. What a comfortable place to be. But I also loved the old, urban cemeteries, with their winding drives. Later in this book I'll share some information I discovered about how that park-like style of cemetery came into being.

The ways in which a culture tends to the body of the deceased may take a variety of approaches. There are so many customs, so many religious beliefs. The rituals associated with the tending of the body are, to me, fascinating. Death is such a dramatic, difficult event for so many. Modern culture brings us images of family members wailing, keening, tearing at their clothing. Family albums hold photos of an earlier generation of those still alive wearing black, comporting themselves with the greatest solemnity, avoiding any sense of levity of faith in the continuity of life. In religion and in literature, death is *dramatic*. Indeed, *Death in Venice*, *Death of a Salesman*, *Deathtrap*, *Death Takes A Holiday* have *death* in their title but oh, the numbers of great, tragic plays in which the death of a character is central to the plot. Would *Romeo and Juliet* have the power it does if, well, Romeo made her quickly drink some Ipecac and, as Juliet vomits, coughing into the wastebasket, we know they will live, happily ever after?

How do we process death as an event? Among the tool box of our instinctive behavior is that quality which leads us to daily believe that everything will always be just fine. Had our species been dominated (genetically) by the great pessimists of humankind, I doubt that we would have survived.

"In *Elements of Social Organization*, Firth (1964:63) observes... that the funeral provides three elements to the living. The first element is the resolution of uncertainties in the behavior of the immediate kin. The funeral provides relatives with an opportunity to display their grief publicly and establishes a period of time for mourning. As such, it is a ritual of closure that also links our understanding of death at the psychological and societal level.

"The second element is the fulfillment of social consequence. This means that the ceremony helps to reinforce the appropriate attitudes of the members of society to each other. Although it focuses on the dead person, the funeral points out the value of the services of the living. Once again, societal and individual comprehensions of death are reflected in everyday ritualistic practices.

"The third element is the economic aspect. Firth explains that every funeral involves the expenditure of money, goods, and services. In this sense, the exchange process is important to the bereaved on a tangible social and economic level. Bereaved people may feel the need to make restitution to the deceased by purchasing such nonabstract items as funeral feasts, funeral merchandise, religious services, and so forth."[53]

Over the years I have sought out information which provides information about attitudes and practices and rituals. One morning while working on this manuscript, a friend came by. We were talking about death in an offhand way, a conversation growing out of my having just undergone lumbar surgery with complete anesthesia the day before. A comment was made by one of us that we'd always found death fascinating. I think it was me, but it could have been either of us for we share a mutual interest in the topic. Jennie commented that she would love to travel the world and see the many, many customs first hand. It would take more than a lifetime and I joked that maybe we're doing just that, one incarnation at a time!

Chapter 5 - Burial and Cremation: What do we do with the body?

That conversation hints, however, at my challenge. There is so vast an amount of information and of diversity in practice and philosophy and in religious belief. There are a few common threads, but we are such a diverse species. We seem to have greater diversity within the human species than do any other species. And, if I take the life-by-life approach, then this book will never seem completion. It's already been nearly 30 years in the writing.

Tibet was the foundation of my exploration of world religions. In *The Tibetan Book of the Dead* it is written that

> "In Tibet itself all known religious methods of disposing of a corpse are in vogue; but, owing to lack of fuel for purposes of cremation, ordinarily the corpse, after having been carried to a hill-top or rocky eminence, is chopped to pieces and, much after the Parsee custom in Persia and Bombay, given to the birds and beasts of prey. If the corpse be that of a nobleman, whose family can well afford a funeral pyre, it may be cremated. In some remote districts earth burial is customary; and it is commonly employed everywhere when death has been caused by a very contagious and dangerous disease, like small-pox... Otherwise, Tibetans generally object to earth-burial, for they believe that when a corpse is interred the spirit of the deceased, upon seeing it, attempts to re-enter it..."[54]

Cultural customs and laws were already in place more than two millennia ago in the Roman world.

> "Various statutory regulations had to be complied with on all occasions of death and burial. Only when a pig had been sacrificed was a grave legally a grave. There were also a number of other acts to be performed by the family. On returning from the funeral the relatives had to undergo the *suffitio*, a rite of purification by fire and water. On the same day there began a period of cleansing ceremonies held at the deceased's house; and again on the same day a funerary feast, the *silicernium*, was eaten at the grave in honour of

the dead. There was also the *cena novendialis* eaten at the grave on the ninth day after the funeral, at the end of the period of full mourning, when a libation to the *Manes* was poured upon the actual burial."[55]

Grief and Sorrow

How different it is to discuss death, to talk about one's own death or the deaths of loved ones, when all who are present for the discussion share this view: *Death is fascinating.* In the late 1980s I was a regular guest speaker at the annual Harvest Moon Celebration held at Pierce College, organized by Lorraine Covenant. Around the time when I began this book I was quite enthusiastic and proposed a workshop on Death and Dying. It was rejected, the topic considered far too gloomy and morbid. I was incredulous. This was a conference bringing a variety of guest speakers and topics and I could not imagine that this was not relevant.

Being young and just a little prone to carrying my soapboxes with me, I wrote a vague proposal which was accepted and scheduled and then... I spoke about Death and Dying anyway. When I read passages from the Ritual for the Dead I had written, it was moving and emotional for everyone. All attending were struck with how beautiful the acknowledgement of a loved one's moving into Union with the Universe would be. Lorraine Covenant accepted my apology and we were all pleased.

Of course, death is one of the greatest mysteries. Only a small percentage of people are restored back to life following death: rescued when so near death that the body and soul were making peace with each other; or those who are already looking about the surgery chamber, aware of the ongoing events even as they can watch the surgical team in crisis mode, turning to tools (pharmaceutical, electrical, even the hands of the physician) to bring the body back to life, usually meaning a sudden, sometimes unpleasant, rush of the spirit back into the struggling body. And when the spirit or soul has left the body, the body is at peace. But those left behind are so often plunged into a deep sense of loss and grief.

Chapter 5 - Burial and Cremation: What do we do with the body?

One of the great attractions of the Christian religion is that Jesus has transcended death. Knowing that one's deity embraced the sacrificial death, and that the death of one's body meant being joined with Jesus and one's loved ones in heaven - a happy place I believe - should alleviate grief.

"In *The Elementary Forms of Religious Life*, Durkheim (1915:435) points out that funeral rites are ceremonies that designate a state of 'uneasiness or sadness.' From this perspective, death produces personal anxieties, which are addressed by the funeral, a ceremony that is indicative of a society's overall comprehension of death. In this sense, then funeral rites mirror a society's interpretation of life and death."[56] From my humorous perspective, there must be a great many religions in which union with Deity must be an unhappy and fearful event!

It is difficult to openly take the point that grief is about the living and not about the one who has passed over. Without wanting to offend anyone nor cause them pain by seeming to diminish the genuine grief they may be feeling, I still continue to counsel people to turn their emotions to growth and to letting go. The Beloved[57] would hopefully have not been the type of person to want those left behind to focus solely upon loss.

Arthur Carr wrote that:

"From the cultural perspective, we have the ideas of the anthropologists Bronislaw Malinowski and Raymond Firth. In *Magic, Science, and Religion*, Malinowski (1948:53) emphasizes that mourning behavior serves to demonstrate the emotions of the bereaved and the loss experienced by the whole group. The rituals of death reinforce as well as reflect the natural feelings of the survivors. Therefore, they help foster and enhance the way people comprehend death.

"In most societies, it is during the funeral ceremony that death reactions reflect our social outlook on life and death. Funeral rites provide bereaved people with a defined social role to help them pass through a period of adjustment following the death. The rites set boundaries on the period of mourning, assist the bereaved by providing the opportunity for the public expression of grief, and help in commemorating an individual's death."[58]

And what is grief?

"In 'Mourning and Melancholia,' Freud (1917:153) refers to grief as a 'painful' state of mind and locates it in terms of the 'economics of the mind.' By bringing in the concept of economics, Freud is able to identify grief as part of the psychological exchange process, with tasks and activities being carried out as 'labour' in exchange for a kind of psychic 'freedom' from the dead person.

"In this vein, Freud (1917:156-161) refers to 'the work of grief' as the need for the bereaved individual to become free from the attachments to the dead person, from the inhibitions of becoming a separate being, and from conflicts and ambivalence over the lost love relationship. Therefore, we comprehend 'the work of mourning' as a temporal process occurring over time."[59]

Rock ... Paper ... Fire?

At what stage in evolution did our ancestors begin to care about the bodies of their kin? We have little in the way of tangible answers. Humans have been placing bodies with intent and with ceremony, with items chosen to carry the body and its spirit beyond death since long before records were being kept, before language was being placed into clay and stone so that truly, the origins of these beliefs may always be a mystery.

Early animal life was a 'food-chain existence' as I like calling it. While today we remain part of the food chain (and by no means, are we at the top - that exalted station is for bacteria and viruses), we have choice. We have some degree of control over what we eat and how we obtain it. It its most carnal form, food chain existence is when a creature is not so fussy. The number of carnivorous and omnivorous species which will take sustenance from the carcass of a dead kin is vast.

Chapter 5 - Burial and Cremation: What do we do with the body?

For some species, including higher mammals, a point in time passed after which they cared for the deceased. I will suggest that some of our earliest options may have been:
1. walking away and abandoning the corpse to decompose, to be eaten by the scavenger species
2. moving the corpse to a more sheltered space, a cave, a crevice
3. adding stones to cover the body, providing some protection but also investing far more effort into the process. This begins to imply caring, the possibility of the deceased being more than compostable material or food for the local vermin.
4. having gained control over fire, *somehow* connecting the ability of enough fuel to consume the body, leaving only remains which might be compost, or might become objects to be carried with the tribe or clan
5. with the advent of tools of metal, digging became more of an option as would hewing timber to construct more elaborate pyres or raised platforms for what may be called *sky burial*

Of these, only the rock cairns would mark the location for future reference, allowing the family and loved ones to seek out the site and have some manner of connection with the memory or spirit of the deceased. It was inevitable that our species would begin to contemplate the meaning of death. As W. Y. Evans-Wentz wrote, "Inasmuch as all mankind must relinquish their fleshly bodies and experience death, it is supremely profitable that they should know how rightly to meet death when it comes."[60]

Just days before working further on this chapter I had a wonderful conversation with a young man who is seeking to further himself on his own journey. At one point he expressed a longing for life back in a time when people lived without technology, lived far more connected to the land. I hear this type of longing from many, usually with a romantic fantasy of living the good life in pre-industrial times. I recalling hearing it a *lot* when I participated in the Minnesota Renaissance Festival back in the 1970s (as a roaming astrologer). Paying guests and Renaissance folk alike would often express the wish that they could live in those times. I would think that I'd hear a medieval version with the folk who re-enact those events (in costume and armor) as well.

I think that many of those people wishing to live closer to the natural rhythms, free of the demands of contemporary life, forget that people of earlier times also lived much closer to death. Life was filled with the unbathed, with your neighbor's raw sewage (and your own), with tainted meat and food poisoning. Most of them would never have survived being born, or never have reached more than a few years of age. Women died in childbirth and most of us, as I like to joke, "would be eaten by the bears." I don't know why I pick on the bears. We could be eaten by wolves, by viruses, too weak or sick or infirm to walk and climb and carry, we'd be abandoned, eventually food for crows and rats.

Houlbrooke wrote, that, prior to the 20th century, "death was much more obviously the companion of life than it is today, because infections and working conditions killed so many more people before they reached old age."[61]

And yet, it is far more complicated than this. Once the belief in the body having a soul (a spiritual counterpart which in some manner endured beyond the body's death) was part of our species' consciousness, there were many new considerations. While burial continued to be far more for the living, there were also aspects of assisting the deceased's soul in achieving the spiritual goals desired by that culture.

> "The four Northern Buddhist methods of disposing of a corpse correspond to those mentioned in various of the sacred books of the Hindus: a human body is said to consist of four elements, - earth, water, air, and fire, - and it should be returned to these elements as quickly as possible. Cremation is considered the best method to adopt. Earth-burial, as among Christians also, is the returning of the body to the element Earth; water-burial is the returning of the body to the element Water, air-burial, to the element Air - the birds which devour the corpse being the denizens of the air; and fire-burial, or cremation, the returning of the body to the element Fire."[62]

Chapter 5 - Burial and Cremation: What do we do with the body?

Air

Just days before working on this element for ritual burial, I happened to hear local travel journalist, author and tour guide, Rick Steves, interviewing a photo journalist. The discussion was about travel today in Tibet and how it is both surviving and being repressed under China. When asked what the most memorable sight he had seen, he spoke about *sky burial*.

Sky burial is most associated with Tibet. Tibetan Buddhism believes in rebirth and, for that reason, the body is considered simply a container for the soul. It is considered credible and acceptable for the body to be placed in a a construction high in the mountains where the dead flesh might be eaten and carried up into the sky by birds. Quick online searching in Wikipedia indicates that one of the oldest known sites dates back more than 11,000 years ago.

"Sky burial or ritual dissection was once a common funerary practice in Tibet wherein a human corpse is cut into small pieces and placed on a mountaintop, exposing it to the elements or the mahabhuta and animals – especially to birds of prey. In Tibetan the practice is known as jhator (Tibetan: བྱ་གཏོར་; Wylie: bya gtor), which literally means, 'giving alms to the birds.'

"The majority of Tibetans adhere to Buddhism, which teaches reincarnation. There is no need to preserve the body, as it is now an empty vessel. Birds may eat it, or nature may let it decompose. So the function of the sky burial is simply the disposal of the remains. In much of Tibet the ground is too hard and rocky to dig a grave, and with fuel and timber scarce, a sky burial is often more practical than cremation.

"Additionally, since no fuel, land, or topsoil is consumed, this way of burial is arguably more ecologically friendly than cremation or interment."[63]

There is something visually eloquent and emotionally satisfying knowing one's body is returning to the element of Air. There is, in a manner which some might find very difficult to accept, a further element of air. In my religious tradition, the ritual blade is associated with the element of air. The process of dissection is a further connection with this element.

Tibet is not the only country to place the body at an elevation. There is evidence that some peoples would place the dead body in a tree, or construct a structure. Wikipedia describes this as "a burial tree or burial scaffold ... a tree or simple structure used for supporting corpses or coffins. They were once common among the Balinese, the Naga people, certain Australian Aborigines, and some North American groups."[64]

Fire

I don't know what it is about fire which seems so ... well ... clean and efficient. My mother vowed for decades that she wished to be cremated. On the one hand she felt it kinder to the pall bearers, having spent most of her adult life morbidly obese. On the other it went against the preferences of her religion. There are religions which teach that the body will be resurrected at some future time. In the end, she opted for embalming and burial by earth. I was disappointed. I cannot even remember why I thought cremation to be my personal ideal. I do know that it was not because of my mother's comments. As I've written, I very much enjoyed visiting graveyards. Being in a burial place seemed peaceful and calming. Facing a wall of nooks for small boxes and urns of cremated remains would be the same as would the catacombs with visible bones.

Two years later I'm editing and proofreading and wanted to add this note. Each year we set up an Ancestors' Altar as part of our Hallows Eve ceremony. Over the years we have small stone boxes, about 18 of them, now, each with perhaps a quarter cup of someone dear to us. Gerry's Mom and brother, my sister... and the rest are Initiates and Novices and Church Members. With the exception of the special altar, they reside on wall shelving in the north - our own wall of remembrance.

I could never understand why the Roman Catholic Church seemed so against cremation but, then, I was never a very good Catholic. The same sentiment is found in most Christian Churches, although some of the clergy did favor cremation. In the late nineteenth century, Leaney writes, "Although the issue of cremation and Christian tradition was an extremely contentious one, the teaching of the Synagogue and the Church, together with the example of the Patriarchs and the Saints, were seen to favour earth sepulture. Earth burial formed 'part of the unwritten code in which so many of the divine ordinances are implied rather than expressed.'[65] Cremation, moreover, was seen as militating against a belief in the resurrection."[66]

Leany continues, "The pro-cremationist Bishop Fraser was quick to respond to these allegations: 'Could they suppose that it would be more impossible for God to raise up a body at the resurrection, if needs be, out of elementary particles which had been liberated by the burning, than it would be to raise-up a body from dust, and from the bodies which had passed into the structure of worms?'[67]"[68] Bishop Fraser, I commend you and applaud even now.

As a child I was reading my mother's lighter fiction upon entering first grade and those books left me ever appreciative of clever repartee. I offer that bit of my background, for I'm unable to resist the next lines:

"The same response was put in a more succinct form by the Earl of Shaftesbury. 'What' he asked, 'would in such a case become of the blessed martyrs?'[69]"[70]

Water

Burial by water is, to me, a beautiful image. This is not to be confused with drowning for, by definition, this elemental approach has the premise that the body is dead, as do the other methods of burial described in this book. Burial by water is no more the same as dying by drowning, as death by conflagration would be the same as cremation.

The practice of burial by water ranges from putting an entire casket into the ocean to laying the deceased's body into a small boat and letting it drift out to sea. The former seems like wasteful littering and, unless the coffin is made of quality biodegradable materials, further pollution of the ocean occurs as well. Many who live the seafaring life opt to have a piece of sail used, the body wrapped in it and the fabric sewn closed. Someone who lives by the Sea, returns to the Sea. This method of burial may leave the more conservative religious mind pretty uncomfortable. My personal, opinionated views are skeptical that even the best embalming would keep a body whole as several centuries pass. Nor would I have any desire to have my soul or spirit returned to such a mess of what was once-living cells. Unless the body has been encapsulated by impermeable metal this brings us to another reality one which is similar to the body being taken away by raptors. I would think that burial in the sea or in a large lake would allow us to extend the gift of our bodies by rejoining the food chain, as is done in the Tibetan sky burial.

Many of the burials at sea were done expediently. Hauling a body for many days without adequate refrigeration is not something most could tolerate. Wouldn't that tempt someone to tout the virtues of cremation?

Fire and water are a combination which is increasingly popular. There are many, many cremated remains (today often called 'cremains') scattered from small airplanes, from ferries, from fishing boats... I would like to believe there have been times when someone paddled a canoe out to the midst of a lake to return the body to the favorite location of the Beloved.

Earth

"The worms crawl in, the worms crawl out..." I recall singing the *Hearse Song* which dates to WWI or earlier and is a classic in folk music, even without a known author. This may also have influenced the appeal of cremation in my mind although I only recall the song being light and humorous. I make the confession that the lack of fear or distaste for death graces me with the ability to see much humor in death and dying even though it would rarely be understood by others.

Burial in the earth is known as interment. I have long thought of this as a word likely derived from something akin to in-terre-ment, as in *within the earth*. The word dates to the 14th century and is thousands of years newer than the practice.

The discovery of an ancient corpse, found during an excavation, in a trench or pit, indicates that this was done on purpose. Were it accidental it would need be from a landslide, and there would be no lowered space into which the body had been placed. Although not accepted among all experts, some maintain that the oldest burials date to the Neanderthal. So early in our human history that the experts can only speculate and make educated guesses, ritual and ceremonial activities had to have taken place, based upon the skeletal posture, objects placed with it, and the like. These customs remain with us today. My mother kept her word to her father and placed a deck of poker cards in his pocket, and he had his many Marine and VFW awards pinned to his suit lapel.

Despite the placing of bodies back into the earth where the natural processes ought bring us back into our origins at a more molecular level, becoming One again with Nature, with the soil, perhaps becoming part of a tree... For reasons I can intellectually understand but with which I feel no kinship is the deep need many humans have to fight against the natural processes. Ah, to be laid in the soil seems so luxurious.

"So many are the peoples who have pictured for themselves an after life beneath the earth that we are not surprised to find the same details at widely different points. About the entrance to the underworld... there are several common beliefs. Most simple and familiar is the view that the grave is the portal... for it is plainly by that gate that the dead themselves have entered. Through the grave, therefore, the living can communicate with the dead. ...inseparable are the merging ideas of a grave home and a wider sphere below where all the dead are met."[71]

Spirit

The fifth classical element is spirit, the most nebulous. I am taking liberties with a stretch of meaning to finish out the classical elements by placing this topic under 'spirit.'

Having looked at the four traditional elements as a way of thinking of the body's disposal, what do you do when there *is* no body? This has been a problem for perhaps the entire history of human civilization. It is not uncommon for a people to be unable to recover all of the dead following a difficult battle or a major natural disaster. Today the recovery of war dead continues to be a significant aspect of diplomatic discussions. We continue to find occasional news stories of the recovery of a body from an early 20th century war.

Many families find it impossible to have a genuine sense of closure without the body and, although its soul or spirit may have been long gone for many decades, the body is still treated with great respect.

The Romans had a fascinating custom described here by Toynbee: "If a person's body was not available for burial, in such eventualities as drowning at sea or death in battle, a *cenotapjhium* was made to provide the soul with a dwelling-place, which it was invited to enter by being called upon by name three times."[72]

The dead, they are always with you

To *embalm* is to use natural substances or balms (herbs, essential oils, etc.) to keep the body from putrefaction, from decaying and beginning to smell. It must be connected with the desire so many have for immortality, to leave a 'legacy' behind, to leave their mark upon their followers. The techniques and skills of mummification in ancient Egypt were remarkable and continue to be a mystery which is not yet duplicated. Thousands of years ago they knew how to perform postmortem surgical techniques and understood how to combine molecular compounds, a science which would have needed a very long time to evolve. The Han dynasty in China also developed techniques with which to keep bodies from decay.

Much of this is based upon beliefs that the body must remain intact in order to again house the soul or spirit at a later time. Is this the basis for the popularity of embalming in Europe? It is believed that embalming had a return to popularity after the 15th or 16th centuries. A German scientist and chemist, August Wilhelm von Hofmann, is credited with the discovery of formaldehyde, which was an astounding way to preserve tissue. I can attest to that. Having dissected a frog for a school project, each organ appropriately labeled and stored in a test tube filled with formaldehyde for preservation, my fingerpads were oddly changed, enough that I could sense tissue preservation from experience.

[Of interest to those who belong to The Rowan Tree Church might be that von Hofmann was able to extract sorbic acid from rowan berries which could then be used to further preserve food.]

Mummification was not limited to Asia, however. I loved some material I found in *National Geographic Magazine* in an article on the role of mummies among the Inca. "Mummies were bound into bundles, which resulted in contorted poses but made them easier to carry."[73]

"The mummies of former rulers sit in the main plaza of Cusco for a symbolic sip of *chicha*, or corn beer, as the current ruler offers a toast from a ritual platform. In his role as host, the ruler served as an intermediary between the present and the past - represented by his deceased ancestors. Each royal mummy was dressed in his finery and carried here from his estate, which he continued to own even after death. This ceremony, held every August before planting season, drew people from the four corners of the empire."[74]

"Even after these [Incan] kings died, they remained the powers behind the throne. 'The ancestors were a key element of Andean life,' says Sonia Guillén, director of Peru's Museo Leymebamba. When Huayna Capac perished of a mysterious disease in Ecuador around 1527, retainers mummified his body and carried it back to Cusco. Members of the royal family frequently visited the deceased monarch, asking his advice on vital matters and heeding the replies given by an oracle sitting at his side. Years after his death, Huayna Capac remained the owner of Quispiguanca and the surrounding estate. Indeed, royal tradition dictated that its harvest keep his mummy, servants, wives, and descendants in style for eternity."[75]

The rise of embalming

The belief in embalming as the most desirable treatment of the body is something that I have never been able to relate to for I have no faith that what would remain in a casket exhumed four centuries later would be anything that my soul would want to embrace as a new body. I must also add, for the side of those not expressing their views in this paragraph, that something I heard within the last ten years in a study reported on Public Radio which indicated the percentages of people in the United States who believed that the rapture could happen in their lifetime. Despite having excellent search engine skills, I could not find the study so can only trust what I recall, having repeated it a number of times and am working on the assumption that the survey was credible. Indicating how prevalent the evangelical movement, the figure for those who believe it *will* happen in their lifetime was smaller, but the response for those who believe it *could* was just under half. The numbers for those who want their body to be ready and waiting is significant.

The concept of embalming came to western culture relatively recently. "Before 1880 most people viewed embalming only as a historical phenomenon, an exotic custom of the ancient Egyptians."[76] In fact, Farrell describes the negative views that the public held regarding this 'grotesque' and 'undesirable' process. Before the U. S. Civil War began in 1861, burial was relatively simple and uncomplicated. By the end of the Civil War in 1865, many events were in motion, from the relocation of numerous people who moved from one area in the United States to another, to former soldiers whose tour of duty took them elsewhere - *not* to return to their homes but to create new homes. Embalming became better known and more widely practiced during the war.

Within a short time, events as diverse as the shifting tides in Christian thought to the emergence of the professional funeral industry led to major changes in public opinion. The continuing trend begun with the Industrial Age led to more people living removed from the rural lives of their forebears. In that earlier time, when people held livestock and cared for them from birth to death, walking through cow dung or cleaning out a stall was simply work, and work of which one could be proud. In that earlier time families lived closer, often several generations in one household and children watched their elders die and then be laid out in the front parlor. All of this was simply life ... and death.

As the people began to more and more earn their income from

Chapter 5 - Burial and Cremation: What do we do with the body?

outside jobs rather than living off the land, they gained better education and more access even to the current cutting edge family medicine of the day. With the continued growth in human population, the burial places of the day did make the news, and not for their cleanliness and beauty.

I am theorizing in the previous paragraph and will sum that up with something I've been known to say now and then, often reflecting upon the prudishness of those in the U.S. when it comes to nudity, or to other social mores more accepted elsewhere. This country was founded by Puritans and is still puritanical. I raise this because it seems appropriate even for this following quotation:

> "The failure of improved burial practices to alleviate the disgust with decay shaped new responses to the troublesome confrontation with death. One response was that of embalming, a practice which, by the end of the [nineteenth] century, had gained almost universal acceptance in North America. The aim of embalming was to preserve the human corpse. The aim of the other response - cremation - was to destroy the corpse. Despite their different methods, both processes advocated human activity ... to dispel the aura of horror surrounding death."[77]

It was not solely the "disgust with decay" for certainly keeping one's deceased family member in the parlor for days would certainly change the household atmosphere. During warmer weather, ice played a major role until embalming took over.

> "Before the advent of embalming, undertakers tried to maintain the appearance of the body by using ice caskets. These 'corpse coolers' surrounded the body with ice or cold air and retarded the onset of putrefaction. ... Unwieldy and unsightly ... the body spoiled if the undertaker did not make frequent trips to the house to drain the casket and replenish the ice. American funeral directors therefor responded favorably to embalming... By 1890 embalming had replaced ice as the main method of preserving the appearance."[78]

Chapter 5 - Burial and Cremation: What do we do with the body?

Embalming: The Facts

I don't know how old I was when I went to the Field Museum in Chicago. I was maybe eleven or twelve. There, in large glass containers, were more than a dozen human fetuses ranging from very tiny to birth size. They looked pretty real. It was then that I learned about formaldehyde. Embalming does not rely solely upon formaldehyde but works with liquids which are a combination of ingredients. The following Wikipedia article describes the content with demographic information from 2007:

> "**Embalming chemicals** are a variety of preservatives, sanitising and disinfectant agents and additives used in modern embalming to temporarily prevent decomposition and restore a natural appearance for viewing a body after death. A mixture of these chemicals is known as **embalming fluid** and is used to preserve deceased (dead) individuals, sometimes only until the funeral, other times indefinitely. Typically embalming fluid contains a mixture of formaldehyde, methanol, and other solvents. The formaldehyde content generally ranges from 5 to 29 percent and the ethanol content may range from 9 to 56 percent. In the United States alone, about 20 million liters (roughly 5.3 million gallons) of embalming fluid are used every year."[79]

And when it comes to the actual procedures, there is a lot of myth. In fact, when I mentioned to a new student the information I was working on for this chapter, I heard another which was very removed from factual information. I could not express it any better, and will again turn to Wikipedia:

> "**Embalming**, in most modern cultures, is the art and science of temporarily preserving human remains (some may preserve for long-term) to forestall decomposition and to make them suitable for public display at a funeral. The three goals of embalming are thus sanitization, presentation and preservation (or restoration) of a corpse to achieve this effect. Embalming

has a very long and cross-cultural history, with many cultures giving the embalming processes a greater religious meaning. "The actual embalming process usually involves four parts:

1. Arterial embalming, which involves the injection of embalming chemicals into the blood vessels, usually via the right common carotid artery. Blood and interstitial fluids are displaced by this injection and, along with excess arterial solution, are expelled from the right jugular vein and collectively referred to as drainage. The embalming solution is injected with a centrifugal pump and the embalmer massages the body to break up circulatory clots as to ensure the proper distribution of the embalming fluid. This process of raising vessels with injection and drainage from a solitary location is known as a single-point injection. In cases of poor circulation of the arterial solution additional injection points (commonly the axillary, brachial or femoral arteries, with the ulnar, radial and tibial vessels if necessary) are used. The corresponding veins are commonly also raised and utilized for the purpose of drainage. Cases where more than one vessel is raised are referred to as multiple-point injection, with a reference to the number of vessels raised (i.e. a six-point injection or six-pointer). As a general rule, the more points needing to be raised, the greater the difficulty of the case. An injection utilizing both the left and right carotids is specifically referred to as a restricted cervical injection (RCI), while draining from a different site to injection (i.e. injecting arterial fluid into the right common carotid artery and draining from the right femoral vein) is referred to as a split (or sometimes cut) injection.
2. Cavity embalming refers to the replacement of internal fluids inside body cavities with embalming chemicals via the use of an aspirator and trocar. The embalmer makes a small incision just above the navel (two inches superior and two inches to the right) and pushes the trocar in the chest and stomach cavities to puncture the hollow organs

and aspirate their contents. He/she then fills the cavities with concentrated chemicals that contain formaldehyde. The incision is either sutured closed or a "trocar button" is secured into place.
3. Hypodermic embalming is a supplemental method which refers to the injection of embalming chemicals into tissue with a hypodermic needle and syringe, which is generally used as needed on a case by case basis to treat areas where arterial fluid has not been successfully distributed during the main arterial injection.
4. Surface embalming, another supplemental method, utilizes embalming chemical to preserve and restore areas directly on the skins surface and other superficial areas as well as areas of damage such as from accident, decomposition, cancerous growth or skin donation.

"A typical embalming takes several hours to complete. An embalming case that requires more attention or has unexpected complications could take substantially longer. The repair of an autopsy case or the restoration of a long-bone donor are two such examples.

"Embalming is meant to temporarily preserve the body of a deceased person. Regardless of whether embalming is performed, the type of burial or entombment, and the materials used – such as wood or metal caskets and vaults – the body of the deceased will eventually decompose. Modern embalming is done to delay decomposition so that funeral services may take place or for the purpose of shipping the remains to a distant place for disposition."[80]

It would seem that the original reasons for embalming combined with a rise in the religious belief that keeping the physical corpse intact was important for being resurrected in the future was promoted by the industry who did not wish to lose business to the cremation movement led to embalming becoming the dominant option in the twentieth century.

Cremation

During my years teaching in Minneapolis, my last home was a lovely duplex on Blaisdell Ave. South. During my time in that home, the *Cremation Society* opened up for business literally a block away (via a crow's flight). The neighbors were *not* thrilled and spoke about the crematorium in italics. Did you know that bits of burnt bodies and ash were landing around the neighborhood? And that you could see smoke coming out of the tall chimney when they were doing it? None of this proved true at all and, in fact, for a very modest lifetime fee I purchased a plan. Many years later, living here in Puget Sound, gerry and I now have a new prepaid plan. But the first time I handled and saw cremated remains?

A very dear friend of mine, Claude Zetty, was the music director at Trinity College in San Antonio, Texas. Claude, a striking, gentle man of considerable height, lost the fight against AIDS-related illnesses in April 1991. I flew to San Antonio as one of the clergy for the memorial service, meeting his three daughters for the very first time. The plan was to have lunch before driving to the college. Despite my years of being pro-cremation, and even having my plan, I was still unenlightened about the actual remains. I knew Claude was to have been cremated and, having had every bit as joyful a time with his lovely daughters as I would have had with Claude, I knew I was safe. I could ask my question.

As we walked across the restaurant parking lot to our cars, I realized that my question would not be unsettling at all. "Metta," I asked, "could I have a little of your Dad's ashes?"

With a cheery, affirmative response, she opened the trunk of her car and pulled out the white, cardboard box. "You can have more than a little," she said, her sisters laughing, "Daddy was a big man." Claude, although slender, was something like 6' 4" tall.

Since then I have seen cremated remains on many occasions. Those of us who embrace cremation as the preferred option may have difficulty with those who maintain embalming to be the best. What might be thought of as the modern cremation movement began during Victorian England according to some experts. In England there remained a reaction against the horrors of the earlier cemeteries. We tend to think of the Victorians, with their bodies hidden beneath so much clothing, as being a bit prudish, despite there being a major surge in births and population. Although cemeteries were becoming increasingly attractive, cremation was growing in popularity. As Leany saw it, "At the base of cremationist thought, and underlying the sanitary and economic motives for advocacy of this method of disposal, was a feeling of intense loathing for the physical remains of the dead. The appalling facts of water, worms, and putrefaction..."[81]

One more image of cremation which I must share with you comes from the beautiful and moving film, *The Emerald Forest*, directed and produced by John Boorman, released in 1985. Although the plot's authenticity is disputed, the death ritual portrayed by the tribal people was deeply moving. The dead are cremated and some of their ashes mixed with those of the ancestors. The living pass around a ceremonial cup and partake of their ancestors. I do not know if this custom comes from the author's imagination or if it is authentic, but either way I find it powerful and moving.

Perhaps my life-long fascination is derived from my destiny. History does seem to imply that it is more appropriate for someone with my religious beliefs: "Cremation, that is, the destruction of the human corpse through burning, had not been practised in Europe since the early Christian era, when, owing to its popularity amongst the Romans, it had acquired the seemingly ineradicable taint of paganism. Since this time, cremation had been practised only in exceptional circumstances: in times of pestilence, and as a form of execution."[82]

In the United States during the late 19th century, not only did the push for embalming increase but "the cremation movement ... competed for converts to its method of disposing bodies. The first crematory in the United States opened in 1876, the year in which the Stein Co. displayed its caskets at the World's Fair, and two years before Auguste Renouard[83] issued the first edition of his *Undertaker's Manual*. The cremation reformers claimed that the process was sanitary, economical, and suited to the spirit of a progressive age."[84]

Despite their promotion of cremation as a far better alternative to the funeral industry and cemeteries, "cremation did not catch on in the United States before 1920."[85] In the United States in 1920, less than one percent of the dead were cremated.

There are two quotations which date back to that earlier time but they express much of what I hear today. Sir Henry Thompson, the British surgeon and social reformer, touted cremation as "'that which is done in all good work of any kind - follow Nature's indication, and do the work she does, but do it better and more rapidly.' He claimed that earth burial unnaturally delayed a needed natural process, the return of nutrients 'to the bosom of Mother Earth.'"[86]

And this one. While I have nothing against worms and love them in the garden and have no qualms about them converting me into nutrients, this person wrote that, "I am a cremationist because I believe cremation is not only the healthiest and cleanest, but also the most poetical, way of disposing the dead. Whoever prefers loathesome worms to ashes possesses a strange imagination."[87]

Burial services are for the living

I have often heard the question asking what does it matter? When one is dead, aren't they dead? There are, as I alluded to above, many reasons that the burial process, including ceremony, is for the living. Ah, those wonderful, joyful family funerals of my youth!

My father descends from a very large family. At one time I literally had over 100 first cousins - and my mother was an only child! In such a large farming family of German descent (and Roman Catholicism for a lifestyle) a funeral meant a huge family gathering. I still remember vividly some of those Beyerl events with family everywhere in the large farmhouse. Those food-filled, card-playing, story-sharing, happy events were part of my life from early childhood until I was finishing elementary school.

My Dad's sisters and their husbands would gather in the huge, old farmhouse. This was the second farm Pa Beyerl (as my Dad's father was called) had built - the first was Pine Lawn Farm where my parents farmed when I was born. Ma Beyerl (Pa Beyerl's third wife, the first two both dying in childbirth) would be cooking on a wood kitchen stove. She could create wonders with it, managing the fuel, the temperatures, and turning out pretty amazing food. The dining room and the parlor were usually where adults played cards. When I was very young, we played and romped and ran through the upstairs bedrooms, none of which were inhabited any longer. And the attic! We could get into the attic and open trunks and explore moth-ball-scented Victorian clothing and old, old hand-stitched woolen quilts. In the summer months, the barn and the outdoor yard were fair game, and in summer weather huge tables would be set up outside.

No matter what tears might have been shed during the days leading up to the funeral, I don't remember ever seeing any great amount of weeping. Some tears at the graveside, to be certain - more when it was military with taps. But then it was a reunion filled with laughter and good memories and a celebration of life. I remember that there *were* tears at the funeral home when the embalmed body was shown, although mostly it was family speaking in whispers about life moving forward.

This was the background for my next story. I had an older brother, Joe. He and his twin, our sister Jeanne, were adopted by my parents when I was four. My brother's pre-orphanage troubled childhood left him a little troubled as an adult, mostly having some difficulty with alcohol. When the third or fourth serious accident happened, this time he did not survive. I went back for the funeral, taking time away from the high school where I was teaching. The night before the funeral, my parents closed all the draperies so the neighbors couldn't see, and we sat around the dining room table and played poker. That was far more consistent with Joe's happiest days.

Now *that* was a celebration of his life, even if muted. Would we have preferred that Joe would have been there with us? Without a doubt. He was a great young man and a huge loss for my parents. And yet, that was a turning point for me, a profound lesson that beating one's breast, gnashing one's teeth and wearing sackcloth over a huge loss is really also about those still living. It does no service for the deceased. I have been grateful on numerous occasions for the valuable lesson from my parents who showed me that we can honor those who have passed away with joy, even in the face of loss.

Chapter 5 - Burial and Cremation: What do we do with the body?

And, finally:
The Cremation of Sam McGee
When in secondary school I had to present a memorized poem. The poem my mother urged me to recite was *The Cremation of Sam McGee*. I might have objected and wanted something of my own choosing but she was correct. It was, well, *different* enough and had an undertone of humor, the type of wry humor that has always brought me delight. Written by Robert W. Service and published in a collection of his in 1907,[88] Sam McGee is a prospector. He freezes to death but has sworn his best friend (the narrator) to cremate him.

The poem opens, "There are strange things done in the midnight sun, By the men who moil for gold..." McGee freezes and the narrator hauls the body to Lake Lebarge where he finds an abandoned boat in the ice. The boiler is used as a crematorium. The next lines were always guaranteed to get a great reaction from an audience:

"I was sick with dread, but I bravely said: 'I'll just take a peep inside

"I guess he's cooked, and it's time I looked;' then the door I opened wide.

"And there sat Sam, looking cool and calm, in the heart of the furnace roar;

"And he wore a smile you could see a mile, and he said: 'Please close that door...'"

Sam, originally from Tennessee, was finally warm. How could I *not* grow up thinking that cremation wasn't such a bad a way to dispose of a corpse?

"A persistent endeavor throughout recorded human history has been the attempt to make life

Chapter 5 - Burial and Cremation: What do we do with the body?

understandable by relating the meaning of death to the meaning of life. In this pursuit, the philosophical and theological outlooks on life and death have been an integral part of the cultural heritage of all societies. To a great extent, it is also the reason societies develop rituals to help cope with the passage from life to death."[89]

Notes for Chapter Five

[53] "Prologue: Principles of Thanatology" by Arthur C. Carr, *Principles of Thanatology*, ed. Kutscher, Carr and Kutscher, Columbia University Press © 1987, pages 13-14

[54] "Introduction: The Death Ceremonies," *The Tibetan Book of the Dead*, compiled and edited by W.Y. Evans-Wentz Oxford University Press © 1960; preface to the paperback edition, W.Y. Evans-Wentz, pages 25-26

[55] *Death and Burial in the Roman World*, J. M. C. Toynbee, The Johns Hopkins University Press, Baltimore © 1971, page 51

[56] "Prologue: Principles of Thanatology" by Arthur C. Carr, *Principles of Thanatology*, ed. Kutscher, Carr and Kutscher, Columbia University Press © 1987, page 15

[57] Within my religion, the word 'Beloved' is one of the words of choice with which to refer to a loved one whose body has passed over.

[58] "Prologue: Principles of Thanatology" by Arthur C. Carr, *Principles of Thanatology*, ed. Kutscher, Carr and Kutscher, Columbia University Press © 1987, page 13

[59] "Prologue: Principles of Thanatology" by Arthur C. Carr, *Principles of Thanatology*, ed. Kutscher, Carr and Kutscher, Columbia University Press © 1987, pages 12-13

[60] *The Tibetan Book of the Dead*, compiled and edited by W.Y. Evans-Wentz Oxford University Press © 1960; preface to the paperback edition, W.Y. Evans-Wentz, page v

Chapter 5 - Burial and Cremation: What do we do with the body?

[61] Houlbrooke, Ralph, ed., *Death, Ritual, and Bereavement*, Routledge in association with the Social History Society of the United Kingdom, London, New York © 1989, page 1

[62] "Introduction: The Death Ceremonies," *The Tibetan Book of the Dead*, compiled and edited by W.Y. Evans-Wentz Oxford University Press © 1960; preface to the paperback edition, W.Y. Evans-Wentz, pages 26-27

[63] http://en.wikipedia.org/wiki/Sky_burial 27 xi 2008 ce

[64] http://en.wikipedia.org/wiki/Burial_tree 5 xi 2012 ce

[65] Quoted from 'Cremation and Christianity,' in the essay "Ashes to Ashes: Cremation and the Celebration of Death in Nineteenth-Century Britain" by Jennifer Leany in *Death, Ritual, and Bereavement*, Routledge in association with the Social History Society of the United Kingdom, London, New York © 1989, page 124

[66] Ref: Eassie, *Cremation of the Dead*, again in the Leany essay "Ashes to Ashes"

[67] Quoted From W. Robinson, *Cremation and Urn-Burial, or The Cemeteries of the Future*, London, 1938 in Leany's essay

[68] "Ashes to Ashes: Cremation and the Celebration of Death in Nineteenth-Century Britain" by Jennifer Leany in *Death, Ritual, and Bereavement*, Routledge in association with the Social History Society of the United Kingdom, London, New York © 1989, page 124

[69] Quoted from Eassie, *Cremation of the Dead*, 3

[70] "Ashes to Ashes: Cremation and the Celebration of Death in Nineteenth-Century Britain" by Jennifer Leany in *Death, Ritual, and Bereavement*, Routledge in association with the Social History Society of the United Kingdom, London, New York © 1989, page 124

[71] James Thayer Addison, *Life Beyond Death In the Beliefs of Mankind*, Houghton Mifflin Co., © 1932, page 61

[72] *Death and Burial in the Roman World*, J. M. C. Toynbee, The Johns Hopkins University Press, Baltimore © 1971, page 55

[73] *The Genius of the Inca*, by Heather Pringle, in National Geographic, April 2011, page 41

[74] *The Genius of the Inca*, by Heather Pringle, in National Geographic, April 2011, page 46

Chapter 5 - Burial and Cremation: What do we do with the body?

[75] *The Genius of the Inca*, by Heather Pringle, in National Geographic, April 2011, pages 55-58

[76] Farrell, James J., *Inventing the American Way of Death, 1830-1920*, Temple University Press © 1989, page 157

[77] "Ashes to Ashes: Cremation and the Celebration of Death in Nineteenth-Century Britain" by Jennifer Leany in *Death, Ritual, and Bereavement*, Routledge in association with the Social History Society of the United Kingdom, London, New York © 1989, page 134

[78] Farrell, James J., *Inventing the American Way of Death, 1830-1920*, Temple University Press © 1989, page 159

[79] http://en.wikipedia.org/wiki/Embalming_solution

[80] http://en.wikipedia.org/wiki/Embalming

[81] "Ashes to Ashes: Cremation and the Celebration of Death in Nineteenth-Century Britain" by Jennifer Leany in *Death, Ritual, and Bereavement*, Routledge in association with the Social History Society of the United Kingdom, London, New York © 1989, page 219

[82] "Ashes to Ashes: Cremation and the Celebration of Death in Nineteenth-Century Britain" by Jennifer Leany in *Death, Ritual, and Bereavement*, Routledge in association with the Social History Society of the United Kingdom, London, New York © 1989, page 118

[83] Renouard "earned a medical degree before the Civil War." In Denver "he used his medical knowledge of anatomical preservation to assist an undertaking firm in embalming... By 1874 undertakers impressed with his work had persuaded Renouard to open a school of embalming." - Farrell, James J., *Inventing the American Way of Death, 1830-1920*, Temple University Press © 1989, page 158

[84] Farrell, James J., *Inventing the American Way of Death, 1830-1920*, Temple University Press © 1989, page 164

[85] Farrell, James J., *Inventing the American Way of Death, 1830-1920*, Temple University Press © 1989, page 164

[86] Farrell, James J., *Inventing the American Way of Death, 1830-1920*, Temple University Press © 1989, page 166

[87] Farrell, James J., *Inventing the American Way of Death, 1830-1920*, Temple University Press © 1989, page 165-4

Chapter 5 - Burial and Cremation: What do we do with the body?

---

[88] *Songs of a Sourdough*. According to Wikipedia, the poem was based on factual people and events Service saw in the Yukon.

[89] "A Healthy outlook on Life Necessarily Comprehends Death" by Vanderlyn R. Pine - *Principles of Thanatology*, ed. Kutscher, Carr and Kutscher, Columbia University Press © 1987, page 1

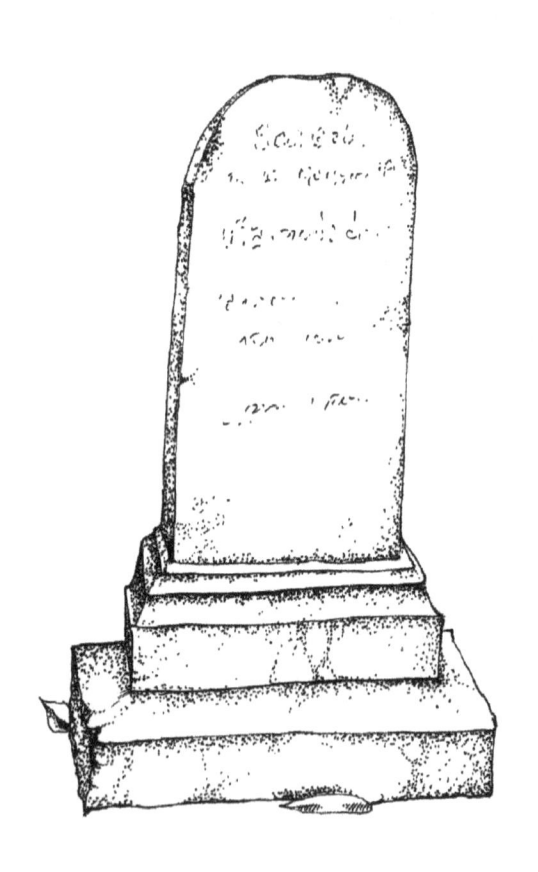

Chapter 6 - An Evolution of Death

The Earliest Times [Before 300 BCE]

- **The background story**
- **Underworlds and Otherworlds**
- **Immortality: Existence beyond the body's death**
- **Early burial practices**
- **Monuments and Markers**

● **The background story**

"'All that lives must die:' Death is an inescapable fact of human existence whose essential nature does not alter in the course of time. But its causes and incidence, understanding of its physical aspects and beliefs about the after-life, the treatment of the dying and their comportment, the disposal of mortal remains and the ritual responses of survivors - all these have clearly changed, and the historian can study the process in a wealth of remaining evidence."[90]

Houlbrooke's musing upon the quote from Hamlet is placed at the beginning of this chapter. The customs and attitudes which have evolved with our species provide us with a profound insight into the beliefs and customs which predate our own.

Originally my notes and attempts to put all of what I have found into print was to be one chapter, but my wish to delve into all the available information on the customs of this period of time is far beyond my grasp. Those who are academics and scientists in this field continue to explore on site. Articles appear. Excavation for a contemporary structure or for infrastructure begins and ... concepts are completely shifted. New burial sites? I have only so much time as my years erode and to bring the information I would wish to cover in this

Chapter 6 - An Evolution of Death - The Earliest Times [Before 300 BCE]

chapter would take two lifetimes of academic research, at least four lifetimes out in the field, uncovering, sitting within the pyramids, meditating at Stonehenge, exploring burial sites from the mounds along the Mississippi to the sites in China, to the shamanic remains found as a glacier recedes to ... well, you see how challenging this is.

For that reason I must lump the data I have found into loose periods of time. This first chapter in this chronology is what I will call the "Early Times." It is not fair to those who lived and died prior to 300 BCE. But, with my limitations acknowledged, I move forward into the past.

"Death is a cultural event and societies as well as individuals reveal themselves in their treatment of death."[91] I have been fascinated with religion and with death for (almost) as long as I can remember. It was easier for me to accept death as normal and natural than it was to embrace an acceptance of religion. Oh, I tried, but it was not an easy journey. One key to the resolution of this conundrum was entering a religious belief system which saw death as I had instinctively felt and experienced it to be, given I had only experienced death indirectly.

In my search for a religion and in my becoming Wiccan - and in that process giving shape to the specific religion[92] which I now practice and represent - I came to become fascinated with what I often refer to as 'the evolution of religion.' In many ways we learn more about the ancient religions by the manner and customs with which they approached death and burial.

In addition to burial and any remnants of customs and rituals, there is also the search for information about what peoples might have believed awaited us after dying. When did our species begin believing that there might be some type of spiritual existence following death? When did we begin to believe that there might be what is called a soul? What about reincarnation? Our distant predecessors did not leave nicely annotated journals answering these questions. They did not record the discussions they had which led to the evolving discussions that ultimately caused our cultural practices to be altered. It was easier for them to create stories for, in those days of the unwritten word, an interesting story was far easier to remember.

- **Underworlds and Otherworlds**

    "You will have noticed that all the races we have dealt with - Egyptians, Babylonians, Greeks and Celts - were believers in two kinds of heaven, an underground heaven, and an island heaven. ... There is the class who love the sea and who would not be happy except on an island, or near the shore. ... There are also those who would be extremely miserable if they were doomed to live within sight of the sea. They could not thrive or be content unless their home was far inland, among hills or mountains."[93]

As the celestial deities of the solar system danced their circles orbiting the Earth around the ancient civilizations, they were perceived literally as moving into the underworld, when the world was plunged into darkness and cooling, and returning back into the above-world, which may be brought life and light. Sunset could be a challenge. "For other races [than the Egyptians] the portals to the lower world were far distant in the west. If the sun can go down through a hole in the west, why not the shades of the departed?"[94] Certainly our genetic heritage as a species would have evolved from a time when darkness was not so safe. Although a clear night with a Full Moon has so much light I can wander in our gardens, when overcast or when the Moon is not above the Earth walking can be perilous even in the open. If beneath a canopy of trees? You might leave your home and not return. What a huge development it must have been when the ability to carry a burning flame for a period of time expanded one's night-time horizon as well as provided protection from predators.

Throughout mythology, legends proliferate in which one descends into that underworld, a realm of existence beneath reality as we know it. In ancient times entering a deep cave was perilous. "Deep caverns have naturally been suggested far and wide as likely entrances to the land of the shades."[95] Unless you could carry fire with you for a period of time with success, you could only travel a modest distance, beyond which was... total darkness. What was there about these deep, dark passages into the Earth's depths which led them to so readily be associated with the land of the dead? The Underworld is not always that hellish environment. "By far the most picturesque underworld is that of the Egyptians. For them it was the realm of Osiris, the god who had died and been restored to life and to whose protection the dead were committed. We learn of it in detail from '*The Book of Him Who is in the Underworld*,' which was written on the walls of sepulchral chambers during the Eighteenth Dynasty (1580-1350 B.C.) and in later times."[96] And this: "The Celtic heaven of Tir Tairngire is subterranean. It might be under a vast plain or hill, especially a fairy hill."[97]

> "As in ancient Canaan and Mesopotamia, in ancient Israel the dead were normally thought to go to 'the land of no return,' which was known in Hebrew as Sheol. This was a place of darkness, dust, and silence. Those who go down to Sheol cannot praise God. ... The biblical Sheol is not yet a hell, but merely a gloomy limbo. This was the normal fate of human beings throughout the biblical period."[98]

When I ask myself if it was due to the darkness, a response I find is questioning that theory. Why darkness? Despite so many stories of 'going toward the light,' the dark imagery for death seems to be far more common. If it were based upon those who had near-death experiences, it would not seem that the dark would be the land of death.

Did the early human note that the deceased usually had their eyelids closed? If I close my eyes, it blocks out much of the light. Would this suggest that the dead are in darkness? Death is often associated with coldness as well with the cold, and yet a deep cavern, while cooler than warmer season temperatures will often be warmer than the winter temperatures. I don't know that cold and dark could alone have led to this belief, but certainly the concept of the Underworld as as old as recorded myths.

> "In that dark region, through which a river ran, the great event was the daily progress of the sun-god Re in his bark. His voyage consumed the twelve hours when it was night on earth, and during each hour his radiance lit up the confines of one of the twelve divisions of the underworld. In each compartment,

entered by a gate, were fields and houses, and along the banks of the stream dwelt all manner of fantastic spirits and demons in human and animal form. Slowly through their midst passed the state barge of Re on which sat the various divinities who were his vassals and the noted dead, fresh from the world above, who were privileged to be in his care. A few of these he leaves behind at each halting place, granting them rich fields to cultivate. In the sixth and seventh compartments dwelt the kings of Upper and Lower Egypt, but even with them there was darkness save for one hour a day."[99]

With sunrise, however, light returned. One could walk without falling over rocks and logs, without stepping off the edge into a chasm, without becoming prey for some predator species with better night vision. Was this why so many cultures developed the dark underworld as the most likely place for the fearful half of the Otherworld and the celestial realm above as the most likely location for the desirable half of the Otherworld? With death unavoidable and the Otherworld having two realms, if we have no control over death, perhaps there is some control over where we will end up. This, then, is also one of the foundations of so many religions: having some control over what happens when the body has reached its expiration date or meets untimely death earlier than what would have been a natural passing. MacDonald's perspective certainly rings true:

"Although there are many paths to hell, the ways to heaven are few but plain. In all the earlier literature of Indian religion - the Vedas and the Brahmanas - the first requirement for eternal reward is to make use of the sacrifices which only the priests could offer to the gods... With the rise of Hinduism, however, which became the dominant religion more than a thousand years ago, the earlier emphasis on 'salvation by works' yielded in large measure to the belief in 'salvation by faith.' ...only through intense personal devotion to his chosen deity... And for the true philosopher ... neither works nor faith were the means to salvation. Salvation could come only through mystical knowledge, and it meant not a heaven of worldly delights but the final peace of union with that impersonal Absolute which is the one reality behind all change."[100]

The word *Underworld* is earth-centric in that it implies it to be lower than the Earth upon which we live. Now that we know our planet better, that would inevitably put it at the center of the Earth which, for me, leads me to prefer *Otherworld*. The concept of the *Otherworld* which can be found as far back as the 13th century in English literature[101] according to my *Merriam-Webster's*. Referring to that vague other-dimensional reality beyond death, the concept, as I found in Wikipedia, was evolved and developed by Lucan, more appropriately known as Marcus Annaeus Lucanus (3 November 39 AD - 30 April, 65 AD). Lucan was a Roman poet better known for his willingness to dissent with Nero. Eventually, Lucan's published comments so inflamed Nero that Lucan was charged with treason and, at the young age of 25, took his own life. A brilliant young man, he also wrote extensively and, as he studied druidic practices, he coined the phrase *orbis alius* which meant *Celtic Otherworld*. Although the concept as such may be dated to Lucan, certainly it was identified by many ancient civilizations. The Egyptians of the fifth and sixth dynasties "believed in an elysium which was situated in the west, where the sun-god descended into his grave each night."[102]

How about this as a desirable state of being following the body's death? "In the tomb-paintings of the sixth and fifth centuries BC the prevailing theme may be said to be Elysium, with the dead imagined as enjoying, either as participants, or as spectators, the jollities, sports, and pleasant pastimes of a well-to-do and cultured people - feasting, fishing and fowling, athletic games, horsemanship, dancing, and music, often portrayed in an idyllic setting of trees, plants, flitting birds, and dangling flower garlands."[103]

> "Perhaps the most popular of all the Egyptian other worlds, the one which is more frequently mentioned, and which reminds us of Tir-nan-Og, is referred to as the Field of Yaru, where the grain grows taller than any ever seen on the banks of the Nile, and the departed enjoyed plenty and

security. The code of ethics which qualified for admittance to those happy elysian fields was lofty. The soul had to recite the ritual confession which gives a list of thirty offences of which he claimed to be innocent. Yaru was surrounded by water, and the waiting soul had to be helped across. Sometimes he was borne there on the pinions of the hawk, or ibis, or the Sun God took him over in his bark... After all is said and done, it was not so much moral purity but ceremonial punctiliousness which secured one a ready passage to Yaru."[104]

Without an extensive study and presentation of the ever-evolving beliefs in Egypt alone, it is important to remember that the religion of Egypt was ever changing and evolving, often because the newest royalty were also divine and the religions were often changed with deities coming and going in prominence.

"There was also the Egyptian nether-world of Amenti, known too as The Hall of Depths; The Land of Knowledge; The Friend of Silence; The Concealer of Resting, etc. The presiding deity was the wife of Osiris, mother of all who die, who receives them into her arms and assigns them their places in her great kingdom."[105]

In the subcontinent beliefs were not so dissimilar:

"In the Vedic heaven of earliest Indian belief, ... Yama, the King of the Dead, rules over all the departed who have lived worthily. His realm is in the radiant light of the outer sky where men may share with his divine associates the unbounded joys of celestial life - food and drink and the pleasures of love. Clothed in glorified bodies that magnify every delight of the senses, the spirits sit at table with the gods, enlivened by the sound of flute and song, quaffing the sacred *soma*, and relishing the milk and honey and melted butter. It is the abode 'where radiance inexhaustible dwells... wherein is movement glad and free, in the third sky, third heaven of heavens, where are the lucid worlds of light....'"[106]

"In most of the ancient world ... the lot of the dead was rather dismal. The inevitability of death for human beings was affirmed alike by the epic of Gilgamesh, Homer, and the Hebrew Bible. Normally, the dead went to the netherworld, where they could not see the light of day. Mesopotamian tradition speaks about the house that those who enter cannot leave, where they dwell in darkness and have dust for food. According to Homer, souls in Hades lack the strength to speak until they are given blood to drink. The Hebrew psalmist complains that the dead cannot even praise God. Only rarely are exceptional individuals exempted from this common fate, The Babylonian flood-hero Utnapishtim was taken off to live with the gods. Homer's Menelaus was admitted to the Elysian Fields. Elijah was taken up to heaven on a chariot. ... In the Semitic world, and in most cases also in the West, the dreariness of the netherworld was punishment enough, regardless of one's behavior in life."[107]

- **Immortality: Existence beyond the body's death**

At the earliest time when we were not yet evolved into human form as we think of it, did we already believe in some manner of afterlife? It is not necessarily a simply philosophical leap to move from belief that all being of the individual ceases to exist at the body's death. That belief in such a finality remains today among individuals. Last year when I was at a gathering with some of our Mystery School students and their spouses, we spoke about our beliefs and a man espoused his firm belief that everything for a person ends with the body's death. He is far from the first that I have heard hold this belief with firm conviction.

Being widely read and having explored these themes and topics throughout my life, my sense is his school of belief may be a minority view. I do not know, for example, that all atheists believe that there is no existence beyond the body's death for, to me, I believe in the Universe, itself, being divine but do not believe in a deity as such. I personally do not believe that the survival of one's soul or spirit is dependent upon a deity. My beliefs arose from experiences I have had which leave me unable to *not* believe in ... the soul's survival. I hesitated because the word immortal suggests that one would last forever and I do not know how long one's astral being might remain intact as 'self.' Whether we survive in some vast, nebulous field of energy or have the ability (or inevitability according to some) to end up in a specific place is something open for discussion but almost impossible to prove. Do we have one incarnation and then the soul survives for a time, or do we continue to incarnate until our learning is done, or are our souls are actually immortal? That also takes me into realms which I cannot define. Time itself is so nebulous and I know that even the Universe undergoes death and rebirth, metaphorically.

Macdonald writes that "belief in an after-life is inherent in man's nature and is practically as ancient as the early dawn of human consciousness."[108] We may not be the only mammal to believe that there is *something* which survives the body's death. The death rituals of elephants could be interpreted in many ways, and we humans have barely begun to understand the intelligence of other species due to the difficulty of communication.

Are these beliefs simply a matter of wishful thinking? Of being unable to accept the finality of corporal death being the end of it all? "A large number of writers on sociology and anthropology, have tried to proves that belief in immortality had its origin in dreams..."[109] I spent many years studying my dreams, *thousands and thousands* of my dreams. Born with a proclivity toward precognitive dreams, dreams so uncanny that more than once I quoted the conversation I brought back from a dream to others who were then present, months later, when suddenly we found ourself in the scenario, with Larry Bradford making the statement which was the key sentence I quoted. I have also had the enormous blessing of having validation from others about my precognition.

My experiences while in the Dreaming did make it difficult to not believe in the metaphysical, and I personally find beliefs in the spiritual and metaphysical leave me unable to not believe that there is *more*. But dreams alone are not, for me, the answer and MacDonald concurs. "The

Chapter 6 - An Evolution of Death - The Earliest Times [Before 300 BCE]

dream theory, while it may yet have a grain of truth in it, is, nevertheless, too anthropocentric and mechanistic to be of any help here. ...dreams alone come infinitely short of explaining mankind's implicit belief in the hereafter."[110]

Was it a fear of the unknown? The civilizations which became the foundation of our western beliefs evolved concepts which have, in a manner, endured yet today. Eschatology is a branch of theology which studies and contemplates the beliefs regarding death and the end of being, as well as related concerns. Despite the many years I've been gathering information, my own book has been often delayed as I look for more detail, attempt to better understand a particular scholar, or am simply distracted by the countless other projects in my busy life. And yet my own contemplation has never ended, whether I have been writing other books, teaching, or tending our sacred gardens.

Just as contemporary science seeks to find and better understand the unifying energy and matter of the Universe, so too do I seek those gems of information which provide for me a unifying concept within religious evolution.

MacDonald describes the Babylonian concept of post-death as being "somewhat sombre, and vague. It lacked the distinctness and certainty of the Egyptian beliefs."[111] If that is true, to me it would seem that the Babylonian eschatology was somewhat earlier, with the Egyptian culture evolving somewhat later than that of the Mesopotamian cultures. In Egypt, which we think of as having a highly evolved eschatology (from the *Egyptian Book of the Dead* to the pyramids and elaborate burial customs), "we find an underworld abode of the dead, and an island, or islands, of the blest. The soul and breath were conceived of as one and man had a double, a semi material shade called ekimmu which bore some resemblance to the Egyptian Ka."[112]

Today we more correctly refer to the *edimmu*, which are somewhat similar to the *utukku* in Sumerian myths. If one was not given the proper burial, consistent with customs and avoid taboos, the spirit would not rest and would hang about and cause problems for the living. These beliefs are so old that one might only speculate about the reasoning for their origin.

As the religion of the Hebrew people underwent change, beginning with the theologically immense shift from polytheism to monotheism for which Moses is the bringer of change, one can see how earlier beliefs are never completely lost but are rather evolved and integrated into the newer version of belief. A similar evolution is the belief in the resurrection of the body at a time after one has died, often considered to be "the great contribution of the Jews to solving the problem of the life beyond death." Addison also adds that "at least four centuries before the Jews had evolved the doctrine it was known in Persia."[113]

Addison writes that "The Persian scheme resembles the Jewish in so many respects, especially in the thought of our bodies living again, that many scholars have seen in Jewish doctrine a direct borrowing from Persian. That conclusion has been all the easier because the Zoroastrian belief is much older than the Hebrew and because the Jews were under Persian rule for some two hundred years before the time of Alexander."[114]

MacDonald's view adds an additional perspective: "The Hebrews borrowed their ideas of angels, devils, and much else, from Persia. Persian eschatology is unique in that it differs from that of any other county. Far from being a paradise, its nether world is the Hell we read of in the Bible. Duzakh, an abyss tenanted by evil spirits and demons, is a place of unrelieved darkness, woe and torment. At death, the soul crosses the Bridge of Chinvat (meaning gatherer or accountant). This bridge is extended over Hell and leads to Paradise. In a particular place, it widens to the length of nine javelins for the souls of the pious, and contracts to a thread for the souls of the wicked, so that they fall off into Hell. The faith of Persia lays more emphasis on future retribution. It is, nevertheless, a religion of hope."[115]

> "By all odds the most familiar ordeal is the famous Bridge Test - a belief so common as to be found (without exhaustive research) among at least forty different tribes and peoples. The main idea is simple: at some point in the journey to the spirit world a river, pool, or chasm must be crossed by a narrow bridge. Those who can pass in safety reach their destination; the others are cast down to a tragic or unknown fate."[116]

Chapter 6 - An Evolution of Death - The Earliest Times [Before 300 BCE]

Similar to many of the heroic stories which become the myths and legends of a culture, one of the means of attaining immortality is by great heroic deeds. Some of the myths become metaphors for values which are to be applied to one's life while still living in order to achieve immortality. As religious beliefs evolved but as far back as prehistoric time, initiation became a process by which the young might become accepted as adults based upon strengths, skills and knowledge; by which children reached puberty and became accepted as entering maturity based upon reproductive status; and by which someone was given access to secretive knowledge only available by means of initiation.

There are initiation rites connected with death and dying as well. "In one of the Solomon Islands... the land of the dead is easily reached only by those who have had their noses pierced. In the New Hebrides it is the ears that must be pierced..."[117] I do not know much about this at all, but it's a wonderful piece of information to ponder. Does one have to bear the tribal marking (i.e. the piercing) in order to be recognized by one's ancestors? In many beliefs we must pass a test following the death of the body before the soul or spirit can reach the destination. What is relevant for this chapter regarding these island practices is the recognition of there *being* a 'land of the dead.' Such a place can only exist if those people believed that there is a soul or spirit which continues on when the body has died.

Yet there are those who feel quite confident that a belief in the ability of one's soul or spirit to exist when the body has died is no more than wishful thinking by those unable to accept the fact that when the body dies, there is nothing more. There is no reunion with one's forebears, no union with deity.

On the other hand there have been a small number of those who work within shamanic lineages, of those who have near death experiences, of those who have out-of-body experiences, of those who learn from direct experience that one's soul or essence or spirit or astral body does have life separate from that of the body. Yet that, too, is a mystery, for words will never fully convey that reality to the many who have ever experienced that state of being.

We really have no recorded history which documents how any religion or culture of old came to believe in immortality, whether the immortality of the deity or of the ability of one's soul to exist beyond the death of the body. Evans-Wentz, when writing about the Tibetan Buddhist beliefs and practices, wrote:

> "As set forth in my first important work, *The Fairy-Faith in Celtic Countries,* forty-four years ago[118], the postulate of rebirth implies a scientific extension and correction of Darwin's conception of evolutionary law - that alone through traversing the Cycle of Death and Birth, as taught by our revered ancestors, the Druids of Europe, twenty-five and more centuries ago, man attains in the spiritual and psychic sphere that destined perfection which all life's processes and all living things exhibit at the end of their evolutionary course, and from which at present man is so far removed."[119]

In ancient Egypt, "evidence for the existence of a developed concept of life after death can be found already in the late predynastic period (ca. 3500-3000 BCE), when corpses were provided with gifts of food, tools, and utensils and were buried in an embryonic posture suggestive of a symbolic return to the womb."[120] Egypt, living with the flood patterns of the Nile and a strong agricultural paradigm, saw nature as a role model. "Life was imagined to follow the cyclic pattern of nature. The sun-god Re and the god Osiris exhibited a pattern of death and resurrection. The transition to the afterlife required certain rituals. The body had to be preserved through mummification, to serve as the basis for the life of the spirit. To reach the realm of the dead, the deceased required special knowledge. From a relatively early period, there was also a judgment, symbolized by the weighing of the heart in a balance."[121]

> "The early Egyptians maintained that there was more to man than a physical, material body. In our spiritual make up they detected three numinous entities, the Ka, the Ba, and the Khu. ... The Ka was the individual's guardian angel who accompanied him into this life when he was born. A material,

Chapter 6 - An Evolution of Death - The Earliest Times [Before 300 BCE]

corporeal being, one's exact double in stature and appearance, this God given comrade, although he had his abode chiefly in the hereafter, continued to befriend a person so intimately and faithfully that the fortunes of both were ever afterwards closely associated."[122]

"... the association of the after-life with the tomb is not confined to the lower races. It was an early belief of the Egyptians from which they never wholly escaped and which prompted them to rear eternal pyramids as homes for their royal dead. Among the ancient Chinese, too, the soul dwelt with the body."[123]

- **Early burial practices**

"That the dead are not usually to be feared is clear enough from the fact that the harmful spirits are always in some fashion exceptional. They are those who have been left unburied or who have died violent deaths or who have met their end by some means unfamiliar, peculiar, or distressing. Rooted in the ancient belief that the soul still haunts the body and somehow depends upon it is the conviction - once universal and widely known today - that the unburied dead are restless and therefore dangerous."[124] The belief that the soul lives beyond the life of the body raises major issues when it comes to religious beliefs about the burial of the body.

What we know of burial among the ancient western cultures tends to be found among civilizations which emerge in and near the Fertile Crescent. This region is often referred to as the *cradle of civilization*, at least for the western world, and is where we find some of the oldest artifacts and remnants of the earliest human cultures. Some of the oldest human settlements were the Pre-Pottery Neolithic in the vicinity of the Euphrates, dating to 9,000 BCE. Information I located was surprisingly extensive yet in the context of this book I can share only a small portion of history from what could be volumes of material from a qualified historian. I will rely heavily upon authors who have provided a wealth of information in the hopes of stirring greater interest. I urge

Chapter 6 - An Evolution of Death - The Earliest Times [Before 300 BCE]

you to consider turning to their texts to learn more about the roots of our beliefs and customs.

Using the three-era system devised by Christian Jürgensen Thomsen, the Bronze age is the second age, following the Stone Age. It will be followed by the Iron Age. Roughly (very), the Bronze age spans 3300 BCE to 1200 BCE.

With human civilization emerging from the Fertile Crescent, the following is among the older insights I found:

> "From time immemorial, the inhabitants of ancient Mesopotamia buried their dead in cemeteries and in private houses, together with meals and personal effects. The archeological finds point to a funerary cult, and the variations suggest differences in the social status of the deceased. The written sources are more explicit about the Mesopotamian conceptions of death and afterlife. Written in Sumerian and Akkadian between the late 3rd millennium and the middle if the 1st millennium BCE, these sources also incorporate much older traditions that were retained by the population."[125]

We do not have a great deal of information older than the Bronze Age. Many of the Neolithic or *new stone age* monuments are believed to have been constructed during the late Stone Age which, in those areas of Europe, saw the Bronze Age emerge later than it appears to have in the Fertile Crescent. The oldest stones at Stonehenge are dated to as early as 3100 BCE. This period of time is described as 'prehistoric,' for prior to the Bronze Age we have almost no recorded history and it remains, even today, a source of mystery, of archaeological debate and uncertainty, and frankly a source of wonder. In recent years excavation has found that there was considerable burial done there, but one theory is that "Stonehenge was a place of healing - the primeval equivalent of Lourdes."[126] If that is the case, then the burial ground is incidental and the megaliths are not indicative of burial practices.

What I found is that by the Bronze Age humans had developed significant regional religions and civilizations. The various customs are more reflective of these beliefs than they are of human evolution. There are significant differences which arise from religious beliefs. When religion and culture began evolving among centers of human population in prehistoric times, differences in climate, differences in which deities had emerged as the more prominent, differences in geography, brought a wide variety of practices. Some of these may have to do with the type of soil, the presence of caves, or other once-pragmatic matters which evolved into religious and ritual traditions.

Ugarit was a port on the Mediterranean across from the island nation of Alashiya, now known as Cyprus. It dates far back into prehistory - enough that it had become a city which was surrounded with a wall as early as 6000 BCE. Archaeological remains "in Late Bronze Age in Ugarit indicate the practice of intramural burials under residential houses and the royal palace. Staircases under the floors led to these vaulted tombs with multiple burials. At Phoenician sites of the Iron Age, cremation and inhumation were both practiced, but in contrast to Ugarit, cemeteries were set far from the living, outside settlements. The Phoenician dead were not to be disturbed."[127] The word *inhumation* means, very simply, to be buried in (*in*) the earth (*hum*). The *hum* syllable is the same as found in humus, or even humble, which means down to earth.

Nearby, just to the north and northwest, in Anatolia, an area which is currently in western and central Turkey, "the cemeteries excavated from the Hittite period [ce. 1650-1150 BCE] convey a fairly uniform picture: inhumation and cremation were practiced simultaneously, and the funeral complexes contain no gifts or any great value. The most valuable depositions consist of bovines and equids - in their entirety or heads only - that sometimes accompany the dead. They were animals in the prime of their lives, constituting considerable wealth."[128]

How were the royalty buried in Anatolia? Obviously, with the most wealth and power, their burial would be the most elaborate and the most likely to endure the ages:

> "One of the most extensive Hittite text compositions concerns a funerary ritual for the Hittite king and queen. ... The ritual lasted for fourteen days and was a rite of passage in

the sense that its goal was to ensure that the inevitable transition would not endanger the country's stability and prosperity, which were embodied by the king. The composition consists of four separate series: a scenario giving a detailed prescription of who should do what where and when; a script with the text of prayers to be spoken with brief directions; a ration list with the materials needed each day; and a summary characterizing each day in a single line. The scenario originally comprised between 3,000 and 3,500 lines of text, half of which can be reconstructed with some confidence. The composition can be dated around 1400 BCE with certainty, but may well be older...

"The body of the deceased was cremated on the night of the first day of the ritual. Then, at dawn, the pyre was quenched with certain liquids. Women collected the remains of the bones, which were then dipped in oil, wrapped in cloth, and brought to the actual tomb or 'Stone House.' There they would be laid out on a bed. That same day, a wooden effigy was made of the deceased: a seated male with weapons in his hands for a king, a seated female with spinning gear for a queen. Eyes and mouth were indicated with gold plaques of inlays. The rest of the second day through the sixth day was filled with offerings that aimed at reconciliation. The latter were probably directed at the powers of the netherworld, the most important of whom was the Sun-goddess of the Earth. The royal body seems to have gone initially to the Stone House, and texts suggest that the king was escorted out from there by his mother.

"The seventh through thirteenth days after death were devoted to rituals concerning particular spheres of life, such as agriculture, viticulture, and animal husbandry, including hunting. For example, among the numerous acts performed, a chunk of sod was cut off and presented to the sun-god for the benefit of the deceased, a plow was used and then burned, a grapevine was brought to the table of the deceased, and some ducks were caught and burned. The seventh day itself probably centered on the theme of kingship, considering the use of 'fine oil' and '[royal] robes,' which recall the ceremony in which a Hittite king was anointed. The thirteenth day was called the day 'of the *lahhanza* birds,' probably some kind of ducks, but the purpose of this day's ritual remains preserved. No text of the fourteenth day has been preserved."[129]

Each morning of the days seven through thirteen, the effigy is brought out and food and drink are given to it as well. Various items are included each day and then burned, symbolic of the various spheres of activity and influence of the deceased.

Even into the Iron Age, we find burial often dependent upon the local terrain. In what is now Israel, "family members were buried together in underground caves; in the Iron Age, the use of caves declined as bench-tombs grew in popularity. Bodies were laid on the benches until they had decomposed, and then the bones were gathered into a repository under one of the benches in a secondary burial. Bench-tombs were the predominant form of burial in Judah during the late 8th through early 6th centuries BCE."[130]

Today Israel and Iran are quite hostile to each other. In what is now Iran, "humans were etymologically mortal... The [Iranians] believed in the resurrection of the dead. Therefore, in eastern Iran (Bactria, Sogdiana) it was recommended that bones be kept carefully after the flesh was gone and collected in bone containers that were often decorated with religious scenes."[131]

As is found in so many of the archaeological sites, often the information which is found through the remaining artifacts and items may raise more questions than are solved. The Etruscan civilization may have emerged as early as the 8th century BCE. The Etruscans, centered in Etruria in what today is in Italy left no history of their own. What we know of them comes from the histories written by the Romans.

> In Etruria "only the elite in Etruscan society had access to formal, and thus archeologically visible, burial, so only an elite world is available for reconstruction. ... The elaborate

Chapter 6 - An Evolution of Death - The Earliest Times [Before 300 BCE]

'houses of the dead' that Etruscans of the 7th century BCE built in monumental mounds, or in the cliff faces of Etruria, testify to the care and wealth that was invested in the treatment of the dead. The discovery of chariots and remains of food in the tombs suggests that elaborate rites (including racing and feasting) accompanied the act of mourning and that the deposition of the corpse was supplemented by complex sets of grave goods."[132]

"The importance of the relationship between the living and the dead is emphasized by the visibility of the monumental cemeteries that formed sacred halos around settlements, like those of Cerveteri or Veii. Roads leading into and out of Etruscan cities of the living passed through the impressive cities of the dead. At the same time, the dead were isolated by the physical separation of forges and valleys ... platforms on or at the side of the tombs were constructed for commemorative rites. Altars for such sacrifices survive inside several tombs at Cerveter"[133]

"There is no direct evidence that beliefs about death and the afterlife had any special bearing on the methods used by the Etruscans for disposing of their dead. The two rites of cremation and inhumation (the term that is used loosely to cover all cases of non-cremation) existed contemporaneously in all regions and the choice of the one or the other would appear to have been determined mainly by family tradition and individual preference. But burning and the burial of unburnt remains, if never mutually exclusive as regards place and period, were not practised everywhere and at all times in the same proportions. The former was, on the whole, less frequent than the latter in the early period, becoming commoner from the fourth to the second centuries, and it prevailed in the central and northern areas; whereas inhumation was chiefly in favour in the south and along the western coast. Any large pot or jar could be used for the ashes of cremated persons. But from the late-eighth to the early-sixth centuries such relics

Chapter 6 - An Evolution of Death - The Earliest Times [Before 300 BCE]

were sometimes put into terracotta vessels that resembled in shape a rudimentary human form esconced in a high-backed chair - the so-called Canopic urns."[134]

Speaking of the Romans, "death, for the Romans, was a communal event. Roman society was built around the family, and Roman death ritual, activated and mediated by the family, perpetuated the foundations of the *res publica* by integrating the newly dead individual into the collectivity of ancestors... whose ways ... provided the paradigm for Roman life."[135]

"When a person died, his or her family and household became *funestus* or *funestatus* (polluted by death) and remained so until the completion of the funerary rites. Just before or immediately after death, the body was placed on the ground outside the house (*depositio*). Ideally a family member caught the last breath. The eyes were closed, and the deceased was called upon by name (*conclamatio*), a procedure that was continued periodically up to the cremation. The corpse was washed in warm water, perfumed (sometimes by a professional *pollinctor*), clothed in finery, and then laid out for viewing in a public area of the house (*collocatio*), with feet pointing toward the door, on a high funerary bed with two mattresses surrounded by incense burners and torches."[136]

With a political system often changing as the city of Rome expanded, accommodating an increasing population, with the Empire, itself, expanding, customs vary widely over throughout the Roman Empire. Toynbee devotes an entire book to the subject. Under the Roman Empire the legal aspects of burial became more defined. "A Roman grave was not a grave until earth had covered the corpse and the heir had sacrificed the sow to Ceres."[137] A forerunner of today's zoning laws, but also applying to the offspring and relatives of any deceased individuals. Of course, in those days "of the three principal ways that Romans disposed of corpses - inhumation, cremation, and (occasionally) embalming ... the first was believed to be the oldest."[138]

Chapter 6 - An Evolution of Death - The Earliest Times [Before 300 BCE]

"In the country districts of the Roman world rich and poor alike could be laid to rest in more or less isolated graves ranging in character from the simplest types of cremation or inhumation burials to those that were marked by, or contained in, elaborately carved or architecturally impressive monuments. A city, on the other hand, has always needed its communal necropolis or necropoleis, at least one dependent city of the dead, more often several such cities, situated on its outskirts. Roman law strictly prescribed that a city's cemeteries should be outside its walls or other formal boundaries."[139]

"All burials, whether of bodies or of ashes, had to take place outside the city. This regulation, laid down in the Twelve Tables, was normally observed until the late Empire... Sanitary precautions and fear of defilement readily explain the law."[140]

It is interesting that already during the Roman Empire there was an awareness of the importance of regulating how and where burial would take place. Compare this with what was happening many centuries later in large European cities further north where cities had grown around cemeteries and there was so little regulation that major health hazards were the result.

Between the Italian peninsula and Anatolia was Greece, a far greater influence upon the Roman Empire than one might think unless you are a student of history.

"In earliest times, the Greeks apparently believed that everyone got the same deal after death. The disembodied soul descended into the underworld, the land of the dead that was ruled by Hades and his queen, Persephone ... There, the souls existed in a state that was not unpleasant but not particularly enjoyable."[141]

I believe it quite possible that the following legal obligation which we also find in Rome was actually adopted from the Greeks:

Chapter 6 - An Evolution of Death - The Earliest Times [Before 300 BCE]

"It was the obligation of surviving kin, especially children, to ensure that the dead received proper funerary rites; if they did not, they were not considered 'fully dead' and their souls would be condemned to wander restlessly between worlds. What constituted proper rites varied from place to place and time to time, but at a minimum, honorable disposal of the corpse by burial or cremation was required. ... If a body were lost at sea or was otherwise irretrievable, rites might be performed for it *in absentia* and a cenotaph erected.

"Ideally, women from the family of the deceased would wash and dress the body as soon as possible after death. A day of mourning would follow... Gifts would be given to the deceased... The body was buried or cremated on the third day... Libations of honey, milk, wine, water, and/or oil were then poured into the grave where the body or ashes had been buried. Libations were repeated periodically, usually for at least a year."[142]

Egypt evolved with a different cosmology, religious hierarchy and with different customs. In earlier times:

"when a death occurred, a period of formal mourning began. The corpse was immediately taken to the place of embalming, where it was treated to preserve it and to transform it into an eternal image... In early burials (predynastic period to early Old Kingdom) the treatment usually consisted of little more than wrapping the body in hides or linen, although attempts at artificial preservation involving evisceration and the use of resin were made as early as approximately 3400 BCE. The corpse was prepared in an embryonic position and laid on its left side in the grave. In the Old Kingdom, with the emergence of true mummification, the body was fashioned into a formal image closely resembling a statue, with the limbs fully extended... This iconography was replaced around 2100 BCE by the classic mummy, in which the body and limbs were cocooned in linen swathings, with only the head emerging..."[143]

Chapter 6 - An Evolution of Death - The Earliest Times [Before 300 BCE]

"The time allotted to the treatment of the corpse varied, but seventy days is most often mentioned as the idea. The manipulations of the body during this period began with cleansings, extraction of the internal organs (except the heart), and desiccation of the corpse and the principal viscera using natron, a natural salt compound."[144]

"The place of burial depended on one's abode and one's rank in society. The king's burials were in cemeteries linked either to the principal royal residence... or associated with major religious centers. Important court members and officials were sometimes buried near the king, but many had tombs in the locality where they lived and worked, and this was the rule for the majority of the population. Cemeteries were usually situated on the west bank of the Nile along the desert fringes. They might develop organically but at important sites there was a high degree of organization, projecting social structures beyond the threshold of death into the next world."[145]

Here is another perspective of the customs of ancient Egypt:

"The ancient Egyptians had an elaborate set of burial customs that they believed were necessary to ensure their immortality after death. These rituals and protocols included mummification, casting of magic spells, and burial with specific grave goods thought to be needed in the afterlife. The burial customs used by the ancient Egyptians evolved throughout time as old customs were discarded and new ones adopted, but several important elements of the process persisted. Although specific details changed over time, the preparation of the body, the magic rituals involved, and the grave goods provided were all essential parts of a proper Egyptian funeral. ...

"After the mummy was prepared, it would need to be re-animated, symbolically, by a priest. The Opening of the Mouth Ceremony was conducted by a priest who would utter a spell and touch the mummy or sarcophagus with a

Chapter 6 - An Evolution of Death - The Earliest Times [Before 300 BCE]

ceremonial adze - a copper or stone blade. This ceremony ensured that the mummy could breathe and speak in the afterlife. In a similar fashion, the priest could utter spells to reanimate the mummy's arms, legs, and other body parts.

"In addition to the Opening of the Mouth ceremony, many mummies were provided with some form of funerary literature to take with them to the afterlife. Most funerary literature consists of lists of spells and instructions for navigating the afterlife. During the Old Kingdom, only the pharaoh had access to this material, which scholars refer to as the Pyramid Texts. The Pyramid Texts are a collection of spells to help the pharaoh in the afterlife. The Pharaoh Unas was the first to use this collection of spells, as he and a few subsequent pharaohs had them carved on the walls of their pyramids. ...

"From the earliest periods of Egyptian history, all Egyptians were buried with at least some burial goods which they thought necessary after death. At a minimum, these usually consisted of everyday objects such as bowls, combs, and other trinkets, along with food. Wealthier Egyptians could afford to be buried with jewelry, furniture, and other valuables, which made them targets of tomb robbers. Mummies were also equipped with the Weres headrest amulet which were magical amulets that were designed to protect the mummy's head. ...

"As burial customs developed in the Old Kingdom, wealthy citizens were buried in wooden coffins and were accompanied by more varied kinds of valuables. Starting in the First Intermediate period, wooden models became very popular burial goods. These wooden models often depict everyday activities that the deceased expected to continue doing in the afterlife. Also, a type of rectangular coffin became the standard, being brightly painted and often including an offering formula.[146]

Chapter 6 - An Evolution of Death - The Earliest Times [Before 300 BCE]

As we near the next stage in history, life in many of these countries was changing. Surrounding the Mediterranean, traffic by sea had grown considerably. The ability to trade goods and the outreach of the shifting empire would have military and political leaders far from home, but this also meant a growth in immigration and of those who would remain.

"Egypt under Ptolemaic and Roman rule was home to an influx of settlers from abroad who brought with them their own distinctive ideas and customs about death and the afterlife. ... the range of funerary beliefs and practices expanded... Greek-style cremations begin to appear in Egypt for the first time. Destruction of the body by fire is a very unEgyptian idea, as it implies disbelief in the notion of the preserved corpse as eternal home."[147]

- **Monuments and Markers**

I've invested a number of years attempting to weave all of the history I wish to share into a linear fabric, hence the "evolution" of Death. This type of history is much like strolling through a cemetery, one which holds many generations interred over centuries. Although we often find a vague sense of the passage of time, a burial ground is not linear. I recall seeing markers from near Civil War times within a very short distance from a memorial stone for someone who died more recently than World War II. The realities of death and burial is that practical matters, issues of kinship, politics, even simply the matter of *space* will often dictate proximity. As I move through the portion of this book which is the "evolution" of Death, I will frequently diverge from a timeline and will mark those shifts in topic and history with one of the handsome markers drawn for me by Dianne Lorden.

Imagine that all of my research and notes and written passage constitute a burial ground, one which has been layered, which has all manner of individual. We might be moving along in discussion of a particular topic when I say, as I might in reality, "But look over here!"

Chapter 6 - An Evolution of Death - The Earliest Times [Before 300 BCE]

Ishtar

My research and knowledge of the evolution of religion so often takes me to the Fertile Crescent. Although this region has lost much of its horticultural fertility due to, some believe, mismanagement of natural resources[148] and improper irrigation, the seeds of those great civilizations were many. Whether I trace my studies of botanical medicine and ethnobotany to the earliest recorded data or think, with wonder, at the ability of the ancient civilizations to discern such incredible information from studying the heavens; when I look at the religious myths which are found throughout region today I see that the seeds of the ancients who lived in the Fertile Crescent have sprouted and taken root right along with the further expansion and exploration by our human species as we came to now inhabit the entire globe.

The religions which held the legend of the Goddess descending into the Underworld, meeting death and returning again to promote fertility in the above world are known to be well-established around 3,000 BCE. There are numerous variations to the myths based upon modern authors and translations. My focus being other than this I simply wish to introduce you to this story, for the religions which worshipped Ishtar and her sister goddesses in other cultures are quite possibly the oldest religions we know to have believed in the transcendence of death as an option for humans - at the very least at a metaphorical level.

There is, undoubtedly, far more information about this period than what I am able to present. At best I am skimming the surface with this overview, historically, of how our views have evolved. I am dependent upon scholars. The following excerpts are taken from MacDonald's work:

> "Much of our knowledge of the Babylonian underworld abode of the dead is derived from the Lay of Istar's Descent to Hades, an extremely interesting mythological poem which has come down to us in Semitic form, but is supposed to be based on earlier Accadian matter. Queen Istar, grief stricken and inconsolable over the death of her beautiful young bridegroom

Tammuz, went on a journey to the underworld in search of the water of life which would restore him to her.

"In Hades, she had to pass through seven gates, and at each one, some article of clothes, crown, jewel, or personal adornment had to be forfeited, and by the time that unfortunate woman got through the seventh gate, its wardens left her naked as at birth.

"But worse was still to come. When she appeared before Hades' rather grim ruler who handed her over to an official called Namtar, all the members of Istar's body were afflicted with diseases as punishment for sins committed on earth.

"After a period of imprisonment, the queen was sprinkled with the water of life and led back to each of the seven gates where all her belongings were restored to her. At the same time the water of life was poured over Tammuz, he was clothed with a purple robe and they put a ring of crystal on his finger."[149]

A goddess of love and war, fertility and sexuality, Ishtar was widely worshipped in areas of Mesopotamia and Assyria. There were numerous shrines and places of religion and worship dedicated to her. In contemporary study she is often equated with the goddess Venus. She is considered to be equated with Astarte of the Arameans and Inanna of the Sumerians.

Her myth is the core of what today in modern Wicca is, for many, known as the Legend of the Descent of the Goddess into the Underworld. As a goddess of regeneration, this myth becomes integral to many of the modern mythology which explains the never-ending cycle of the fertile Goddess of Nature descending into the Underworld where She conquers death and returns so that the earth is again green and lush and ready for the pollination - the sexual life of the plant world.

The Eleusinian Mysteries

In my varied reading of neopagan and Wiccan literature as a Wiccan Priest, I have come across references to the

Chapter 6 - An Evolution of Death - The Earliest Times [Before 300 BCE]

Eleusinian Mysteries on many occasions and also in a variety of contexts. Eleusis was a city located northwest of modern Athens. Archaeological research shows that Eleusis may have been a sacred site as early as 1700 BCE and remained functional until nearly 400 CE. The Eleusinian Mysteries have much to do with an initiatory tradition which holds at its center the sacred myth of the descent of Demeter into the Underworld to bring back her daughter Persephone. I believe it *possible* (I am not adequately educated in this field) that this legend has as its earlier source the religious myths which date back to the Fertile Crescent, to the Assyrian and Babylonian goddess Ishtar, and the Aramean goddess Astarte. There were variations of legends of the Descent of the Goddess into the Underworld, which would have aided the understanding of the way in which life returned to the agrarian surface following the winter death. Ishtar may be in the oldest surviving fragments of the *Epic of Gilgamesh* which dates back to the 18th century BCE.

"The famous Eleusinian Mysteries were known in Greece before Orphism arose. They began on a small scale among certain noble families at Eleusis; but when Eleusis was annexed by Athens in the seventh century before Christ the mysteries became a branch of the Attic state religion. ... Like Orphism, these mysteries of Eleusis were founded on a myth. In their beliefs the central figure was Demeter, the goddess of soil and crops. While her daughter Persephone was once gathering flowers with her maidens, she was seized by the god Hades and carried off to his kingdom below the earth. In deep mourning for her lost child, Demeter neglected her divine duties as the earth mother, so that there was no seed-time or harvest in the world and mankind was faced with starvation. Responding to human prayers, Zeus intervened, and sent Hermes to bring Persephone back to earth. But since she had tasted the food of Hades, she must return to him each year for four months. Yet always in springtime she would reappear from the gloomy realm below. The myth is a familiar kind of story which aims to account for the death of vegetation in the winter and its miraculous return in spring; but if it had meant no more than that, there would have been no mysteries. The worship of Demeter, however, had been specially associated with Eleusis, and at that centre there arose a series of rites which interpreted the myth to be a promise of immortal happiness to all who could win, through initiation, the favor and promise of Demeter."[150]

Not only is the Eleusinian mythos of interest, but it also carries with it a broader view of death and dying. The belief that following a specific religious practice, of becoming an Initiate, would bring one to immortal happiness has some implied information along with it. There are two unspoken aspects to this which I'd like to address.
- First, there is the concept of immortality, of there being some essence of the self which survives the death of the body.
- The second is that we have some control over the outcome by changing the course of events in our incarnate life.

Death had become a motivating factor for living one's life more in conformity with the recommended practices of one's cultural religion. Religion informs us regarding the nature of reality and of the nature of deity as believed by that religion and, as a consequence, guides us in living our lives based upon a belief that when the body passes away, that relationship with our religion will now be shaped by how well we have followed the ethics and morals and lifestyle indicated by the religion.

Humans grew in their knowledge and skills and began to expand their own range learning to adapt to climates less temperate. As the center of civilization was shifted from Mesopotamia to Egypt to Greece, the beliefs and religious practices also stayed the same and yet changed and adapted at the same time.

Despite the beauty and hope promised for those who became initiates within the Eleusinian mystery tradition, it could still be said that the "Greeks of Homer's time regarded death as the greatest calamity that could overtake a human being."[151]

And yet, the same can be said for religions and people in most times. Death is looked upon with fear and dread. Truly, the Mysteries are not for everyone. Had I the time and far more resources, I would be so pleased to have some concept of what the demographics might have been for the Eleusinian Initiates. Were they as small a segment of the population as it seems those who embrace the deepest Mysteries usually are?

"It was due to the influence of the mystery schools that the Greek eschatology made such an advancement in the poetry of Pindar." According to Pindar, the future life is a life of happiness and knowledge for the initiated. 'Blessed is he,' Pindar says, 'who has beheld the mysteries and descends under the hollow earth; he knows the end; he knows the divine origin of life.'"[152]

Orphism

Orpheus was, in many ways, a Bard but in a different world. To the ancient Greeks he was musician, poet, and prophet. As an artist, he had the "ability to charm all living things and even stones with his music" but, alas, when his wife Eurydice died and went to the Underworld, his music was unable to bring her back. In ancient Greek culture, Orpheus is often considered the founder of the Mysteries of Dionysus. The Mysteries of Orpheus have to do with his having descended into Hades, into the Underworld, and been able to return.

Orphism evolved into a Mystery Religion which included Initiation. Among their beliefs was that humans had souls which survived the death of the body. The soul had aspects of divinity and also immortality. The usual pattern for the soul following the body's death was to reincarnate in what was called a "'grievous circle' of successive bodily lives."[153] By choosing to live an ascetic life and pursuing the necessary training and education and living the appropriate lifestyle one could become an Initiate which would enable one to achieve a communion with deities. "The Orphics taught that the purity of life was not enough. The believer must be initiated into the sect by mystic rites and sustained in his growth by sacraments in which he could share the divine nature."[154]

The *Derveni papyrys* is a roll discovered in 1962. Found in Derveni in northern Greece, it enables scholars to date the scroll itself

Chapter 6 - An Evolution of Death - The Earliest Times [Before 300 BCE]

to 340 BCE, but also indicates the beliefs to be significantly older. According to Addison (whose book was published thirty years prior to the discovery of the oldest European manuscript), "...there arose, sometime before the sixth century (B.C.), a second tide of Dionysiac religion. The new movement was associated with the name of Orpheus whom legend called a prophet of Dionysus. ...this Orphic religion was not absorbed and controlled by the state. Growing up outside the official cultus, it kept and refined its original mystic meaning and began to flourish in the form of *sects*. For the first time in Europe there had appeared a missionary religion of salvation whose adherents were grouped in little churches. ...their teaching became a controlling element in all the later thought of Greece about the life beyond death. For the worship of Dionysus was no longer on the level of riotous barbarism; it had been purified and transformed into a system of belief with a message for the soul of man and a way of life by which he might achieve a blessed immortality."[155]

There is a close link with the Mysteries of Dionysus as well, as Dionysus (Bacchus) was also to have descended into the Underworld and returned. Orphism represents a significant shift in attitudes toward death and dying. "Hitherto... the Greeks had looked forward to nothing better than a dismal Hades for all men. Only the immortal gods could enjoy eternal blessedness, and no way was open to man by which he could share their joys. Now, at length, ...there was proclaimed a path to immortality. By sharing in the divine nature of Dionysus, through sacraments and mystic experience, all believers might themselves become divine and win the heritage of a deathless bliss. Through a god who had once died and lived again, men too might die only to live again. Purified by the proper rites, the devout need have no fear of death."[156]

Many scholars believe that the Orphic Mysteries were so influential that, "In Plato [Orphic teaching] received its highest expression, and through Plato it passed into the philosophy of the Greco-Roman world and even helped to mould the doctrine of the Christian Church."[157]

Ancient Group Believed Departed Souls Lived in Stone Monuments

"Archaeologists in southeastern Turkey have discovered an Iron Age chiseled stone slab that provides the first written evidence in the region that people believed the soul was separate from the body. University of Chicago researchers will describe the discovery, a testimony created by an Iron Age official that includes an incised image of the man, on Nov. 22-23 at conferences of biblical and Middle Eastern archaeological scholars in Boston.

"The Neubauer Expedition of the Oriental Institute at the University of Chicago found the 800-pound basalt stele, 3 feet tall and 2 feet wide, at Zincirli (pronounced "Zin-jeer-lee"), the site of the ancient city of Sam'al. Once the capital of a prosperous kingdom, it is now one of the most important Iron Age sites under excavation.

"The stele is the first of its kind to be found intact in its original location, enabling scholars to learn about funerary customs and life in the eighth century B.C. At the time, vast empires emerged in the ancient Middle East, and cultures such as the Israelites and Phoenicians became part of a vibrant mix.

"The man featured on the stele was probably cremated, a practice that Jewish and other cultures shun because of a belief in the unity of body and soul. According to the inscription, the soul of the deceased resided in the stele.

"'The stele is in almost pristine condition. It is unique in its combination of pictorial and textual features and thus provides an important addition to our knowledge of ancient language and culture,' said David Schloen, Associate Professor at the Oriental Institute and Director of the University's Neubauer Expedition to Zincirli. ...

"According to Schloen, the stele vividly demonstrates that Iron Age Sam'al, located in the border zone between Anatolia and Syria, inherited both Semitic and Indo-European cultural traditions. Kuttamuwa and his king, Panamuwa, had non-

Semitic names, reflecting the migration of Indo-European speakers into the region centuries earlier under the Hittite Empire based in central Anatolia (modern Turkey), which had conquered the region. But by the eighth century B.C., they were speaking the local West Semitic dialect and were fully integrated into local culture. Kuttumuwa's inscription shows a fascinating mixture of non-Semitic and Semitic cultural elements, including a belief in the enduring human soul— which did not inhabit the bones of the deceased, as in traditional Semitic thought, but inhabited his stone monument, possibly because the remains of the deceased were cremated. Cremation was considered to be abhorrent in the Old Testament and in traditional West Semitic culture, but there is archaeological evidence for Indo-European-style cremation in neighboring Iron Age sites, although not yet at Zincirli itself.

"In future excavation campaigns, the Neubauer Expedition, under Schloen's direction, plans to excavate large areas of the site in order to understand the social and economic organization of the city and its cultural development over the centuries. Schloen hopes to illuminate Iron Age culture more widely, of which Zincirli provides a richly documented example."[158]

"That the living do come from the dead, as Socrates intuitively perceived as he was about to drink the hemlock and experience death, this treatise maintains, not in virtue of tradition or belief, but on the sound basis of the unequivocal testimony of yogins who claim to have died and re-entered the human womb consciously."[159]

Chapter 6 - An Evolution of Death - The Earliest Times [Before 300 BCE]

Notes for Chapter Six

[90] Houlbrooke, Ralph, ed., *Death, Ritual, and Bereavement*, Routledge in association with the Social History Society of the United Kingdom, London, New York © 1989, page 1, quote from W. Shakespeare, Hamlet I ii 72

[91] Farrell, James J., *Inventing the American Way of Death, 1830-1920*, Temple University Press © 1989, page 3

[92] The Tradition of Lothloriën which is the core of The Rowan Tree Church

[93] Rev. Norman MacDonald, *The After-Life in Celtic and Oriental Folklore*, pub. 1970 by the author in Cachan Locheport, page 20

[94] James Thayer Addison, *Life Beyond Death In the Beliefs of Mankind*, Houghton Mifflin Co., © 1932, page 62

[95] James Thayer Addison, *Life Beyond Death In the Beliefs of Mankind*, Houghton Mifflin Co., © 1932, page 62

[96] James Thayer Addison, *Life Beyond Death In the Beliefs of Mankind*, Houghton Mifflin Co., © 1932, page 60

[97] Rev. Norman MacDonald, *The After-Life in Celtic and Oriental Folklore*, pub. 1970 by the author in Cachan Locheport, page 7

[98] in *Religions of the Ancient World: A Guide*, Johnston, Sarah Iles (ed.), The Belknap Press of Harvard University Press, Cambridge and London, © 2004, page 479 by John J. Collins

[99] James Thayer Addison, *Life Beyond Death In the Beliefs of Mankind*, Houghton Mifflin Co., © 1932, pages 60-61

[100] James Thayer Addison, *Life Beyond Death In the Beliefs of Mankind*, Houghton Mifflin Co., © 1932, pages 183-184

[101] Mish, Frederick C. (ed. in chief), *Merriam-Webster's Collegiate Dictionary*, 11th edition, Merriam-Webster, Inc., Springfield, MA © 2005

[102] Rev. Norman MacDonald, *The After-Life in Celtic and Oriental Folklore*, pub. 1970 by the author in Cachan Locheport, page 11

[103] *Death and Burial in the Roman World*, J. M. C. Toynbee, The Johns Hopkins University Press, Baltimore © 1971, page 12

[104] Rev. Norman MacDonald, *The After-Life in Celtic and Oriental Folklore*, pub. 1970 by the author in Cachan Locheport, page 12

[105] Rev. Norman MacDonald, *The After-Life in Celtic and Oriental Folklore*, pub. 1970 by the author in Cachan Locheport, page 11

Chapter 6 - An Evolution of Death - The Earliest Times [Before 300 BCE]

[106] James Thayer Addison, *Life Beyond Death In the Beliefs of Mankind*, Houghton Mifflin Co., © 1932, pages 248-249

[107] in *Religions of the Ancient World: A Guide*, Johnston, Sarah Iles (ed.), The Belknap Press of Harvard University Press, Cambridge and London, © 2004, page 470 *Introduction* by John J. Collins

[108] Rev. Norman MacDonald, *The After-Life in Celtic and Oriental Folklore*, pub. 1970 by the author in Cachan Locheport, page 5

[109] Rev. Norman MacDonald, *The After-Life in Celtic and Oriental Folklore*, pub. 1970 by the author in Cachan Locheport, page 5

[110] Rev. Norman MacDonald, *The After-Life in Celtic and Oriental Folklore*, pub. 1970 by the author in Cachan Locheport, page 5

[111] Rev. Norman MacDonald, *The After-Life in Celtic and Oriental Folklore*, pub. 1970 by the author in Cachan Locheport, page 16

[112] Rev. Norman MacDonald, *The After-Life in Celtic and Oriental Folklore*, pub. 1970 by the author in Cachan Locheport, page 16

[113] James Thayer Addison, *Life Beyond Death In the Beliefs of Mankind*, Houghton Mifflin Co., © 1932, page 133

[114] James Thayer Addison, *Life Beyond Death In the Beliefs of Mankind*, Houghton Mifflin Co., © 1932, page 135

[115] Rev. Norman MacDonald, *The After-Life in Celtic and Oriental Folklore*, pub. 1970 by the author in Cachan Locheport, pages 17-18

[116] James Thayer Addison, *Life Beyond Death In the Beliefs of Mankind*, Houghton Mifflin Co., © 1932, pages 92-93

[117] James Thayer Addison, *Life Beyond Death In the Beliefs of Mankind*, Houghton Mifflin Co., © 1932, pages 88-89

[118] Evans-Wentz wrote that in 1955.

[119] *The Tibetan Book of the Dead*, compiled and edited by W.Y. Evans-Wentz Oxford University Press © 1960; preface to the third edition, W.Y. Evans-Wentz, page x

[120] in *Religions of the Ancient World: A Guide*, Johnston, Sarah Iles (ed.), The Belknap Press of Harvard University Press, Cambridge and London, © 2004, page 471 by John Taylor

Chapter 6 - An Evolution of Death - The Earliest Times [Before 300 BCE]

[121] in *Religions of the Ancient World: A Guide*, Johnston, Sarah Iles (ed.), The Belknap Press of Harvard University Press, Cambridge and London, © 2004, page 470 by John J. Collins

[122] Rev. Norman MacDonald, *The After-Life in Celtic and Oriental Folklore*, pub. 1970 by the author in Cachan Locheport, pages 12-13

[123] James Thayer Addison, *Life Beyond Death In the Beliefs of Mankind*, Houghton Mifflin Co., © 1932, pages 10-11

[124] James Thayer Addison, *Life Beyond Death In the Beliefs of Mankind*, Houghton Mifflin Co., © 1932, page 44

[125] in *Religions of the Ancient World: A Guide*, Johnston, Sarah Iles (ed.), The Belknap Press of Harvard University Press, Cambridge and London, © 2004, page 477 by Dina Katz

[126] http://en.wikipedia.org/wiki/Stonehenge

[127] in *Religions of the Ancient World: A Guide*, Johnston, Sarah Iles (ed.), The Belknap Press of Harvard University Press, Cambridge and London, © 2004, page 479 by Tawny L. Holm

[128] in *Religions of the Ancient World: A Guide*, Johnston, Sarah Iles (ed.), The Belknap Press of Harvard University Press, Cambridge and London, © 2004, page 483 by John J. Collins

[129] in *Religions of the Ancient World: A Guide*, Johnston, Sarah Iles (ed.), The Belknap Press of Harvard University Press, Cambridge and London, © 2004, pages 483-484 by Theo van den Hout

[130] in *Religions of the Ancient World: A Guide*, Johnston, Sarah Iles (ed.), The Belknap Press of Harvard University Press, Cambridge and London, © 2004, page 480 by John J. Collins

[131] in *Religions of the Ancient World: A Guide*, Johnston, Sarah Iles (ed.), The Belknap Press of Harvard University Press, Cambridge and London, © 2004, page 486 by Philippe Gignoux

[132] in *Religions of the Ancient World: A Guide*, Johnston, Sarah Iles (ed.), The Belknap Press of Harvard University Press, Cambridge and London, © 2004, page 488 by Vedia Izzet

[133] in *Religions of the Ancient World: A Guide*, Johnston, Sarah Iles (ed.), The Belknap Press of Harvard University Press, Cambridge and London, © 2004, page 489 by Vedia Izzet

Chapter 6 - An Evolution of Death - The Earliest Times [Before 300 BCE]

[134] *Death and Burial in the Roman World*, J. M. C. Toynbee, The Johns Hopkins University Press, Baltimore © 1971, pages 14-15

[135] in *Religions of the Ancient World: A Guide*, Johnston, Sarah Iles (ed.), The Belknap Press of Harvard University Press, Cambridge and London, © 2004, pages 489-490 by John Bodel

[136] in *Religions of the Ancient World: A Guide*, Johnston, Sarah Iles (ed.), The Belknap Press of Harvard University Press, Cambridge and London, © 2004, page 490 by John Bodel

[137] in *Religions of the Ancient World: A Guide*, Johnston, Sarah Iles (ed.), The Belknap Press of Harvard University Press, Cambridge and London, © 2004, pages 490 by John Bodel

[138] in *Religions of the Ancient World: A Guide*, Johnston, Sarah Iles (ed.), The Belknap Press of Harvard University Press, Cambridge and London, © 2004, pages 492 by John Bodel

[139] *Death and Burial in the Roman World*, J. M. C. Toynbee, The Johns Hopkins University Press, Baltimore © 1971, page 73

[140] *Death and Burial in the Roman World*, J. M. C. Toynbee, The Johns Hopkins University Press, Baltimore © 1971, page 48

[141] in *Religions of the Ancient World: A Guide*, Johnston, Sarah Iles (ed.), The Belknap Press of Harvard University Press, Cambridge and London, © 2004, page 486 by Sara Iles Johnston

[142] in *Religions of the Ancient World: A Guide*, Johnston, Sarah Iles (ed.), The Belknap Press of Harvard University Press, Cambridge and London, © 2004, page 488 by Sara Iles Johnston

[143] in *Religions of the Ancient World: A Guide*, Johnston, Sarah Iles (ed.), The Belknap Press of Harvard University Press, Cambridge and London, © 2004, page 473 by John Taylor

[144] in *Religions of the Ancient World: A Guide*, Johnston, Sarah Iles (ed.), The Belknap Press of Harvard University Press, Cambridge and London, © 2004, page 473 by John Taylor

[145] in *Religions of the Ancient World: A Guide*, Johnston, Sarah Iles (ed.), The Belknap Press of Harvard University Press, Cambridge and London, © 2004, page 474 by John Taylor

[146] http://en.wikipedia.org/wiki/Ancient_Egyptian_burial_customs 27 xii 2008 ce

Chapter 6 - An Evolution of Death - The Earliest Times [Before 300 BCE]

[147] in *Religions of the Ancient World: A Guide*, Johnston, Sarah Iles (ed.), The Belknap Press of Harvard University Press, Cambridge and London, © 2004, page 475 by Dominic Montserrat

[148] David Montgomery, *Dirt: The Erosion of Civilization*

[149] Rev. Norman MacDonald, *The After-Life in Celtic and Oriental Folklore*, pub. 1970 by the author in Cachan Locheport, pages 16-17

[150] James Thayer Addison, *Life Beyond Death In the Beliefs of Mankind*, Houghton Mifflin Co., © 1932, page 114

[151] Rev. Norman MacDonald, *The After-Life in Celtic and Oriental Folklore*, pub. 1970 by the author in Cachan Locheport, page 18

[152] Rev. Norman MacDonald, *The After-Life in Celtic and Oriental Folklore*, pub. 1970 by the author in Cachan Locheport, page 19

[153] http://en.wikipedia.org/wiki/Orphic#Burial_rituals_and_beliefs

[154] James Thayer Addison, *Life Beyond Death In the Beliefs of Mankind*, Houghton Mifflin Co., © 1932, page 110

[155] James Thayer Addison, *Life Beyond Death In the Beliefs of Mankind*, Houghton Mifflin Co., © 1932, pages 108-109

[156] James Thayer Addison, *Life Beyond Death In the Beliefs of Mankind*, Houghton Mifflin Co., © 1932, page 110

[157] James Thayer Addison, *Life Beyond Death In the Beliefs of Mankind*, Houghton Mifflin Co., © 1932, page 111

[158] http://www.newswise.com/articles/view/546481/ - Released by the University of Chicago news office November 18, 2008.

[159] *The Tibetan Book of the Dead*, compiled and edited by W.Y. Evans-Wentz Oxford University Press © 1960; preface to the paperback edition, W.Y. Evans-Wentz, page v

Chapter 7 - An Evolution of Death

The Classical times [300 BCE - 450 CE]

- **The background story**
- **Death & burial in the Roman Empire**
- **Changing Values**
- **Monuments and Markers**

The background story

This chapter encompasses what I see as really two periods in history. The Changing Times, as I call them, begin around 300 BCE as Alexander takes this huge swath of the western world. This coincides with the end of the dynastic era in Egypt (and please, scholars, I am aware of being loose with my historical eras, which I need do for convenience in this book), and encompasses the birth and life of Jesus and the arrival of Christianity.

In my thinking I have this information divided into a similar division as the actual calendar. The word *classical* itself is problematic. Classical Greece, for example, is the period of the 5th and 4th centuries BCE. In music, by contrast, which evolved its forms as we know them later, the classical period is from the mid-1700s and runs about a century. Wikipedia refers to *Classical Antiquity* as a period dated from early Greek literature as early as 700 BCE to as late as 600 CE.

Over the past decades I've found various scholars who have published their findings. I almost feel as if I am a *print* archaeologist who, every so often, finds these wonderful shards of published information. Try as I might, I am unable to put all of these pieces together into as unified a whole as I had once thought possible.

Chapter 7 - An Evolution of Death - The Classical Times [300 BCE - 450 CE]

In July 356 BCE King Philip II of Macedonia and Olympias, princess of Epirus, had a son. It was the 20th or 21st of July, depending upon the historian. Philip had a long history of conducting successful battles and expanded his empire with often violent but successful battles. According to Plutarch, "the night before the consummation of their marriage Olympias dreamed that a thunderbolt fell upon her womb and a great fire was kindled, its flames dispersed all about and then were extinguished. After the marriage Philip dreamed that he put a seal upon his wife's womb, the device of which was the figure of a lion."[160] Alexander's parents fell in love while studying at the Sanctuary of the Gods on Samothrace where they both were being initiated into the Mysteries of Cabeiri. Although the records are not clear, according to Athenaeus, a scholar of their era, this was his *fourth* wife and she was not so pleased when he continued collecting wives! Philip was assassinated in 336 BCE and Alexander, having been a student of Aristotle for some years, stepped into his father's role as King.

Alexander was one of the most successful tacticians and so successful in battles that within ten years he had put together one of the largest empires of the ancient world and ... never lost a battle.

The Changing Times is a phrase that I use to describe an approximate period of time which runs from roughly Alexander the Great until near the birth of Jesus. What led me to this phrase was a question I was asked repeatedly in the late 1970s. As someone who studied astrology - much more akin to Jungian astrology and not what I humorously call *newspaper* astrology - people of that era liked to ask me when the Age of Aquarius would be starting. I knew that an astrological age would not begin at a specific date but there would be a period of change. I spent several years developing my theory (for nearly every astrologer has a personal theory and there is no collective agreement). I felt that the front edge of a cusp for the current period of change (hence, the *Changing Times*) might well be placed in the late 19th century, based upon social, economic, scientific and other events in - addition to unusual positions of planets within the solar system. Unexpectedly, my theory of a 300 year cusp put the previous era of

Chapter 7 - An Evolution of Death - The Classical Times [300 BCE - 450 CE]

change from the Age of Aries into the Age of Pisces from roughly Alexander the Great to Jesus. The former brought to an end dynastic Egypt, for whom the ram and the staff had been highly symbolic. And Jesus brought us into the symbol of the fish.

This period of time which had begun already under Philip, represented a tremendous shift in the religious, economic and political paradigms for what grew into the western world. Not only was Alexander forging his empire, but the political center of the western world would be shifting, ending up in Rome. Ten years before the birth of Alexander was the infamous earthquake which destroyed much of Crete, creating a huge tsunami which washed away vast areas along the Mediterranean coast.

During this same period there was another major earthquake in 226 BCE which devastated the island of Rhodes, destroying the famous Colossus. The near end of this period, just a few decades following the death of Jesus, was the eruption of Mount Vesuvius in 79 CE.

The amount of change during these few centuries struck me as dramatic, even if it did not seem quite as major during those times. The western world was, as we moved into the first decades of the Common Era, poised to embark upon a completely different direction for the next two millennia.

The second half of the Classical Times (as *I* have limned it) brings the strength and then decline of the Roman Empire, and I mark the change into the next period of time with Constantine, who was Emperor from 306-337 and brought yet another major change, this time in religion, which would become the constant religious theme (with untold variations) during the Age of Pisces.

Much of our western culture (as well as philosophy) comes down to us from the western empires. As far as death and the soul, "with the Romans, as with the Etruscans, the survival of the soul after death was an ancient, deep-seated belief. It is true that during the first centuries BC and AD the skeptical attitude to immortality of the Epicurean and Stoic systems had its repercussions in Rome and Italy and elsewhere in the Roman world."[161] It is not as if there are extensive written records and histories left behind for us to study. "The bulk of our evidence, written

Chapter 7 - An Evolution of Death - The Classical Times [300 BCE - 450 CE]

and archaeological, for Roman afterlife ideas is not earlier than the first century BC. For the preceding period Plautus (*c.* 250-184 BC) is our chief literary authority."[162]

To repeat, "In the country districts of the Roman world rich and poor alike could be laid to rest in more or less isolated graves ranging in character from the simplest types of cremation or inhumation burials to those that were marked by, or contained in, elaborately carved or architecturally impressive monuments. A city, on the other hand, has always needed its communal necropolis or necropoleis, at least one dependent city of the dead, more often several such cities, situated on its outskirts. Roman law strictly prescribed that a city's cemeteries should be outside its walls or other formal boundaries."[163]

"Early Roman ideas as to where the *Manes* dwelt, after the body had received due burial, are not explicitly recorded. It is, however, likely that they were thought of as being underground, at or near their burial place, where they could be given nourishment. From later periods there is, indeed, abundant evidence of an urge to keep the dead 'alive' by offerings made to them of food and drink, oil, and even blood and by their share in the funerary meals partaken of at the tomb by the survivors... For this purpose holes were pierced and pipes provided so that the offerings and portions allotted to the dead could penetrate to the burials... There the departed were believed to rest in the kindly bosom of maternal Earth, to whom they had descended. Hence the representations of Terra Mater in sepulchral art. Hence the reiterated prayer of the epitaphs 's(it) t(ibi) t(erra) l(evis).'[164] Hence, too, the notion of immortality as union with the Earth-Goddess - *'cinis sum cinis terra est terra dea est ergo ego mortua non sum;'*[165] and the imagery of bones or ashes giving birth to flowers: *'hic iacet Optatus pietatis nobilis infans/cui precor ut cineres sint ia sintque rosae, terraque quae mater nunc est sibi sit levis oro/namque gravis nulkli vita fuit pueri'* ('Here lies Optatus, a child noble and dutiful. I pray that his ashes may become violets and roses and that the Earth, who is his mother now, rest lightly on him, who in life weighed heavily on no man'). There would seem to be no reason to hold that such thoughts deny individual survival or involve 'renunciation of personality,' absorbed into the pure life-essence of earth. Rather they imply the continuance of the dead's identity."[166]

This was a complex period of time. The vastness of empires combined with extensive trade led to ever-larger cities. Not only were religious values changing, but there was considerable growth in science as well. The Hippocratic School of Medicine, founded just ahead of Alexander, revolutionized medicine at the time. Plato and Socrates were, at the same time as Hippocrates, changing the social and political arena so much that these are names well known today, even if today's citizen is weak on the actual historical reality.

The social, political, and legal structure of Rome had become far more defined. *The Law of the Twelve Tables*, which took considerable political debate and discussion, was initially begun a century before Alexander. This was a prototype which might be a forerunner of what we have today, which defined procedures, rights, and how to deal with such things. Many of these customs or procedures were followed until the late Empire.

One of the conflicts came from the recognition that bodies were, in fact, something which polluted the environment and yet, at the same time, there were strong beliefs about caring for one's ancestors and treating the dead with respect. Thus we find that "all burials, whether of bodies or of ashes, had to take place outside the city. This regulation, laid down in the Twelve Tables, was normally observed until the late Empire... Sanitary precautions and fear of defilement readily explain the law."[167]

- **Death & burial in the Roman Empire**

This period of time has left us far more recorded history than we previously had. Scholars have been able to provide us with some

Chapter 7 - An Evolution of Death - The Classical Times [300 BCE - 450 CE]

detailed descriptions of the practices during these times. Toynbee, to whom I am deeply indebted for the information I bring to this chapter, wrote the following:

"When death was imminent relations and close friends gathered round the dying person's bed, to comfort and support him or her and to give vent to their own grief. The nearest relative present gave the last kiss, to catch the soul, which, so it was believed, left the body with the final breath. The same relative then closed the departed's eyes (*oculos premere*, etc.), after which all the near relatives called upon the dead by name (*conclamare*) and lamented him or her, a process that continued at intervals until the body was disposed of by cremation or inhumation. The next act was to take the body from the bed, to set it on the ground (*deponere*), and to wash it and anoint it. Then followed the dressing of the corpse - in a toga, in the case of a male Roman citizen, the laying of a wreath on its head, particularly in the case of a person who had earned one in life, and the placing of a coin in the mouth to pay the deceased's fare in Charon's barque."[168]

While this may have been appropriate for the common people (like we are, most likely), those with status rated far better.

"In Ancient Rome, important people of the time had elaborate funerals. The funerals themselves were part of a tradition from the early Roman Republic, whereby the achievements of the dead man were celebrated alongside those of his ancestors. Hired mourners were at the front of the procession. These mourners would wear the masks (imagines) of the dead's descendants who had served as magistrates. The emphasis of the funeral therefore, was put on the achievements of the dead. The body of the dead person was behind the mourners. A eulogy (praise for the dead person) was read during the procession. After the funeral, the body was buried or cremated (burnt). If the body was cremated, the ashes were put in a container and the container was buried. If a family did not have enough money to afford a proper funeral, they simply put the corpse in a casket and threw it in a creek where other poor dead people had been thrown. The Egyptian goddess Isis promised the Romans life after death, but this was a much later addition to the Roman belief system, and was not present during the Republican period.

"During the first and second centuries AD, cremation was the most common burial practice in the Roman Empire. Ultimately, inhumation would replace cremation; a variety of factors, including the rise of Christianity among Romans and changes in attitudes to the afterlife, would contribute to this marked shift in popular burial practices.

"Also, coins would be placed in the mouth to ensure a safe journey to the underworld. This was, so we are informed by several ancient sources, most notably Virgil in *Aeneid* Book 6, to pay the boatman Charon, to take them across the river Styx into the underworld itself. There would be food and drink offerings to the dead, for it was thought that the dead could impact the living. Festivals would be held for important members of the family."[169]

"The desire for sanitation, concerns for space and the religious philosophies had led cremation to be the most common burial practice in the Mid- to Late Republic and the Empire into the 1st and 2nd centuries AD."[170]

- **Changing Values: Setting the Stage**

In the centuries leading into this period of time there were a number of shifts in the religious paradigms. During the changing Classical Times themselves, there was a significant alteration in values although I don't know that someone living during those times would have fully grasped the import. Our lives are so short that the events during our lifetimes often seem far greater than they will appear to later generations or are often underestimated, being a catalyst for a far greater degree of change than a might have been imagined. In our brief and fragile human lives we so often believe that our decisions and accomplishments will be of great import, but overall, time moves along.

For me, this has proven to be one of the more difficult periods of time. The transition taking place left the older practices still dominant but within a few more centuries, many of the older practices would be left behind. I found myself returning to the previous periods of time in order to assess this span. We enter this time with Alexander the Great, but by the time we move into the Middle Times (loosely, the Medieval Period), there is a considerable amount of internal turmoil.

Please, however, allow me to back up and take a new start. What I have found through my research leaves me believing that prior to the Classical Times, the assessment made by MacDonald may well have prevailed. Although there were some Mystery Traditions which set the tone for other beliefs, the Mystery Religions have always been for a smaller number of people and not the masses. When it came to the prevailing beliefs under Homer, "Greeks of Homer's time regarded death as the greatest calamity that could overtake a human being."[171] Homer lived 850 BCE, roughly, according to Herodotus although many scholars believe Homer lived more in the 7th or 8th centuries BCE. Affirming this, Addison writes that,"…throughout the whole history of Israel, till the last two centuries before Christ, men viewed with dread this prospect… of endless negative misery…"[172]

It was during the second half of the classical times that Christianity was in the process of, well, becoming *Christianity*. There were discussions and there were disagreements. There were many versions of the history of the life of Jesus written down and, for the sake of having a consistent and cohesive religion, those who emerged as the early leaders of this growing religion had to establish their beliefs even while frequently facing major persecution and prejudice.

One of the theological beliefs which greatly influences death and burial up to and including our contemporary times is the resurrection of the body. And yet, as MacDonald indicates, this is not a new concept but one which the early Christians found compatible in the religions they were replacing:

Chapter 7 - An Evolution of Death - The Classical Times [300 BCE - 450 CE]

> "As we find it today in orthodox Christianity and Mohammedanism, [the belief in the resurrection of the body] may properly be counted the great contribution of the Jews to solving the problem of the life beyond death. But at least four centuries before the Jews had evolved the doctrine it was known in Persia."[173]

In addition, many of the myths and stories found in the Hebrew bible (for most of us, the Old Testament) have been shown to have striking similarities with those of other, much older religions which emerged in the Fertile Crescent. As I quoted earlier:

> "The Hebrews [had] borrowed their ideas of angels, devils, and much else, from Persia. Persian eschatology is unique in that it differs from that of any other county. Far from being a paradise, its nether world is the Hell we read of in the Bible. Duzakh, an abyss tenanted by evil spirits and demons, is a place of unrelieved darkness, woe and torment. At death, the soul crosses the Bridge of Chinvat (meaning gatherer or accountant). This bridge is extended over Hell and leads to Paradise.
>
> "In a particular place, it widens to the length of nine javelins for the souls of the pious, and contracts to a thread for the souls of the wicked, so that they fall off into Hell.
>
> "The faith of Persia lays more emphasis on future retribution. It is, nevertheless, a religion of hope."[174]

If the body is to somehow come to life again, what do we do with it when it has died? This very concept is often the divisive issue when it comes to those making choices between cremation or earth burial. In so many ways all of these later economic and theological issues have much earlier roots, for in later times when funeral technology makes enormous advances, embalming and burying the body as if it is 'sleeping' in appearance, in highly expensive and tightly sealed burial coffins and caskets becomes the norm. ... Addison dates these origins which come down to early Christianity through the Jewish beliefs of the day to more than 500 years before the time of Jesus. To quote again:

"The Persian scheme resembles the Jewish in so many respects, especially in the thought of our bodies living again, that many scholars have seen in Jewish doctrine a direct borrowing from Persian. That conclusion has been all the easier because the Zoroastrian belief is much older than the Hebrew and because the Jews were under Persian rule for some two hundred years before the time of Alexander."[175]

- **Changing Values: The Mysteries**

In addition to the beliefs and practices of the average person, for the population at large, there was also a smaller number of those who saw reality from a more mystical or esoteric perspective. "It was due to the influence of the mystery schools that the Greek eschatology made such an advancement in the poetry of Pindar. According to Pindar, the future life is a life of happiness and knowledge for the initiated. 'Blessed is he,' Pindar says, 'who has beheld the mysteries and descends under the hollow earth; he knows the end; he knows the divine origin of life.'"[176]

Pindar is one of the most notable of poets dating to ancient Greece. He was so respected that when Alexander, highly displeased that Thebes did not eagerly embrace his desire to include it in his empire, demolished it but left Pindar's house intact as Pindar had written poetry praising his namesake. Why is Pindar important? We see in his work much about society in Greece during his lifetime.

Looking back again, we see that even earlier than Pindar:

"... there arose, sometime before the sixth century (B.C.), a second tide of Dionysiac religion. The new movement was associated with the name of Orpheus whom legend called a prophet of Dionysus. ... This Orphic religion was not absorbed and controlled by the state. Growing up outside the official cultus, it kept and refined its original mystic meaning and began to flourish in the form of *sects*. For the first time in Europe there had appeared a missionary religion of salvation whose adherents were grouped in little churches. ... their teaching became a controlling element in all the later thought of Greece about the life beyond death. For the worship of Dionysus was no longer on the level of riotous barbarism; it had been purified and transformed into a system of belief with a message for the soul of man and a way of life by which he might achieve a blessed immortality."[177]

"Hitherto... the Greeks had looked forward to nothing better than a dismal Hades for all men. Only the immortal gods could enjoy eternal blessedness, and no way was open to man by which he could share their joys. Now, at length, ... there was proclaimed a path to immortality. By sharing in the divine nature of Dionysus, through sacraments and mystic experience, all believers might themselves become divine and win the heritage of a deathless bliss. Through a god who had once died and lived again, men too might die only to live again. Purified by the proper rites, the devout need have no fear of death."[178]

"Among the Greeks and Romans, both cremation and burial were practiced. However, the Jews buried their dead. Even God himself is depicted in the Torah as performing burial: "And [God] buried him (Moses) in the depression in the land of Moab, opposite Beth Peor. No man knows the place that he was buried, even to this day." (Deuteronomy 34:6). Early Christians used only burial, as can be demonstrated from the direct testimony of Tertullian and from the stress laid upon the analogy between the resurrection of the body and the Resurrection of Christ (1 Corinthians 15:42)."[179]

"Little is known with regard to the burial of the dead in the early Christian centuries. Early Christians did practice the use of an Ossuary to store the skeletal remains of those saints at rest in Christ. This practice likely came from the use of the same among Second Temple Jews. Other early Christians likely followed the national customs of the people among whom they lived, as long as they were not directly idolatrous. St. Jerome, in his account of the death of St. Paul the Hermit, speaks of the singing of hymns and psalms while the body is carried to the grave as an observance belonging to ancient Christian tradition."[180]

The "Christians" were not Christians initially, but were, as was Jesus, Jews who wanted reform. It would take time for them to decide what their identity would be.

- **Changing Values: Emerging Christianity**

The second half of the Classical Times is often about the latter portion of classical Rome, but for this book I wish to explore the emergence of Christianity. There are few early customs regarding Christian burial because the earliest Christians were still Jewish, as I mentioned just above. It was not until near the "end of the 1st century, [that] Christianity began to be recognized internally and externally as a separate religion from Rabbinic Judaism which itself was refined and developed further in the centuries after the destruction of the Second Jerusalem Temple."[181] As noted above, earth-burial would have predominated and, as their beliefs became cohesive, the belief in resurrection made cremation an undesirable option.

There was considerable internal difficult taking place. In the Roman Empire there were problems with the rapid expansion of Christianity.

> "Rodney Stark estimates that the number of Christians grew by approximately 40% a decade during the first and second centuries. This phenomenal growth rate forced Christian communities to evolve in order to adapt to their changes in the nature of their communities as well as their relationship with their political and socioeconomic environment. As the number of Christians grew, the Christian communities became larger, more numerous and farther apart

Chapter 7 - An Evolution of Death - The Classical Times [300 BCE - 450 CE]

geographically. The passage of time also moved some Christians farther from the original teachings of the apostles giving rise to teachings that were considered heterodox and sowing controversy and divisiveness within churches and between churches."[182]

But within Christianity itself, there was also dissension. Following the death of Jesus, the Apostles set out to spread the word. Initially they carried the word to the Hellenistic (Greek) world and then throughout the Roman Empire and beyond. Following the death of the Apostles, what is often called the 'Apostolic Age' came to an end. Now, without the strong leadership and direct continuity, what was called Christianity went off in all manner of directions. Their message was heard. "According to Will Durant, the Christian Church prevailed over Paganism because it offered a much more attractive doctrine and because the church leaders addressed human needs better than their rivals."[183]

Christianity began to emerge as increasingly separate from Judaism. This was in part as the early Christians adopted and Christianized practices. Baptism, which today seems so very Christian to us, predated Christianity as it was Jewish. Paul, one who shaped Christianity in so many ways, "likened baptism to being buried with Christ in his death (Romans 6:3,4; Colossians 2:12)."[184]

Christians faced persecution at various times. The issue which was the most problematic was that the Roman Emperor was considered to be a divinity and should be treated with the appropriate type of honor. As a targeted minority but also as a growing faith which would be perceived as a threat by the ruling aristocracy, persecution had increased significantly by the second century. Earlier, under Nero, the earliest documented persecution led by the imperial class was waged. When Rome was devastated by the fire in 64 CE, Nero laid all blame upon the Christians. As Wikipedia describes it, "Nero fastened the guilt and inflicted the most exquisite tortures on a class hated for their abominations, called Christians [or Chrestians by the populace (Tacit. Annals XV, see Tacitus on Jesus)."[185]

Chapter 7 - An Evolution of Death - The Classical Times [300 BCE - 450 CE]

The degree of persecution at times would have to have added to the shaping of theology within the emerging Christian church. Early Christian history contains remarkable stories of martyrs, those willing to die for their faith. It was not until my research into this period of time that I had any concept about the extent of persecution. For so many, to be Christian meant a willingness to face death.

By the closing of this early Christian era, Christianity within the Roman Empire was as diverse as it is today. There were many leaders (hundreds of bishops alone) and variations of belief.

Christianity was growing fast, and the Roman Empire and then Constantinople, would become the setting for what would shape the western world for the Age of Pisces. Global domination would ultimately come from ruling the seas and the religion of Christianity became symbolized by the fish.

The times were right, people were ready for a change, and the message they heard from the Christians had considerable appeal. Buddhist beliefs had spread throughout much of Asia with the same rapidity. These were the Changing Times. When the world is filled with change, there is much anxiety and, as we see in our own lifetime, that often leads to persecution and fear of those who are different and who represent change.

"The persecutions culminated with Diocletian and Galerius at the end of the third and beginning of the 4th century. The Great Persecution is considered the largest. Beginning with a series of four edicts banning Christian practices and ordering the imprisonment of Christian clergy, the persecution intensified until all Christians in the empire were commanded to sacrifice to the gods or face immediate execution. Over 20,000 Christians are thought to have died during Diocletian's reign. However, as Diocletian zealously persecuted Christians in the Eastern part of the empire, his co-emperors in the West did not follow the edicts and so Christians in Gaul, Spain, and Britannia were virtually unmolested."[186]

For many, the fear of death by persecution ended with Constantine when Christianity was declared legal and was moving toward Theodosius I who would make it the official, state religion.

There are widely differing figures for the number of Christians thought to have died for their faith, from a lower estimate of 10,000 to ten times that many. Christians were persecuted not only in the Roman Empire. In the Persian Sassanid Empire Shapur II, a Zoroastrian, declared that all Christians should be put to death. Athanaric, who was the king of the Goths, was fiercely opposed to Christianity, ordering Christians to be persecuted.

It did not end. In Najran, that area today known as Saudi Arabia, the king, Dhu Nuwas, is said to have persecuted and killed as many as 20,000 Christians according to records written by the Bishop of Beth Arsham in 524 CE. This was a tribal area as I understand it, with the people predominately practicing a variant of the Jewish religion.

- **Monuments and Markers**

Christian Expansion

"Early Christianity spread from city to city throughout the Hellenized Roman Empire and beyond into East Africa and South Asia. The Christian Apostles, said to have dispersed from Jerusalem, traveled extensively and established communities in major cities and regions throughout the Empire. The original church communities were founded in northern Africa, Asia Minor, Armenia, Arabia, Greece, and other places by apostles (see Apostolic see) and other Christian soldiers, merchants, and preachers. Over forty were established by the year 100, many in Asia Minor, such as the seven churches of Asia. By the end of the 1st century, Christianity had spread to Greece and Italy, even India.

"In 301 AD, the Kingdom of Armenia became the first state to declare Christianity as its official religion, following the conversion of the Royal House of the Arsacids in Armenia.

Chapter 7 - An Evolution of Death - The Classical Times [300 BCE - 450 CE]

The Armenian Apostolic Church is the world's oldest national church.

"Despite sometimes intense persecutions, the Christian religion continued its spread throughout the Mediterranean Basin.

"There is no agreement on an explanation of how Christianity managed to spread so successfully prior to the Edict of Milan. For some Christians, the success was simply the natural consequence of the truth of the religion and the direct intervention of God. However, similar explanations are claimed for the spread of, for instance, Islam and Buddhism. In *The Rise of Christianity*, Rodney Stark argues that Christianity triumphed over paganism chiefly because it improved the lives of its adherents in various ways. Another factor, more recently pointed out, was the way in which Christianity combined its promise of a general resurrection of the dead with the traditional Greek belief that true immortality depended on the survival of the body, with Christianity adding practical explanations of how this was going to actually happen at the end of the world. For Mosheim the rapid progression of Christianity was explained by two factors: translations of the New Testament and the Apologies composed in defence of Christianity. Edward Gibbon, in his classic *The History of the Decline and Fall of the Roman Empire*, discusses the topic in considerable detail in his famous Chapter Fifteen, summarizing the historical causes of the early success of Christianity as follows: '(1) The inflexible, and, if we may use the expression, the intolerant zeal of the Christians, derived, it is true, from the Jewish religion, but purified from the narrow and unsocial spirit which, instead of inviting, had deterred the Gentiles from embracing the law of Moses. (2) The doctrine of a future life, improved by every additional circumstance which could give weight and efficacy to that important truth. (3) The miraculous powers ascribed to the primitive church. (4) The pure and austere morals of the Christians. (5) The union and discipline of the Christian republic, which gradually formed an independent and increasing state in the heart of the Roman empire.'"[187]

The Druids left no artifacts

"A druid was a member of the priestly class among the Celtic peoples of Gaul, Britain, Ireland, and possibly elsewhere during the Iron Age. Very little is known about the ancient druids. They left no written accounts of themselves and the only evidence is a few descriptions left by Greek, Roman and various scattered authors and artists, as well as stories created by later medieval Irish writers. While archaeological evidence has been uncovered pertaining to the religious practices of the Iron Age people, 'not one single artefact or image has been unearthed that can undoubtedly be connected with the ancient Druids.' Various recurring themes emerge in a number of the Greco-Roman accounts of the druids, including that they performed human sacrifice, believed in a form of reincarnation, and held a high position in Gaulish society. Next to nothing is known about their cultic practice, except for the ritual of oak and mistletoe as described by Pliny the Elder.

"The earliest known reference to the druids dates to 200 BCE, although the oldest actual description comes from the Roman military general Julius Caesar in his Commentarii de Bello Gallico (50s BCE). Later Greco-Roman writers also described the druids, including Cicero, Tacitus and Pliny the Elder. Following the Roman invasion of Gaul, druidism was suppressed by the Roman government under the 1st century CE emperors Tiberius and Claudius, and it had disappeared from the written record by the 2nd century.

"In about 750 CE the word druid appears in a poem by Blathmac, who wrote about Jesus, saying that he was '...better than a prophet, more knowledgeable than every druid, a king who was a bishop and a complete sage.' The druids then also appear in some of the medieval tales from Christianized Ireland like the Táin Bó Cúailnge, where they are largely portrayed as sorcerers who opposed the coming of Christianity. In the wake of the Celtic revival during the 18th and 19th centuries, fraternal and Neopagan groups were founded based on ideas about the ancient druids, a movement which is known as Neo-Druidism. Many popular modern notions about Druids have no connection to the Druids of the Iron Age, and are largely based on much later inventions or misconceptions."[188]

The Celts
"Celtic polytheism, commonly known as Celtic paganism, comprises the religious beliefs and practices adhered to by the Iron Age peoples of Western Europe now known as the Celts, roughly between 500 BCE and 500 CE, spanning the La Tène period and the Roman era, and in the case of the Insular Celts the British and Irish Iron Age.

"Celtic polytheism was one of a larger group of Iron Age polytheistic religions of the Indo-European family. It comprised a large degree of variation both geographically and chronologically, although 'behind this variety, broad structural similarities can be detecte' allowing there to be 'a basic religious homogeneity' amongst the Celtic peoples.

"The Celtic pantheon consists of numerous recorded theonyms, both from Greco-Roman ethnography and from epigraphy. Among the most prominent ones are Teutatis, Taranis and Lugus. Figures from medieval Irish mythology have also been adduced by comparative mythology, interpreted as euhemerized versions of pre-Christian Insular deities. The most salient feature of Celtic religion as reflected in Roman historiography is their extensive practice of human sacrifice. According to Greek and Roman accounts, in Gaul,

Chapter 7 - An Evolution of Death - The Classical Times [300 BCE - 450 CE]

Britain and Ireland, there was a priestly caste of 'magico-religious specialists' known as the druids, although very little is definitely known about them.

"Following the Roman Empire's conquest of Gaul (58–51 BCE) and southern Britannia (43 CE), Celtic religious practices began to display elements of Romanisation, resulting in a syncretic Gallo-Roman culture with its own religious traditions with its own large set of deities, such as Cernunnos, Artio, Telesphorus, etc.

"In the later 5th and the 6th centuries, Christianity became the dominant religion in the Celtic area, supplanting earlier religious traditions. However, it left a legacy in many of the Celtic nations, influencing later mythology, and served as the basis for a new religious movement, Celtic Neopaganism, in the 20th century...

"Literary evidence for Celtic religion also comes from sources written in Ireland and Wales during the Middle Ages, a period when traditional Celtic religious practices had become extinct and had long been replaced by Christianity. The evidence from Ireland has been recognised as better than that from Wales, being viewed as 'both older and less contaminated from foreign material.' These sources, which are in the form of epic poems and tales, were written several centuries after Christianity became the dominant religion in these regions, and were written down by Christian monks, 'who may not merely have been hostile to the earlier paganism but actually ignorant of it.' Instead of treating the characters as deities, they are allocated the roles of being historical heroes who sometimes have supernatural or superhuman powers, for instance, in the Irish sources the gods are claimed to be an ancient tribe of humans known as the Tuatha Dé Danann. Because they were written in a very Christian context, these sources must be scrutinised with even more rigor than the classical sources in assessing their validity as evidence for Celtic religion.

"While it is possible to single out specific texts which can

Chapter 7 - An Evolution of Death - The Classical Times [300 BCE - 450 CE]

be strongly argued to encapsulate genuine echoes or resonances of the pre-Christian past, opinion is divided as to whether these texts contain substantive material derived from oral tradition as preserved by bards or whether they were the creation of the medieval monastic tradition.

"Various Greek and Roman writers of the ancient world commented on the Celts and their beliefs. Barry Cunliffe stated that 'the Greek and Roman texts provide a number of pertinent observations, but these are at best anecdotal, offered largely as a colourful background by writers whose prime intention was to communicate other messages. The Roman general (and later dictator) Julius Caesar, when leading the conquering armies of the Roman Republic against Celtic Gaul, made various descriptions of the inhabitants, though some of his claims, such as that the Druids practiced human sacrifice by burning people in wicker men, have come under scrutiny by modern scholars.'

"However, the key problem with the use of these sources is that they were often biased against the Celts, whom the classical peoples viewed as 'barbarians.' In the case of the Romans who conquered several Celtic realms, they would have likely been biased in favour of making the Celts look uncivilised, thereby giving the 'civilised' Romans more reason to conquer them.

"Celtic burial practices, which included burying food, weapons, and ornaments with the dead, suggest a belief in life after death.

"The druids, the Celtic learned classes which included members of the clergy, were said by Caesar to have believed in reincarnation and transmigration of the soul along with astronomy and the nature and power of the gods.

"A common factor in later mythologies from Christianised Celtic nations was the otherworld. This was the realm of the fairy folk and other supernatural beings, who would entice humans into their realm. Sometimes this otherworld was claimed to exist underground, whilst at other times it was said to lie far to the west. Several scholars have suggested that the otherworld was the Celtic afterlife, though there is no direct evidence to prove this."[189]

"By various means [men] can encourage] spirits to appear. One of the favorite methods (applied to gods as well as souls of the dead) is that of 'incubation' - sleeping on the right spot. In various parts of Greece, for instance, there were thought to be chasms communicating with the underworld through which the shades could rise. At these spots were sanctuaries where inquirers would offer sacrifice and then lie down to sleep. And in their dreams the dead, without fail, would appear. The Christian Tertullian [160-225 CE] records a like practice among the Celts of his time, who would seek hidden knowledge by sleeping on graves, to be inspired by the spirits of those within. The very same custom is known today on the island of Kiwai in New Guinea, where the natives will dig up the skulls of the dead and sleep beside them and win their reward by learning much useful information."[190]

⚘

"In the light of the dogma of the resurrection of the body as well as of Jewish tradition, the burial of the mortal remains of the Christian dead has always been regarded as an act of religious import. It is surrounded at all times with some measure of religious ceremony."[191]

Notes for Chapter Seven

[160] http://en.wikipedia.org/wiki/Olympias

[161] *Death and Burial in the Roman World*, J. M. C. Toynbee, The Johns Hopkins University Press, Baltimore © 1971, page 34

Chapter 7 - An Evolution of Death - The Classical Times [300 BCE - 450 CE]

---

[162] *Death and Burial in the Roman World*, J. M. C. Toynbee, The Johns Hopkins University Press, Baltimore © 1971, page 34

[163] *Death and Burial in the Roman World*, J. M. C. Toynbee, The Johns Hopkins University Press, Baltimore © 1971, page 73

[164] As near as I can translate on my own, it has to do with a rapid union with the Earth. When I put that phrase into my search engine the only source I found was an archaeologist's work with a tomb ... with that epitaph ... and in a Latin language I did not recognize.

[165] Toynbee's translation, provided in an endnote: "I am ash, ash is earth, earth is a goddess, therefore I am not dead."

[166] *Death and Burial in the Roman World*, J. M. C. Toynbee, The Johns Hopkins University Press, Baltimore © 1971, page 37

[167] *Death and Burial in the Roman World*, J. M. C. Toynbee, The Johns Hopkins University Press, Baltimore © 1971, page 48

[168] *Death and Burial in the Roman World*, J. M. C. Toynbee, The Johns Hopkins University Press, Baltimore © 1971, pages 43-44

[169] http://en.wikipedia.org/wiki/Roman_funerals_and_burial - 1 i 2011 ce

[170] http://en.wikipedia.org/wiki/Roman_funerals_and_burial - 12 ii 2014 ce

[171] Rev. Norman MacDonald, *The After-Life in Celtic and Oriental Folklore*, pub. 1970 by the author in Cachan Locheport, page 18

[172] James Thayer Addison, *Life Beyond Death In the Beliefs of Mankind*, Houghton Mifflin Co., © 1932, page 58

[173] James Thayer Addison, *Life Beyond Death In the Beliefs of Mankind*, Houghton Mifflin Co., © 1932, page 133

[174] Rev. Norman MacDonald, *The After-Life in Celtic and Oriental Folklore*, pub. 1970 by the author in Cachan Locheport, pages 17-18

[175] James Thayer Addison, *Life Beyond Death In the Beliefs of Mankind*, Houghton Mifflin Co., © 1932, page 135

[176] Rev. Norman MacDonald, *The After-Life in Celtic and Oriental Folklore*, pub. 1970 by the author in Cachan Locheport, page 19

[177] James Thayer Addison, *Life Beyond Death In the Beliefs of Mankind*, Houghton Mifflin Co., © 1932, pages 108-109

Chapter 7 - An Evolution of Death - The Classical Times [300 BCE - 450 CE]

[178] James Thayer Addison, *Life Beyond Death In the Beliefs of Mankind*, Houghton Mifflin Co., © 1932, page 110
[179] http://en.wikipedia.org/wiki/Christian_burial#Early_historical_evidence
[180] http://en.wikipedia.org/wiki/Christian_burial#Early_historical_evidence
[181] http://en.wikipedia.org/wiki/Early_Christianity
[182] http://en.wikipedia.org/wiki/Early_Christianity
[183] http://en.wikipedia.org/wiki/Early_Christianity
[184] http://en.wikipedia.org/wiki/Early_Christianity
[185] http://en.wikipedia.org/wiki/Persecution_of_Christians
[186] http://en.wikipedia.org/wiki/Diocletian_Persecution
[187] http://en.wikipedia.org/wiki/Early_Christianity
[188] http://en.wikipedia.org/wiki/Druid
[189] http://en.wikipedia.org/wiki/Celtic_polytheism#Burial_and_afterlife
[190] James Thayer Addison, *Life Beyond Death In the Beliefs of Mankind*, Houghton Mifflin Co., © 1932, page 40
[191] http://en.wikipedia.org/wiki/Christian_burial#Early_historical_evidence

Chapter 8 - An Evolution of Death:

The Middle Times [450 - 1500 CE]

- The background story
- The European Church
- The Art of Dying
- Returning to the Earth
- Theological Transition: Courtrooms and Purgatory
- Urbanization
- Monuments and Markers

● The background story

"The [Middle Ages] apparently experienced an increasing concern with death and the after-life, evident in the emergence of the *ars moriendi*, a growing demand for intercessory prayers, and the appearance of artistic themes such as the *danse macabre*."[192]

What are the *Middle Ages*?

"In European history, the Middle Ages, or Medieval period, lasted from the 5th to the 15th century. It began with the collapse of the Western Roman Empire and at its end merges into the Renaissance and the Age of Discovery. The Middle Ages is the middle period of the three traditional divisions of Western history: Antiquity, Medieval period, and Modern period."[193]

When setting aside this period of history and research for Chapter 8, I wished to have it encompass the Medieval period of time. Little did I know how historical events would so shape this period of time. I had come across numerous references to this period of time being erroneously referred to as the Dark Ages, with those historians indicating clearly that there were so many reasons that they were not 'dark' at all.

Literally within two days of my returning to this chapter to begin weaving the disparate parts into a single fabric I heard some striking stories on the international (BBC) radio news.

The first took me to an event which was recorded as having taken place in 536 CE. The planet was plunged into a severe period of cold, one which perplexed historians and scientists for a long time. Chinese astronomers, perhaps the most advanced of any culture, noted that Halley's Comet was the brightest ever noted. On the other hand, the period of darkness suggested a major volcanic eruption. The study of ice core samples, an aspect of contemporary research, shows that there was, indeed, a volcanic eruption. In January 2014 CE there were a number of studies and published works by experts who believe that both took place, the volcano and a large chunk of comet ice striking the Earth, leading to the severe cold and lack of sunlight, both of which led to severe famine.

This was very near the beginning of a period of time which indeed began with darkness.

In a curious way, this same period of time - the Middle Times as I will call them - may be dated from one period of pandemic death to another historic period of pandemic death, from the great plague which took the Byzantine Empire known as the Plague of Justinian, to The Black Death which began in the 14th century. Many historians consider this Plague of Justinian to be the first major recorded outbreak of the bubonic plague. Again, interestingly, the morning after I began writing about the Justinian Plague, a report was published in the *Lancet Infectious Diseases Journal* by a group who had studied the genetic makeup of the Justinian Plague, having sequenced the DNA from two teeth of plague victims buried at that time.

In 541 CE, a pandemic considered among the most deadly in history overtook the Eastern Roman Empire, including Constantinople. Worldwide in scope, including devastation in Asia, the Arabian countries, and the northern half of Africa, a Wikipedia article indicates that there were as many as 5,000 people who died *every day* and that as

Chapter 8 - An Evolution of Death - The Middle Times [450 - 1500 CE]

much as 40% of all of the population of Constantinople died from this plague. The plague came and went in waves until around 750 CE, and then seems to have gone underground. Until the aforementioned *Lancet* study, it was believed that this was the same genetic strain as the plague known as the Black Death, "but the genetic fingerprint of the Black Plague is sufficiently distinct from the Justinian Plague that researchers concluded it is highly unlikely that they are related, or that one of the Justinian strains evolved into the strains that caused the 'Black Death.'"[194]

The Black Death was the emergence of another major pandemic of the bubonic plague. In just the short time of roughly 1346-1353 as many as 75 million to 200 million people died. The total loss of population is estimated to be between 30-60% in Europe and caused a major loss of global population.

There was no historical event which began the Middle Times, nor is there any event or date which indicates the end of the Middle Times. What I found interesting, however, is that the end of this era (various dates are thought of as climatological records were not accurate) there was another period of cooling. François E. Matthes used the phrase 'The Little Ice Age' which, although it was not a genuine ice age, the phrase has survived.

The Middle Times (loosely) spans the period from unusual cold to unusual cold. It also spans a period of time from a major period of plague-by-death to an even worse plague-by-death.

If that wasn't enough, politically Europe was not a happy place for many. A century earlier, under Constantine the Great (272-337 CE) the Roman Empire was moved into a major religious conversion, whether willing or not. History suggests that there was enough dissatisfaction with the previous way of doing things that reform was welcome. Constantine created a new social order in the western world. Although a new convert to the Christianity, he also promoted religious tolerance throughout the empire even while working to establish Christianity. Christianity was given a strong assist when Constantine also created dynastic succession for the empire. A religion which is given control over such vast geographical and economic wealth becomes very

Chapter 8 - An Evolution of Death - The Middle Times [450 - 1500 CE]

political. The Catholic Church consolidated its power and frequently treated dissension within its ranks as as heresy. During the twelfth century, the sentencing for those convicted of heresy increasingly brought far more than imprisonment. It was under Pope Innocent IV's papal bull of 1252 that torture became acceptable. As we move out of the Middle Times into more advanced times, we also encounter the Witch trials. This troubling period of persecution and of false accusations led to the deaths of as many as a hundred thousand people, most of them women. Many believe the numbers are far higher, but many scholars also place it at half of what I give as a figure.

In trying to find some simple ways in which to understand some of the prevalent attitudes toward death and dying during this time, we need also remember that, following Constantine, and "prior to 1500, the cosmos of Western culture was essentially Roman Catholic."[195]

- **The European Church**

Why *European*? I must preface what I am about to say with a repeat of my disclaimer. I am not a historian. This has been a very challenging chapter for me. My comment about not being a historian? I am reminded of a course I took in University in the 1960s. Majoring in music performance I was still required to take a course from one category and I chose medieval history. I enjoyed listening to the professor. I found much of the required text interesting but not enough to stir my passion for learning, nor was it interesting enough to be retained by my memory. I was good when it came to dialogue during the lectures if called upon or, at times, to ask a question. I barely survived a long paper we had to write, and then upon learning that the entire final would be three hours of exam suitable only for a trivia fanatic, I knew I was sunk. I have never had a memory which could store names and dates and locations and facts. This was also a class for which my attendance record showed academic anemia.

Emboldened with the knowledge that I would fail the course, I raised my hand and, when called upon, stated that I did not believe that the scheduled exam was capable of measuring whether or not we

Chapter 8 - An Evolution of Death - The Middle Times [450 - 1500 CE]

understood that period of history or not. I made some comment about memorizing names and dates not being what history was about. And then I left the class. During the final I did what I could and submitted my papers after 20 minutes (of a three hour exam). I know that I had clearly turned in a failed exam. When the grades came out, I was given a C. That passing grade could only have been acknowledgement that history is not about names and dates.

For decades I made references to Medieval History as an example of a course I was required to take which had no value for me and yet, here I am today, completely engrossed in this vast period of time, so filled with the very trivia which was my bane. I have gathered up armloads of data which I interpret and include to provide historical content when it comes to the evolution of our beliefs. Clearly, I am not a historian.

One of my premises is that, until the divisions which led to Christianity being Catholic (primarily Roman Catholic from the western perspective) *and* Protestant, the average person may not have thought of their religion or of their church as Christian or as Catholic or as Roman. In western Europe if you were Christian, that's the church to which you belonged. The absence of choice may well have meant an absence of questioning. And what type of person was the 'average' person? Who was this common person?

The average person was not likely to have access to education. Learning meant one had resources and one had time. Time and money were the domain of the ruling class, both politically and also within the monastic and clerical church. The average person's life was dominated by the need to survive, to have food on the table, to have good shelter where one could have a family, to have furniture which met one's needs and for some provided comfort (comfort was rare). Meeting one's needs likely consumed most of one's life.

And yet, death was not prejudiced by class or by economic status. Wars were fought. The working class of the day lived simple lives, hard lives. They were subjected to the rule of the landed, the politically more-powerful, and the church.

Chapter 8 - An Evolution of Death - The Middle Times [450 - 1500 CE]

Although education was kept in the hands of the powerful, the customs brought into being by the church were the law of the land for many. Even the poor and the peasantry, attending their churches, were reminded of the importance of being prepared for death. I wonder if it was not what we call 'preaching to the choir,' given that it was the upper class who lived more removed from death while, for the poor, it was a daily fact of life.

As W. Y. Evans-Wentz writes:

"Throughout the Middle Ages, and during the Renaissance that followed, Europe still retained enough of the Mystery teachings concerning death to understand the paramount importance of knowing how to die; and many treatises, hereinafter referred to, on the Art of Dying were then current there."[196]

Within the Catholic Church the Requiem Mass, or Mass for the Dead, evolved over time. Parts of this liturgy date back to the twelfth century, if not older. The nature of this period of time, with its cold and darkness and death, contributed greatly to the overall dark and negative view of death.

In the article on *Christian Burial* and its history, the entry in Wikipedia states:

"Little is known with regard to the burial of the dead in the early Christian centuries. Early Christians did practice the use of an Ossuary to store the skeletal remains of those saints at rest in Christ. This practice likely came from the use of the same among Second Temple Jews. Other early Christians likely followed the national customs of the people among whom they lived, as long as they were not directly idolatrous. St. Jerome, in his account of the death of St. Paul the Hermit, speaks of the singing of hymns and psalms while the body is carried to the grave as an observance belonging to ancient Christian tradition. Several historical writings indicate that in the fourth and fifth centuries, the offering of the Eucharist was an essential feature in the last solemn rites. These writings include: St. Gregory of Nyssa's detailed description of the funeral of St. Macrina, St. Augustine's references to his mother St. Monica, the Apostolic Constitutions (Book VII), and the Celestial Hierarchy of Dionysius the Areopagite. Probably the earliest detailed account of funeral ceremonial [sic] which has been preserved to us is to be found in the Spanish Ordinals of the latter part of the seventh century. Recorded in the writing is a description of 'the Order of what the clerics of any city ought to do when their bishop falls into a mortal sickness.' It details the steps of ringing church bells, reciting psalms, and cleaning and dressing the body."[197]

Christopher Daniell, in his very helpful book on *Death and Burial in Medieval England* provides a very succinct overview of the medieval paradigm:

"The key to medieval religion is the fate of the individual's soul after death. Death was defined as the moment when the immortal soul left the mortal body and joined with an incorruptible, sexless, immortal body, often depicted in art as a small naked person."[198]

The Roman Church was the predominate Christian Church. Not until the Middle Times had ended do we see Martin Luther's defiance in 1520, King Henry VIII's breaking away to form what becomes the Church of England, John Calvin's publication of *Institutes of the Christian Religion* in 1536, and a further movement with newer forms of Christianity which were the further breakup of the overall dominance of the Roman Church in the western world. I have found too little material from those parts of the world where the Orthodox Christian churches held sway to write from a knowledgeable base. In this context, then, I use *European Christianity* as a phrase to indicate that I am not including the Orthodox Christian beliefs in my generalization. I use the phrase as well in acknowledgement that to most of my readers the word *Europe* brings western Europe to mind. Let those more learned provide some basis.

Chapter 8 - An Evolution of Death - The Middle Times [450 - 1500 CE]

"The East-West Schism of 1054 formally separated the Christian church into two parts: Western Catholicism in Western Europe and Eastern Orthodoxy in the east. It occurred when Pope Leo IX and Patriarch Michael I excommunicated each other, mainly over disputes as to the existence of papal authority over the four Eastern patriarchs"[199] with additional disagreements.

"The Catholic Church, the only centralized institution to survive the fall of the Western Roman Empire intact, was the sole unifying cultural influence in the West, selectively preserving some Latin learning, maintaining the art of writing, and preserving a centralized administration through its network of bishops ordained in succession. The Early Middle Ages are characterized by the urban control of bishops and the territorial control exercised by dukes and counts. The rise of urban communes marked the beginning of the High Middle Ages."[200]

"The centuries from 500 to 1000 saw the emergence of a fully developed ritual process around death, burial, and the incorporation of souls into the otherworld that became a standard for Christian Europeans until the Reformation, and for Catholics until the very near present. The multitude of Christian kingdoms that emerged in the West as the Roman Empire declined fostered the development of local churches. In the sixth, seventh, and eighth centuries, these churches developed distinctive ritual responses to death and dying. In southern Gaul, Bishop Caesarius of Arles (503–543) urged the sick to seek ritual anointing from priests rather than magicians and folk healers and authored some of the most enduring of the prayers that accompanied death and burial in medieval Christianity. Pope Gregory the Great (590–604) first promoted the practice of offering the mass as an aid to souls in the afterlife, thus establishing the basis for a system of suffrages for the dead."[201]

Thus, for the average person, the customs and rituals and practices of the dominant church, of Christianity, were evolving.

- **The Art of Dying**

In many ways, my life has been a study of the "Art of Dying," in a manner of speaking. My father's side of the family was very large and there were numerous family funerals, always joyous during the post-funeral family reunion. The adults played cards, the young ran about wildly having fun in a huge, sturdy farm house and everyone shared news and caught up on life.

By age twelve I was actively involved in the Roman Catholic Church, now attending a religious elementary school. I loved ritual and was good at it. Plus, I lived within walking distance, convenient to schedule. I was an 'altar boy' which meant wearing religious robes, assisting the Priest, and chanting the Latin responses to the officiating Priest which kept things moving forward. When not in that role, I sang in the school choir up in the loft by a magnificent pipe organ[202] which I had the privilege of playing as well.

Death and dying were such a part of my life from my earliest days, and then I began taking note of my paternal grandfather's death, my brother's accidental death, my godmother Juanita's death, my grandmother's death. I learned early on that having foreknowledge of dying was preferable in my mind than dying in a horrific accident or in a fire, where one's emotions and soul and mind would be terrorized by pain and suffering, unable to have one's thoughts in order.

Although I grew into my teens within a religion and made many attempts to fully embrace it, I remained unfulfilled. When I began my intense Quest in the early 1970s, where I landed (so to speak) was in the Evans-Wentz edition of *The Tibetan Book of The Dead*. I read and reread the text and the footnotes and felt that book at a deep level. Although from a different culture and of a different language, the *Bardo Thödol* held light for me. That book became, for me, something tangible that allowed me to begin having my own Art of Dying.

Chapter 8 - An Evolution of Death - The Middle Times [450 - 1500 CE]

As the years passed and I grew into my Priesthood, it was with amazement that I learned that the Art of Dying had been part of western culture for so very long. But what happened? Why had it seemingly disappeared, no longer found in a culture which had grown puritanical and squeamish about death and focused upon being young forever?

During the Classical Times - and even before - there was emphasis placed upon remembering that we ought live our lives in preparation for death. I do not claim that this would have been the mindset of the people at all levels of society. Many were likely far more focused upon survival, anguish, or for a few, luxury and debauchery. In the European Church's early years, I believe that many Christians were also focused primarily upon the same issues if not more, given that their chosen belief system often made them targets of horrific persecution. In the time following Constantine, the Roman Church had tremendous growth with political and financial success. This stability allowed it to begin developing many beliefs and practices. As the following Wikipedia article describes:

> "However difficult the contemplation (or moment) of death became, the living continually invented new ways of aiding the passage of souls and maintaining community with the dead. In one of the most important developments of the age, Christians began to revere the remains of those who had suffered martyrdom under Roman persecution. As Peter Brown has shown, the rise of the cult of the saints is a precise measure of the changing relationship between the living and the dead in late antiquity and the early medieval West. The saints formed a special group, present to both the living and the dead and mediating between and among them. The faithful looked to them as friends and patrons, and as advocates at earthly and heavenly courts. Moreover, the shrines of the saints brought people to live and worship in the cemeteries outside the city walls. Eventually, the dead even appeared inside the walls, first as saints' relics, and then in the bodies of those who wished to be buried near them. Ancient prohibitions against intramural burials slowly lost their force. In the second

Chapter 8 - An Evolution of Death - The Middle Times [450 - 1500 CE]

half of the first millennium, graves began to cluster around both urban and rural churches. Essentially complete by the year 1000, this process configured the landscape of Western Christendom in ways that survive until the present day. The living and the dead formed a single community and shared a common space. The dead, as Patrick Geary has put it, became simply another 'age group' in medieval society."[203]

Survival was difficult and death awaited all. It was only a question of how long before death claimed you. Truly, I cannot imagine just how present death would have been. I was born into a world just as penicillin emerged as a miracle drug, saving countless lives even as it sowed the seeds for a future of antibiotic-resistant mutants which cause great anxiety in today's world.

"Death was at the centre of life in the Middle Ages in a way that might seem shocking to us today. With high rates of infant mortality, disease, famine, the constant presence of war, and the inability of medicine to deal with common injuries, death was a brutal part of most people's everyday experience. As a result, attitudes towards life were very much shaped by beliefs about death: indeed, according to Christian tradition, the very purpose of life was to prepare for the afterlife by avoiding sin, performing good works, taking part in the sacraments, and keeping to the teachings of the church. Time was measured out in saint's days, which commemorated the days on which the holiest men and women had died. Easter, the holiest feast day in the Christian calendar, celebrated the resurrection of Christ from the dead. The landscape was dominated by parish churches - the centre of the medieval community - and the churchyard was the principal burial site."[204]

The above passage gives me pause to think that it was not only a fear of dying, but perhaps more a fear of what one would encounter *after* dying. The issue of sin and of living a life *without* what was deemed sin was twofold. On the one hand, it does prepare a person for

Chapter 8 - An Evolution of Death - The Middle Times [450 - 1500 CE]

what follows life. To some degree, I believe that any path that includes a consciousness and awareness of death shapes a person's life. Add to this the potential for fear lest one steps off the path of proscription, of becoming one of *those*, a person who may have been so vile and cruel, a person known to have transgressed - or worse. The population of the day would not have had an exceptional education and are quite likely to have been superstitious as well. What a simple matter to stir fear in the public with visions of horror of what one's afterlife could be.

In the Middle Times one struggled for survival. Death did not always take place surrounded by family and prayers in one's home. Death by disease, by accident, death at the hands of others... The awareness that death could happen at any moment and, if one wished to escape the horrors which could then be encountered, you could make changes in how you lived your life! I doubt that the average person felt that she or he had much control over life. Every so often war or invaders or conflicts between those striving to rule the land... and death, death from childbirth, from what are today minor infectious diseases... If you could not live so well and your life was controlled by the ruling class, perhaps you could take some control over what would be awaiting you at your death.

"The dying person was not a spectator, but a key player. To die well was so important that manuals (called *Ars Moriendi*) were written to describe the 'craft' of a 'good' death so that it would profit the soul. These manuals were very popular and followed many of the same themes, although there could be differences of content between them."[205]

It is difficult for the modern person to grasp the role that death held in earlier times. For much of the Middle Times, life was more agrarian, even as urban areas grew and then sometimes diminished through family, war, and disease with some undefinable tidal rhythm with Death as the Lord Overseer. The desire of the people and the knowledge of the learned class, which is nearly always those who were church-educated in some manner, led to a gradual refining and shaping of the beliefs and practices.

Chapter 8 - An Evolution of Death - The Middle Times [450 - 1500 CE]

"The death-bed scenes and burial of the body followed definite procedures, though these changed over time and some parts are much better understood and documented than others. Ultimately liturgy and procedures concerning Christian death and burial were derived from late Roman practice and were then further developed in France by the Frankish kings between 750 and 850. The monastic movement of the eleventh and twelfth centuries then spread a more standardised burial liturgy across Europe."[206]

We know far more about the the arts of dying and the practices for those who were leaving behind wealth, whether in land or possessions or other matters of substance which could not be taken along. I must believe that today's phrase that 'you can't take it with you' had its counterpart in the phrases familiar to those in the Middle Times. It is unknown whether it arose from seeing acrimonious disputes among those left behind, whether it arose as the times changed and it was no longer the oldest child (son, most often) who automatically inherited it all, or as the cynic might say, whether it arose as people were more and more encouraged to leave money to the church in order to better ensure a good afterlife. In the theatre of the afterlife, wouldn't you rather have a comfortable seat with a good view than to be in the standing-only area which is unheated and crowded with the disease-ridden rabble?

"The dying person was responsible for leaving both the material and spiritual estates in good order by the writing of a will. ... The will and testament allowed the deceased to gain spiritual benefits for the soul and control the distribution of funds to family and friends."[207]

Beliefs and practices continued to evolve. Around the time of the twelfth century, the evolution of liturgical structure and societal conditioning was such that

"at the point of death there were two conflicting views. The first was that the behavior at the time of death was crucial to the destination of the soul. This 'Final Moment' (often so with capitals), depended upon the dying person's mental attitude as to whether the soul wold be saved or damned. ... One mental lapse at the point of death could result in despair, raging, blaspheming and swearing: ammunition enough for the Devil to seize the soul. ... A 'good death' - emphasized by the popular *Ars Moriendi* - accepted bodily suffering patiently and without complaint, which in turn led to salvation."[208]

Although the soul will not be affected by any disease of the body, it is able to be seriously damaged and corrupted by the individual who has sinful ways. To avoid eternal damnation, the Church "had to correct sins by confession, repentance and penance ... In the worst cases of heresy or witchcraft burning was used to help save the individual (fire was a cleansing agent for souls) and stop the infection spreading to other souls."[209]

- **Returning to the Earth**

It took money, or its equivalent, to provide for burial of one's kindred. Population grew, despite the occasional contraction of numbers from disease, famine, pestilence and war. Those with money and enough status were buried with some degree of pomp and ways to remember them. Those who died in religious communities had the benefit of a community and of some means which provided for burial or for the means of tending to the dead.

> "Evidence for burial practices within monastic communities is substantial, which contrasts sharply with the paucity of documentary evidence for lay burial practices in the eleventh, twelfth and thirteenth centuries. Some evidence has survived that the more holy and penitent laity did at least lie down on sack-cloth and ashes."[210]

For the common soul, life was not so generous. Cemeteries had been part of the Roman world, and the customs of the Classical Times were the foundation for the Middle Times. Increasingly over the centuries western European culture and the Roman Church reshaped the practices. Yet, one might conclude that the burial process had more

Chapter 8 - An Evolution of Death - The Middle Times [450 - 1500 CE]

to do with the living, or that the remains of the dead diminished in spiritual value over time. According to Daniell, it was not unheard of for an older burial site to give way to current uses. Upon "the foundation of a new church in an area; or an outlying chapel being granted its own burial rights from the parish church, once permission had been granted, the wholesale clearance of the land might then take place. At Mitre Street, in London, the Roman remains were completely cleared in the tenth century to make space for a Saxon graveyard."[211] In truth, this may be something which is simply the way our species functions.

Just as cities were built upon the remains of cities, there were times that people were buried on top of previous graveyards. Cities came and went, and so too did burial places. London under Roman rule had flourished as an outpost with a population estimated to be 45,000. There was a significant decline and then, "by the early 12th century the population of London was about 18,000,"[212] according to Davis Ross, editor for the Britain Express. The Roman Church held a strong influence, most of which today is noteworthy only by the names which have survived: Greyfriars, Whitefriars, and Blackfriars are areas of London dating to a period of the Middle Times when there were 13 monasteries in the city. Mind you, it was *not* a large city at the time.

As London grew, the infrastructure did not grow nor improve. Wandering the streets of London in the areas dating to the Middle Times is a fascinating lesson of the times. Every few blocks the street makes a bend and ... has a new name. Many of the names reflect the nature of that segment of street when it was added. Although so much of Medieval London would be destroyed in the Great Fire of 1666, many of the the street names survived.

We know so little of the daily lives and daily beliefs. Daniell writes that:

> "Once the graveyard was in existence the position of the burials became an issue. The physical placing of bodies depended on the marking of other graves and how much space remained in the cemetery. At Kellington it was discovered that a major shift in the care of burial took place in the twelfth

Chapter 8 - An Evolution of Death - The Middle Times [450 - 1500 CE]

century before that date, bodies were carefully laid out and any bones which were discovered were treated with reverence. After that date less care was taken about cutting through existing graves and many bones were incorporated into the backfill without any reverence shown. If this trend was discovered in other twelfth century cemeteries, it could be argued that it reflected the change in belief from the Day of Judgement to Purgatory."[213]

In England we continue to learn about the Middle Times from modern excavations. Kellington, in North Yorkshire, has St. Edmunds, parts of which date to 1185 CE. A stunning Master's thesis by Robert O'Hara submitted to the UCD School of Archaeology in 2010, *An Iron Age and Early Medieval Cemetery at Collierstown 1, Co. Meath: Interpreting the changing character of a burial ground,"* studies a burial site in Ireland dating to the Iron Age.

London, situated on the Thames, was crowded, disease-ridden, and subject to recurrent fires and plagues. London's history is, in fact, datable by its fires. During Classical Times Queen Boudica burned Londinium to the ground. The fire was so intense and complete that modern archaeologists use a distinct layer of ash to separate the historical periods before and following the fire. A massive fire followed the visit of the Roman emperor Hadrian. This may even have been a series of fires, but only a few of the sturdiest of Roman buildings survived.

A major fire in 1087 destroyed most of the Norman area of London. St. Paul's Cathedral went down in the fire.

The Great Fire of London took place on Pentecost Sunday, May 26th, 1135. Most of the city from St. Paul's to Westminster was destroyed. And less than a century later, The Great Fire of Suthwark began on July 10th, 1212. In addition to a very large area, it is believed that as many as 3,000 people died on London Bridge alone, trying to escape the conflagration. Given the size of London, it may have been less. There were other fires, but so often a major fire in a city like this meant a complete restart. Construction began anew, and there would be many bodies to inter.

Chapter 8 - An Evolution of Death - The Middle Times [450 - 1500 CE]

And there were other significant fires. In the 12th century there were fires in 1130 and 1132, and following the Great Fire of 1212, there were additional fires in 1220, 1227, and 1299. Thatch (straw) remained the primary roofing material for the crowded buildings. Fighting fires was primarily up to those living in the immediate area, but in that era, London life was in a city always ready to go up in flames.

The fires of London did not much seem to care whether they burned the homes of the wealthy or those of the poor although the areas of wealth had more at their disposal for protection. Despite the economic barriers between various areas, the entire city was still dry and flammable. During this time the wealthy lived on Fleet Street and near the Strand. Their money elevated their stature so that they were considered important enough so that their lives and their deaths and customs became part of recorded history.

The poor and the working poor were not valued in the same way and today their lives and deaths are studied only by the remnants left behind. A body was wrapped in a shroud and buried. Good Christians to the core, nothing else was placed with the body. The ancient custom of adding coins was abhorrent to the Christian mindset of the day, and they thoroughly practiced the "can't take it with you" lifestyle.

> "The burial of objects in graves in the Middle Ages is a problem. The situation should be straight forward for the fast majority of graves have no grave-goods, or occasionally a simple pin to hold the shroud together. ... This lack of finds can be replicated across the country in medieval cemeteries. This absence of grave-goods is hardly surprising, as England was nominally Christian and Christians were not expected to be buried with objects."[214]

Religion rarely seems to be straightforward with an absence of complexity. One truth I have seen in studying the evolution of religion is that a new religion supplants the old by occupying the same sacred spaces, often taking on the older customs and then applying new labels while, at the same time, attempting to label the former as very bad if not evil incarnate, and the new religion as supremely desirable, even when the deities of the former have simply been co-opted.

Daniell describes this well:

"The horror of Christian writers against placing coins in the grave may be a reaction against pagan burials. Roman burial practice occasionally included coins as grave-goods, either in the mouth of the person or near them, in a container. These have been related to pagan practices, and one early Christian writer wrote 'certain sorcerers, acting against the Faith, place five *solidi* on the chest of the dead, thus imitating the gentiles who put a *denarius* in the mouth of the dead.'"[215]

And yet, just pages later comes something of a contradiction. Perhaps, if you had enough wealth and religious status, you *could* take it with you!

"The absence of grave-goods in Christian graves is a truism, and any items found are normally commented upon at length in archaeological reports. However, there is a massive problem with the general statement that there are no grave goods in Christian graves; it was the Christian hierarchy who were buried with the most elaborate grave goods. At the bottom of the scale were clerks who were buried with chalice and paten. At the top of the scale were the bishops and archbishops who were buried in full ceremonial robes."[216]

And for the moment, this:

"Until the twelfth and thirteenth centuries the commemoration of the dead was almost entirely based in the monasteries. This emphasis grew with the monastic reforms of the tenth and the eleventh centuries. The new and spiritually pure orders of the Cluniacs and Cistercians vied with each other over the number and quality of prayers..."[217]

Prayers are not good historical information when looking for information about the burial of the average person.

Chapter 8 - An Evolution of Death - The Middle Times [450 - 1500 CE]

- **Theological Transition: Courtrooms and Purgatory**

By the time of the schism which divided Roman Church from the Eastern Orthodox, the Roman Church had considerable emphasis upon death and dying. Live your life following the morality defined by the Church, or following your death you will face the divine courtroom and your eternal fate will be judged. "Throughout the twelfth and thirteenth centuries the imagery of the courtroom as the Last Judgement grew in strength."[218]

I do not know whether this growing view of standing trial for one's human foibles would have encouraged one to practice the Art of Dying, living life accordingly, or have growing increasingly fearful of Death.

Fearful of Death? Fearful of the God of the Middle Times. "By the twelfth century this imagery was changing to signify a more judgemental [sic], legalistic, attitude. God was depicted as a fearsome judge passing sentence on the soul. Intercessors on the soul's behalf included Christ or the saints, whilst the Devil was the prosecutor and attempted to get the soul damned ..."[219]

I know in today's world I often state that I have difficulty believing that I know any person who has never broken the law. Certainly in the United States, if you do everything completely legal while driving, you are treated as a pariah, some fool of a driver who is holding up traffic. It would be a very rare driver who drives within the speed limit at *all* times, who makes a complete stop at every appropriate place. Did I say *complete* stop?

Knowing the nature of our species, I would wager that most people living during the Middle Times would have broken the laws of their God now and then as well. Knowing that you are likely to face a losing courtroom hearing before this 'fearsome judge' would have led many to increased prayer and I wager would have increased the stature and power of the clergy of the dominant Church.

> "The period of the late eleventh, twelfth and early thirteenth centuries (a period sometimes described as the twelfth-century renaissance) had a profound effect upon attitudes to death and burial. At the beginning of the twelfth

century the Church's attitude towards the dead was, broadly, as follows: at the Last Judgement souls would be judged and then divided into the saved and the damned, depending on their life on earth. If a person had done good works, then in all probability salvation would follow: if a person had led an evil life, then the soul would be condemned to Hell."[220]

The Christian God's courtroom was a pretty grim place. There was no in between. If you conform to the church's rules and do "good works," then you are saved. If you don't qualify, then you're in the "evil" group and that is deathly discouraging. As if people didn't have enough difficulty in their lives already, now they had significant worry over whether or not they would qualify as good or whether they would be shipped off to Hell.

During this period of time the concept of Purgatory gained strength.

"It was a logical step for the idea of Purgatory as a place, rather than just a concept, to develop at a time when there was increasing interest in what happened to the soul after death and before the Last Judgement. The date that purgatory was 'born' as a place in Christian theology was ... between 1170 and 1180... at the 'school' of Notre-Dame in Paris. Between those dates Peter Comestor use the noun *purgatorium* to denote the place of Purgatory, and not some abstract idea."[221]

In the thirteenth century, however, Purgatory now offers many an in-between, more realistic option.

"This defining of Purgatory as a place caused a revolution in the geography of the other world. .. The popularity of Purgatory as a place quickly grew and in 1254 Pope Innocent IV gave the first papal definition of Purgatory ... which is still authoritative."[222]

"The history of death and burial in England between 1066 and 1600 may be divided into three broad sections: the eleventh to mid-fourteenth century, the period between the

Chapter 8 - An Evolution of Death - The Middle Times [450 - 1500 CE]

Black Death and the Reformation (1348 to mid-sixteenth century), and the Reformation. The importance of these divisions is that they allow analysis of important themes concerning death and burial, of which the most important is theological change. In the twelfth century Purgatory was, for the first time, clearly defined, which led to a change in burial practice. The second major theological change was the Reformation, when many of the medieval religious beliefs were swept away and the emphasis was on the individual, the Bible and his or her faith. Almost exactly half-way between these changes was the Black Death, which arrived in England in 1348. The Black Death was possibly the worst catastrophe that the human population has ever suffered, and from then on mortality was given a much more prominent role in art and the population's consciousness..."[223]

- **Urbanization**

"In the longer term, change in funeral practices may have come about through increasing urbanisation and individualism. The joint processes of migrations into towns and plague led to a separating of people from their ancestral graveyards, a subsequent dislocation and isolation. To reassert their own identity within towns a new flamboyant and more macabre funeral ceremony developed which emphasized the role of the individual."[224]

Based upon simply my understanding of human nature with little to document this theory, living in increasing proximity to more and more of one's species, death remained a mystery.

"French scholars have also suggested that there were remnants of ancient pre-Christian beliefs which filtered down and became incorporated into medieval burial practice... One potential example is that the 'charcoal' burials in England reflected pagan cremations, or that shoes in the graves followed Roman customs."[225] However there are many who see this as not necessarily the case. There are periods of time when this doesn't happen and there are other customs which emerge. Just as those who visit lands with other customs are quick to return with new information regarding botanicals and other possible solutions to illness and disease, it would follow that customs regarding death and burial might also be culled as a means of better understanding the mysteries and roles of death.

While death has been an absolute, how we choose to deal with it is in our hands. I feel compelled to believe that our species understood that death was inevitable from the earliest times that we know burial was done with intention, as shown in Chapter 6, yet what happened once the physical body ceased to be alive remains one of the great Mysteries and one which has defined religions and customs throughout our history. Were there to suddenly emerge irrefutable proof of what happens to one's *intangible* self ... to our emotional self, mental self, spiritual self ... the impact upon our belief systems and those global institutions and churches who all claim to hold the answer, would be radical and perhaps even politically catastrophic.[226]

Because we do not know, or because we follow a belief system which provides us an answer yet those beliefs being inconsistent with each other, humans will often hold on to a belief with an unrelenting inflexibility while others, at the far end of the spectrum, will metaphorically grasp at straws, choosing to move to the next realm of existence based upon the movement of celestial bodies, the number of offspring, what one is wearing, or how much money one has given. Along with this whether to cremate or have earth burial or sky burial, whether one must attempt to preserve the corpse or quickly dispose of it, whether to let others come and stare at the corpse or have it immediately taken away never to be seen by the family... The customs and beliefs which accompany death are anything but consistent over time.

> "By the middle of the fourteenth century many theological beliefs and burial practices had changed radically since the twelfth century. How these would have developed is unknown for in the mid-fourteenth century a sudden catastrophe further changed people's perception of death. The

Black Death arrived in England in 1348 and killed between one-third and half of the entire population." [227]

Between 1430 and 1480 there were eleven outbreaks and eighteen years of national epidemics.

"Around 1300, centuries of prosperity and growth in Europe came to a halt. A series of famines and plagues, such as the Great Famine of 1315–1317 and the Black Death, reduced the population to around half of what it was before the calamities. Along with depopulation came social unrest and endemic warfare. France and England experienced serious peasant uprisings: the Jacquerie, the Peasants' Revolt, as well as over a century of intermittent conflict in the Hundred Years' War. To add to the many problems of the period, the unity of the Catholic Church was shattered by the Western Schism."[228]

"Throughout the Middle Ages, and during the Renaissance that followed, Europe still retained enough of the Mystery teachings concerning death to understand the paramount importance of knowing how to die; and many treatises, hereinafter referred to, on the Art of Dying were then current there."[229]

- **Monuments and Markers**

    ### Burial
    "An associated issue is that of the orientation of the grave and the body within it. There are numerous possibilities as to what controls orientation, even in a Christian context: some event of religious significance (in Christian belief the Last Judgement and the Resurrection of the body), paths or roads (so that the memorial or grave could be seen) or holy buildings, such as the alignment of a church. ... By the Middle Ages the orientation of graves was consistent: the heads point west, the feet east.

The explanations for the orientation given in medieval texts include: that Christ would appear from the east on the Day of Judgement; the cross of Cavalry faced west, so those looking at Christ faced east; the west is the region of shadows and darkness and the east is the region of goodness and light... All these reasons, and others, were probably attempts to explain the existing practice and no reason is given before the ninth century."[230]

"During the Middle Ages a practice arose among the aristocracy that when a nobleman was killed in battle far from home, the body would be defleshed by boiling or some such other method, and his bones transported back to his estate for burial. In response, in the year 1300, Pope Boniface VIII promulgated a law which excommunicated ipso facto anyone who disembowelled bodies of the dead or boiled them to separate the flesh from the bones, for the purpose of transportation for burial in their native land. He further decreed that bodies which had been so treated were to be denied Christian burial."[231]

Vikings

"It was common to leave gifts with the deceased. Both men and women received grave goods, even if the corpse was to be burnt on a pyre. A Norseman could also be buried with a loved one or house thrall, who were buried alive with the person, or in a funeral pyre. The amount and the value of the goods depended on which social group the dead person came from. It was important to bury the dead in the right way so that he could join the afterlife with the same social standing that he had had in life, and to avoid becoming a homeless soul that wandered eternally.

"The usual grave for a thrall was probably not much more than a hole in the ground. He was probably buried in such a

Chapter 8 - An Evolution of Death - The Middle Times [450 - 1500 CE]

way as to ensure both that he did not return to haunt his masters and that he could be of use to his masters after they died. Slaves were sometimes sacrificed to be useful in the next life. A free man was usually given weapons and equipment for riding. An artisan, such as a blacksmith, could receive his entire set of tools. Women were provided with their jewelry and often with tools for female and household activities. The most sumptuous Viking funeral discovered so far is the Oseberg ship burial, which was for a woman (probably a queen or a priestess) who lived in the 9th century.

"A Viking funeral could be a considerable expense, but the barrow and the grave goods were not considered to have been wasted. In addition to being a homage to the deceased, the barrow remained as a monument to the social position of the descendants. Especially powerful Norse clans could demonstrate their position through monumental grave fields. The Borre mound cemetery in Vestfold is for instance connected to the Yngling dynasty, and it had large tumuli that contained stone ships.

"Jelling, in Denmark, is the largest royal memorial from the Viking Age and it was made by Harald Bluetooth in memory of his parents Gorm and Tyra, and in honour of himself. It was only one of the two large tumuli that contained a chamber tomb, but both barrows, the church and the two Jelling stones testify to how important it was to mark death ritually during the pagan era and the earliest Christian times.

"On three locations in Scandinavia, there are large grave fields that were used by an entire community: Birka in Mälaren, Hedeby at Schleswig and Lindholm Høje at Ålborg. The graves at Lindholm Høje show a large variation in both shape and size. There are stone ships and there is a mix of graves that are triangular, quadrangular and circular. Such grave fields have been used during many generations and belong to village like settlements."[232]

Chapter 8 - An Evolution of Death - The Middle Times [450 - 1500 CE]

The ibn Fadlan Account

"A 10th-century Arab Muslim writer named Ahmad ibn Fadlan produced a description of a funeral of a Scandinavian, probably Swedish, chieftain who was on an expedition on the eastern route. The account is a unique source on the ceremonies surrounding the Viking funeral of a chieftain.

"The dead chieftain was put in a temporary grave, which was covered for ten days until they had sewn new clothes for him. One of his thrall women volunteered to join him in the afterlife and she was guarded day and night, being given a great amount of intoxicating drinks while she sang happily. When the time had arrived for cremation, they pulled his longship ashore and put it on a platform of wood, and they made a bed for the dead chieftain on the ship. Thereafter, an old woman referred to as the "Angel of Death" put cushions on the bed. She was responsible for the ritual.

Then they disinterred the chieftain and gave him new clothes. In his grave, he received intoxicating drinks, fruits and a stringed instrument. The chieftain was put into his bed with all his weapons and grave offerings around him. Then they had two horses run themselves sweaty, cut them to pieces, and threw the meat into the ship. Finally, they sacrificed a hen and a cock.

"Meanwhile, the thrall girl went from one tent to the other and had sexual intercourse with the men. Every man told her: 'Tell your master that I did this because of my love to him.' In the afternoon, they moved the thrall girl to something that looked like a door frame, where she was lifted on the palms of the men three times. Every time, the girl told of what she saw. The first time, she saw her father and mother, the second time, she saw all her relatives, and the third time she saw her master in the afterworld. There, it was green and beautiful and together with him, she saw men and young boys. She saw that her master beckoned for her. By using intoxicating drinks, they thought to put the thrall girl in an ecstatic trance that made her psychic and through the symbolic action with the door frame, she would then see into the realm of the dead. The same ritual also appears in the Icelandic short story 'Völsa þáttr,' where two pagan Norwegian men lift the lady of the household over a door frame to help her look into the otherworld.

"Thereafter, the thrall girl was taken away to the ship. She removed her bracelets and gave them to the old woman. Thereafter she removed her finger rings and gave them to the old woman's daughters, who had guarded her. Then they took her aboard the ship, but they did not allow her to enter the tent where the dead chieftain lay. The girl received several vessels of intoxicating drinks and she sang and bade her friends farewell.

"Then the girl was pulled into the tent and the men started to beat on the shields so her screams could not be heard. Six men entered the tent to have intercourse with the girl, after which they put her onto her master's bed. Two men grabbed her hands, and two men her wrists. The angel of death put a rope around her neck and while two men pulled the rope, the old woman stabbed the girl between her ribs with a knife. Thereafter, the relatives of the dead chieftain arrived with a burning torch and set the ship aflame. It is said that the fire facilitates the voyage to the realm of the dead.

"Afterwards, a round barrow was built over the ashes, and in the centre of the mound they erected a staff of birch wood, where they carved the names of the dead chieftain and his king. Then they departed in their ships."[233]

The Norse Expansion

"Norse society was based on agriculture and trade with other peoples and placed great emphasis on the concept of honour, both in combat and in the criminal justice system. It was, for example, unfair and wrong

Chapter 8 - An Evolution of Death - The Middle Times [450 - 1500 CE]

to attack an enemy already in a fight with another.

"It is unknown what triggered the Norse expansion and conquests. This era coincided with the Medieval Warm Period (800–1300) and stopped with the start of the Little Ice Age (about 1250–1850). The start of the Viking Age, with the sack of Lindisfarne, also coincided with Charlemagne's Saxon Wars, or Christian wars with pagans in Saxony. Historians Rudolf Simek and Bruno Dumézil theorise that the Viking attacks may have been in response to the spread of Christianity among pagan peoples. Professor Rudolf Simek believes that 'it is not a coincidence if the early Viking activity occurred during the reign of Charlemagne.' Because of the penetration of Christianity in Scandinavia, serious conflict divided Norway for almost a century.

"With the means of travel (longships and open water), their desire for goods led Scandinavian traders to explore and develop extensive trading partnerships in new territories. It has been suggested that the Scandinavians suffered from unequal trade practices imposed by Christian advocates and that this eventually led to the breakdown in trade relations and raiding. British merchants who declared openly that they were Christian and would not trade with heathens and infidels (Muslims and the Norse) would get preferred status for availability and pricing of goods through a Christian network of traders. A two-tiered system of pricing existed with both declared and undeclared merchants trading secretly with banned parties. Viking raiding expeditions were separate from and coexisted with regular trading expeditions. A people with the tradition of raiding their neighbours when their honour had been impugned might easily fall to raiding foreign peoples who impugned their honour.

"Historians also suggest that the Scandinavian population was too large for the peninsula and there was not enough good farmland for everyone. This led to a hunt for more land. Particularly for the settlement and conquest period that followed the early raids, internal strife in Scandinavia resulted

Chapter 8 - An Evolution of Death - The Middle Times [450 - 1500 CE]

in the progressive centralisation of power into fewer hands. Formerly empowered local lords who did not want to be oppressed by greedy kings emigrated overseas. Iceland became Europe's first modern republic, with an annual assembly of elected officials called the Althing, though only goði (wealthy landowners) had the right to vote there."[234]

⊙

And out of darkness comes light.

Notes for Chapter Eight

[192] Houlbrooke, Ralph, ed., *Death, Ritual, and Bereavement*, Routledge in association with the Social History Society of the United Kingdom, London, New York © 1989, page 25

[193] http://en.wikipedia.org/wiki/Middle_Ages

[194] Reported in the *Los Angeles Times*, January 28, 2014

[195] Farrell, James J., *Inventing the American Way of Death, 1830-1920*, Temple University Press © 1989, page 3

[196] *The Tibetan Book of the Dead*, compiled and edited by W.Y. Evans-Wentz Oxford University Press © 1960; preface to the second edition, W.Y. Evans-Wentz, page xiv

[197] http://en.wikipedia.org/wiki/Christian_burial

[198] Daniell, Christoper, Death and Burial in Medieval England, Routledge © 1997, page 1

[199] http://en.wikipedia.org/wiki/High_Middle_Ages

[200] http://en.wikipedia.org/wiki/Early_Middle_Ages

[201] http://www.deathreference.com/Ce-Da/Christian-Death-Rites-History-of.html

Chapter 8 - An Evolution of Death - The Middle Times [450 - 1500 CE]

[202] That small town Catholic church managed to install a Kilgen pipe organ made by the famous family dating to Sebastian Kilgen in the 17th century.

[203] http://www.deathreference.com/Ce-Da/Christian-Death-Rites-History-of.html

[204] http://www.bl.uk/learning/histcitizen/medieval/death/medievaldeath.html

[205] Daniell, Christoper, Death and Burial in Medieval England, Routledge © 1997, page 37

[206] Daniell, Christoper, Death and Burial in Medieval England, Routledge © 1997, page 30

[207] Daniell, Christoper, Death and Burial in Medieval England, Routledge © 1997, page 32

[208] Daniell, Christoper, Death and Burial in Medieval England, Routledge © 1997, page 39-40

[209] Daniell, Christoper, Death and Burial in Medieval England, Routledge © 1997, page 1

[210] Daniell, Christoper, Death and Burial in Medieval England, Routledge © 1997, page 31

[211] Daniell, Christoper, Death and Burial in Medieval England, Routledge © 1997, page 145

[212] http://www.britainexpress.com/London/medieval-london.htm

[213] Daniell, Christoper, Death and Burial in Medieval England, Routledge © 1997, page 146

[214] Daniell, Christoper, Death and Burial in Medieval England, Routledge © 1997, page 150

[215] Daniell, Christoper, Death and Burial in Medieval England, Routledge © 1997, page 150

[216] Daniell, Christoper, Death and Burial in Medieval England, Routledge © 1997, page 153

[217] Daniell, Christoper, Death and Burial in Medieval England, Routledge © 1997 pp. 178-179

[218] Daniell, Christoper, Death and Burial in Medieval England, Routledge © 1997, page 176

Chapter 8 - An Evolution of Death - The Middle Times [450 - 1500 CE]

[219] Daniell, Christoper, Death and Burial in Medieval England, Routledge © 1997, page 176

[220] Daniell, Christoper, Death and Burial in Medieval England, Routledge © 1997 pp. 175-176

[221] Daniell, Christoper, Death and Burial in Medieval England, Routledge © 1997, page 178

[222] Daniell, Christoper, Death and Burial in Medieval England, Routledge © 1997, page 178

[223] Daniell, Christoper, Death and Burial in Medieval England, Routledge © 1997, page 175

[224] Daniell, Christoper, Death and Burial in Medieval England, Routledge © 1997, page 181

[225] Daniell, Christoper, Death and Burial in Medieval England, Routledge © 1997, page 183

[226] It is this potential that led to part of the premise of the movie *Brainstorm*.

[227] Daniell, Christoper, Death and Burial in Medieval England, Routledge © 1997, page 189

[228] http://en.wikipedia.org/wiki/Late_Middle_Ages

[229] *The Tibetan Book of the Dead*, compiled and edited by W.Y. Evans-Wentz Oxford University Press © 1960; preface to the second edition, W.Y. Evans-Wentz, page xiv

[230] Daniell, Christoper, Death and Burial in Medieval England, Routledge © 1997, page 148

[231] http://en.wikipedia.org/wiki/Christian_burial

[232] http://en.wikipedia.org/wiki/Norse_funeral

[233] http://en.wikipedia.org/wiki/Norse_funeral

[234] http://en.wikipedia.org/wiki/Viking_Age

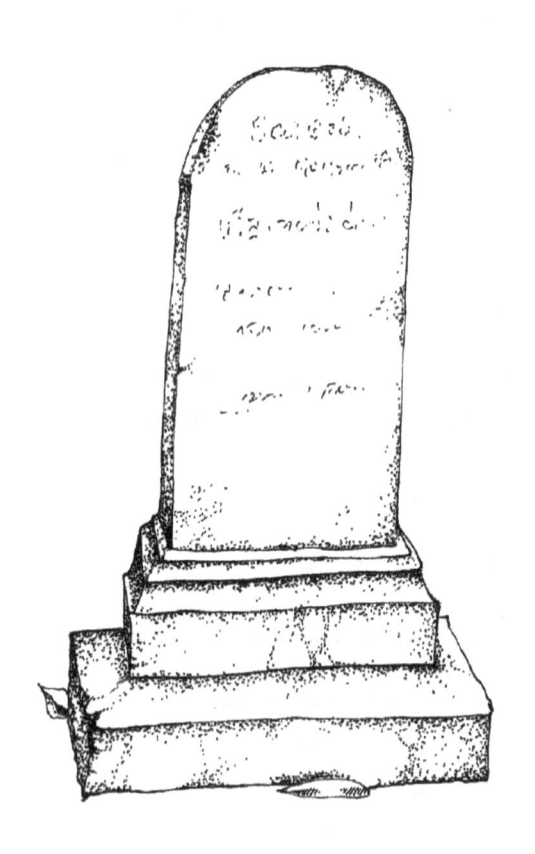

Chapter 9 - An Evolution of Death

Enlightenment and Romance [1500 - 1850 CE]

- The background story
- Notable Religious Reformers
- The Renaissance
- The Age of Enlightenment
- The first Industrial Revolution
- Romanticism
- Monuments and Markers

The background story

"The ideal pattern of dying set out in the thanatography of the period [between the late 15th and early 18th centuries] was one of patience in the face of trial, arduous but ultimately successful struggle with fleshly pains and spiritual temptations, and final quiet sleep in the Lord. Dr. Beier points out... how important prior preparation and a 'cooperative' malady were for the successful practice of the *ars moriendi*. By no means all deaths, even among the godly, conformed in every point to the ideal pattern."[235]

The span of time described above by this chapter's subtitle provided me with a framing for a period of time that reached from the ending of the Middle Ages to the beginning of what could be seen as modern times, modern at least in terms of electrification and the technologies which, as they evolved, defined the twentieth century. This span of over three centuries has several periods of time, each with enough distinctive qualities that they are named. There are other events as well. In a broad, general sense this is a transitional period of time, one in which we see change from the upper social strata eventually changing all levels of society.

Chapter 9 - An Evolution of Death - Enlightenment and Romance
[1500 - 1850 CE]

In my studies of religious, medical, and social evolution, I find myself brought back, on many occasions, to the magnitude of the development of what we often think of as the Gutenberg printing press. Five centuries[236] before my birth, Johannes Gutenberg, of Mainz Germany, developed the ability to make metal movable type. With books taking months or years to be completed by hand, or those printed with wood blocks having many limitations, the printing of books achieved a sense of liberation never before known. Gutenberg and his fellow printers also developed oil-based inks, the direct predecessors of inks used today.

Ink from the classical period of Greece and Rome was a mixture of soot, glues, and water. Around the time that Gutenberg (and others) began developing the cast metal type, there was also a formula of gall, gum, and water with ferrous sulfate. These older formulas worked when writing with a quill pen, but did not provide clarity on the printed page. The metal type was only one component which led to the massive information explosion of this era. We rarely hear of about the changes in ink technology which also were needed. Various experiments led to an ink which was oily, containing soot, turpentine, and walnut oil. The printing press was but one component, as workable ink was just as essential. Together, these developments created a revolution. When you put the next toner cartridge into your printer, think of this history.

In 1457, Gutenberg had a single press in Mainz, Germany, but within 23 years there were 110 presses in use, 45% of them in Italy, with Venice becoming the center of publishing for Europe. This major evolution in printing led to a huge growth in the dissemination of information never before experienced on our planet. I have been known for many years as a Master Herbalist, a field of study which is a daily adventure. The number of herbal books which appeared following soon after the printing developments and the material in them changed medical care of the day and made information far more available to ever greater numbers of people. I must assume that with the sudden growth in the number of books, the value placed on the ability to read and to write must have led to a growth in education as well.

Chapter 9 - An Evolution of Death - Enlightenment and Romance
[1500 - 1850 CE]

Life in Mainz at this time also reflected the growing dissatisfaction within the Christian (Roman Catholic) Church. In 1461, Mainz found itself with two archbishops. The role of Archbishop of Mainz was very important politically when it came to electing the German emperor and remained so for the duration of the Holy Roman Empire. It also holds exceptional prominence within the Church. Just as Gutenberg was bringing the press into functioning and was printing the Bible, Mainz was struggling. One archbishop had been elected by the cathedral, and the public wanted him in that position. A competing archbishop had been established in his position by the pope, who held the authority to name the official for that position. Growing dissatisfaction with problems within the Catholic Church can be seen in this scenario. The archbishop appointed by the pope raided Mainz, and hundreds of citizens were killed.

It may seem inappropriate to a knowledgeable historian that this aging author places these three separate periods, those of the Renaissance, the age of Enlightenment, and then the Romantic period all in one chapter. The perspective that I have sees the Renaissance as a strong shift from the way things had been for so many centuries. I note the emergence of Christian churches who no longer followed the Roman leadership, but who sought change, reform, and a marked shift in how the Christian faith would be interpreted and practiced.

The Renaissance represents a significant shift as well, with creative minds busy, through art, stirring the exploratory mind toward invention. Is it not likely that the Renaissance set the stage for the onset of the first Industrial Revolution? Dissatisfaction, even with the creative momentum of the Renaissance, set change in motion. This momentum appears to have gained speed during these transitional centuries for, although Romanticism continues to be a major presence in art and literature and music, it passed quickly in linear time.

All of this would seem to set the stage for the Victorian and modern eras. Thus, I see the years of this chapter as transition and transformation, the beginning of time speeding up, presaging our modern times. In a broad sense (with my redundant non-historian disclaimer), the Western tradition had remained somewhat intact from the end of the Classical Times until the religious reformers changed the

Chapter 9 - An Evolution of Death - Enlightenment and Romance
[1500 - 1850 CE]

monolithic face of Western Christianity for the rest of time. With the European Church controlling education, medicine, and the arts to such an extent, not to mention how much control was also had with politics and finance, the amount of influence from the Roman center was enormous. It may be posited that this was also a source of stability as the political and royal wars redefined countries and boundaries in between plagues and unseasonable temperatures.

In addition to the major changes the printing evolution must have brought to life, there are other significant periods and events which can be identified. Moving into this stage in our history, the cauldrons of change were simmering and bubbling away, and some would come along to stir the broth of revolution. All of this provides the understory for the evolving changes in attitudes and practices regarding death, dying, and burial.

- **Notable Religious Reformers**

Because I am looking for signposts in the evolution of attitudes and customs regarding death and dying, religion is a preeminent topic. There were plagues in the field of epidemiology, but there were plagues of corruption within the European Church as well.

The Protestant Reformation is usually dated as starting in 1517 with Martin Luther (10 November 1483 - 18 February 1546) publishing his *Theses*. Luther was born in Eisleben, Saxon. Following a harrowing experience with a lightning strike near him, Luther entered an Augustinian friary in Erfurt in 1505. A dozen years later, his disagreements with some policies and practices led Luther to write what is known as *The Ninety-Five Theses*. Academic scholars tend to maintain that there is no historical evidence that Luther ever posted these upon the door of the All Saints Church in Wittenberg. Whether Luther actually nailed them to that church door or not, what we do know is that the new printing presses made a huge difference. Copies of Luther's work were widely distributed, and in 1521 he was defrocked and excommunicated.

Others became involved in the reformist movement, one of the

Chapter 9 -An Evolution of Death - Enlightenment and Romance
[1500 - 1850 CE]

more notable being John Calvin (10 July 1509 - 27 May 1564), whose work led to the development of what became Calvinism. Calvin left the Roman Catholic Church when he was 21 amid the growing religious strife as the various religions struggled with each other and Protestants in France were met with violence. He fled to Basel, Switzerland for safe refuge and wrote his work *Institutes of the Christian Religion* in 1536. Along with William Farel, Calvin's attempt to bring reform led to them both being expelled from Basel, and he next went to Strasbourg, where he formed a church. Calvin's writings led to what we know of as the Reformed, the Congregational, and the Presbyterian churches.

Henry VIII (28 June 1491 - 28 January 1547) was crowned King of England in 1509. Henry also played a major role in the religious struggles the Roman Catholic Church was having. His reasons, however, were not to reform the Church as much as to satisfy his penchant for attractive young women in hopes of having a male child. Not only did he have no faith in a daughter of his having the ability to rule England, his attitudes toward women led to a series of marriages and mistresses which make even contemporary television soap operas seem tame by comparison. As some sources state, "Henry cultivated the image of a Renaissance man."[237] In order to have his way, in the 1530s he separated England from the church in Rome, ending the influence and leadership of the country by the Roman Catholic Church. The Church of England represented yet another major shift in the hold of the Roman Church in Europe.

Thomas More (7 February 1478 - 6 July 1535) was another significant figure. More did not favor the Protestant Reformation and was not a fan of Luther nor of Tyndale. Although More remained true to the Roman Church until beheaded for not following Henry VIII's wishes, More was clearly a Renaissance humanist, easily seen in his book *Utopia*, published in 1516. More was a critical thinker whose reach is felt even today.

Erasmus of Rotterdam (27 October 1466 - 12 July 1536) was also a Catholic priest, and a scholar known as a Dutch Renaissance humanist. He managed to be highly influential as a social critic and yet maintain a middle ground, while keeping his Roman priesthood. Erasmus, as he is

Chapter 9 - An Evolution of Death - Enlightenment and Romance
[1500 - 1850 CE]

known, fought against the monasticism which he felt contributed to the rigidity of church doctrine. When it came to the New Testament, Erasmus included the Greek text to allow a careful study and comparison of his accuracy.

Whether one thinks favorably of the Roman Church's fairly exclusive rule in Western Europe, certainly the emergence of differing religious paradigms and philosophies and increasingly different interpretations of the primary Christian doctrines left the masses no longer able to hold onto a relatively stable and unified approach to death and dying and burial.

"The last rites underwent important changes during the Reformation. Beforehand, the part played by the priest had been crucially important. ....Extreme Unction disappeared altogether, and though the main outlines of the rest of the last rites survived successive liturgical revisions, they were drastically simplified, and the confession of sins became optional. .... Meanwhile the art of dying well had been expounded in a stream of tracts and sermons. ... For many people, the Visitation of the Sick and the reception of the last Communion remained important. ... But ... death without priestly help grew more common. The Reformation changes left more initiative in the hands of the dying and enhanced the importance of their role as the leading actors in the culminating drama of their lives; but this role could impose heavy burdens."[238]

- **The Renaissance**

The first of the intellectual and cultural shifts that took place in response to the changing tides was the Renaissance. I worked on my notes and concepts regarding the religious and philosophical evolution which rippled and surged through these three and a half centuries and they remain, for me, so interwoven that I cannot address them in a separate and detached manner. My belief is that the same social reasons which led the reformers to seek a new way to bring religious ideals to the people also led to the Renaissance. It was time for change. There

Chapter 9 - An Evolution of Death - Enlightenment and Romance
[1500 - 1850 CE]

are times when an individual has felt a need for growth, a need to become free of the rut, no matter how comfortable, and the desire and need are put into action. When we multiply this by the population of the Western world in counterpart to those who are inevitably apt to resist change, change will win out.

During the Middle Times, power and control were in the hands of those who held the political, financial, and educational reins of the realm. In our Western world, that meant the European Church, by which I reference the Catholic Church centered in Rome. I can imagine that those who had the luxury of restlessness were the educated and those who could afford it. The working classes were not educated, had poor access to quality health care, and were genuinely the working poor whose lives were far more about survival.

The opening sentence of this Wikipedia article says it all:

> "The Renaissance was a cultural movement that profoundly affected European intellectual life in the early modern period. Beginning in Italy, and spreading to the rest of Europe by the 16th century, its influence was felt in literature, philosophy, art, music, politics, science, religion, and other aspects of intellectual inquiry. Renaissance scholars employed the humanist method in study, and searched for realism and human emotion in art."[239]

The Renaissance is also considered to have brought forth the first in a line of Renaissance humanist movements. "The 19th-century German historian Georg Voigt (1827–91) identified Petrarch as the first Renaissance humanist."[240] Petrarch is considered the first to have turned to the Classical times as being the model of greatness. Petrarch referred to the period between Rome's fall (the ending of the Classical Times as I call them) and the new ways of viewing reality, including the relationship between humans and deity, as the age of darkness. From Petrarch forward this period became the Dark Ages in common language.

In music, for example, music moves into a new tonality, a polyphonic style of music which is far more familiar to our ears than earlier liturgical music. Gregorian chant, a monophonic tonality, creates

Chapter 9 - An Evolution of Death - Enlightenment and Romance
[1500 - 1850 CE]

a strong sense of religion and piety, even today. But the rise of humanism and the flowering of music led to musical works being created for the public, with printed music now far more widely available thanks also to the new presses.

When I look at the Renaissance and religion, it is as if the new humanism of the Renaissance emerges from the long-simmering cauldron of discontent.

"The Renaissance began in times of religious turmoil. The late Middle Ages saw a period of political intrigue surrounding the Papacy, culminating in the Western Schism, in which three men simultaneously claimed to be true Bishop of Rome. While the schism was resolved by the Council of Constance (1414), the 15th century saw a resulting reform movement known as Conciliarism, which sought to limit the pope's power. Although the papacy eventually emerged supreme in ecclesiastical matters by the Fifth Council of the Lateran (1511), it was dogged by continued accusations of corruption, most famously in the person of Pope Alexander VI, who was accused variously of simony, nepotism and fathering four children (most of whom were married off, presumably for the consolidation of power) while a cardinal.

"Churchmen such as Erasmus and Luther proposed reform to the Church, often based on humanist textual criticism of the New Testament. It was Luther who in October 1517 published the 95 Theses, challenging papal authority and criticizing its perceived corruption, particularly with regard to instances of sold indulgences. The 95 Theses led to the Reformation, a break with the Roman Catholic Church that previously claimed hegemony in Western Europe. Humanism and the Renaissance therefore played a direct role in sparking the Reformation, as well as in many other contemporaneous religious debates and conflicts.

"In an era following the sack of Rome in 1527 and prevalent with uncertainties in the Catholic Church following the Protestant Reformation, Pope Paul III came to the papal throne (1534–1549), to whom Nicolaus Copernicus dedicated

Chapter 9 - An Evolution of Death - Enlightenment and Romance
[1500 - 1850 CE]

De revolutionibus orbium coelestium (On the Revolutions of the Celestial Spheres) and who became the grandfather of Alessandro Farnese (cardinal), who had paintings by Titian, Michelangelo, and Raphael, and an important collection of drawings and who commissioned the masterpiece of Giulio Clovio, arguably the last major illuminated manuscript, the Farnese Hours."[241]

The Renaissance is considered by many scholars to have had its initial growth spurt as early as the 12th century. The renewed interest in using the technology of the day to learn more about the world around them came to a halt with the plague.

"When the Black Death came, it wiped out so many lives it affected the entire system. It brought a sudden end to the previous period of massive scientific change. The plague killed 25–50% of the people in Europe, especially in the crowded conditions of the towns, where the heart of innovations lay. Recurrences of the plague and other disasters caused a continuing decline of population for a century."[242]

It took time for the world of science to gain the momentum that the cultural Renaissance experienced. The seeds which provided that growth came from the Fall of Constantinople. Many of the top minds used that collapse to relocate into the West, bringing their knowledge with them. Figures like Paracelsus, a learned physician and alchemist whose works have been deeply influential for me, was a product of the Renaissance, not only as an explorer of the sciences but in terms of where he spent his early years as a physician, exposed to so many of the richly embroidered esoteric views of the natural world he brought back from that eastern haven of wisdom: tapestries of enlightenment.

The study of the celestial world took the existing studies of astronomy - and for many astrology - and underwent considerable evolution which culminated with Copernicus. The view put forth in Wikipedia is that even Copernicus "was in many ways a Renaissance scientist rather than a revolutionary, because he followed Ptolemy's methods and even his order of presentation. In astronomy, the

Chapter 9 - An Evolution of Death - Enlightenment and Romance
[1500 - 1850 CE]

Renaissance of science can be said to have ended with the truly novel works of Johannes Kepler (1571–1630) and Galileo Galilei (1564–1642)."[243]

In medicine doctors and their students honed their ability to dissect and study human anatomy. Here we find the advance of science to have a direct influence in the care of the dead. "Patents were taken out for special iron coffins with secure locks...."[244] In fact,

> "the fear of bodysnatching was extremely pervasive... During the entire period from about 1700 and reaching a peak in the early nineteenth century - in parallel with the growth of private anatomy tuition - bodysnatching was both widespread and lucrative. The only legal source of corpses for dissection during the entire period was the gallows... Most of the corpses the resurrectionists supplied to anatomists were stolen from graves..."[245]

Meanwhile, the movement toward early globalization led to the Age of Discovery. The ability to find new worlds filled with the unknown potential for resources and plunder. These new lands could be used to grow supplies for the existing markets. All of this fueled changes from which the world could never turn back.

- **The Age of Enlightenment**

Also referred to as the Age of Reason, this was a movement more intellectual than political. But again I see this as something which, if I were part of the working poor, I would remain quite unaffected. Once again this is a *cultural* movement and clearly not one of the working class people.

> "The **Age of Enlightenment** (or simply the **Enlightenment** or **Age of Reason**) was a cultural movement of intellectuals beginning in the late 17th and 18th century Europe emphasizing reason and individualism rather than tradition. Its purpose was to reform society using reason, challenge ideas grounded in tradition and faith, and advance

Chapter 9 - An Evolution of Death - Enlightenment and Romance
[1500 - 1850 CE]

knowledge through the scientific method. It promoted scientific thought, skepticism, and intellectual interchange. It opposed superstition and intolerance, with the Catholic Church a favorite target. Some Enlightenment *philosophes* collaborated with Enlightened despots, who were absolute rulers who tried out some of the new governmental ideas in practice. The ideas of the Enlightenment have had a long-term major impact on the culture, politics, and governments of the Western world."[246]

Without political or significant economic events, there is not a consensus regarding the actual span of time. Some believe that the Age of Enlightenment can be dated to the publishing of *Discourse on Method* by Rene Descartes in 1637 CE while others would see Sir Isaac Nerwton's *Principia Mathematica* published in 1687 CE as the beginning of the era. Generally, the Age of Enlightenment is perceived by many as ending when the French Revolution broke out in 1789 CE, and some see it as lasting until the Napoleonic Wars started in 1805.

The way of thinking which emerged with the Enlightenment disdained what was considered superstition. What were some of the superstitions which the Enlightened often wished to disparage?

What a challenging time for the average person. Despite the ups and down of monarchies and empires, at least one could depend upon the Church remaining stable in life. Surely there were changes, but those upper level disputes and decisions took time to filter down to the local church and even then change was rarely with drama. Life remained far more about survival. The surviving offspring were baptized. If the very young survived, they received the wafer of bread representing the body of Jesus and then were later initiated into the Church through Confirmation. The Council of Trent met in the mid-16th century (1545-1563), alarmed by the Protestant Reformation, perhaps not so much simply by the Reformers as much as by how *popular* they were among the general public.

In addition to those three sacraments, which the Church maintains were handed down to them directly by Jesus the Christ, the average person would have access to Penance (confession) and Matrimony

Chapter 9 - An Evolution of Death - Enlightenment and Romance
[1500 - 1850 CE]

(should they wish to be wed within the Church). Holy Orders is only for those entering the priesthood. And last we have the Anointing of the Sick which, for the average person, became that visit by the priest which indicated that the anointing (*unction*) was an indication that the patient was *in extremis* or near death.

It is believed that Peter of Lombardy (1096-1164 - date of birth uncertain), a noted Catholic theologian and Bishop of Paris, was the first to use the phrase *Extreme unction*. Within a few decades it was among the most common phrases for the Final Anointing.

It was under the Council of Trent in 1551 that the authority to administer this sacrament in ministering to the dying was placed firmly within the hands of the Roman clergy. For all these centuries there was basically one Church. Feeling remorse over your sinful ways? Your nearby parish priest would sit down with you (although it may be on the other side of a screen for privacy) and intercede on your behalf with Deity.

However, now when you neared the Gates of Death, it was not a simple matter. No longer was being a good Christian easy access to this wonderful state of existence after the passing of your body. Now there were increasing varieties of Christian practices, and the wrong choices might bar you from heaven. Death and dying were becoming far more complicated.

> "The last rites underwent important changes during the Reformation. Beforehand, the part played by the priest had been crucially important. .... Extreme Unction disappeared altogether, and though the main outlines of the rest of the last rites survived successive liturgical revisions, they were drastically simplified, and the confession of sins became optional. .... Meanwhile the art of dying well had been expounded in a stream of tracts and sermons. ... For many people, the Visitation of the Sick and the reception of the last Communion remained important. ... But ... death without priestly help grew more common. The Reformation changes left more initiative in the hands of the dying and enhanced the importance of their role as the leading actors in the

Chapter 9 -An Evolution of Death - Enlightenment and Romance [1500 - 1850 CE]

culminating drama of their lives; but this role could impose heavy burdens."[247]

"The attendance of supportive family and neighbours at the bedside forms part of our picture of death... Their spiritual role probably became more important among the godly after the Reformation. ...."[248]

Meanwhile, the Western world was becoming more mechanical, more scientific, and knowledge was changing.

- **The first Industrial Revolution**

It was during this period of time that the first steam engine was patented by Jerónimo de Ayanz y Beaumont a Spanish inventor. His patent in 1606 gave him the credit for the first functional device able to convert steam into usable energy. Improvements were made and in 1698 the English inventor Thomas Savery patented a steam engine utilizing a vacuum pump. The first steam engine using pistons to drive activity is credited to another English inventor, Thomas Newcomen. It was not until the Scottish James Watt improved on Newcomen that an engine generated a continuous motion. Patented in 1781, this new technology revolutionized industry which could now drive far more powerful machinery than was previously done with water and gravity, or team animals, or humans.

Changes were taking place in many ways. An English philosopher and true Renaissance man, Francis Bacon (22 January 1561 - 9 April 1626) was known for many things. Until Bacon metaphysical sciences were interwoven with the emerging sciences. Bacon was arguably the most prominent voice for the Scientific Method. He was the Attorney General and the Lord Chancellor of England, but he was also a scientist and author, and his work was eminently influential. Although born into privilege, he was home schooled due to poor health. While at Cambridge he met Queen Elizabeth. Politically, it was a dangerous world in England and he did see the Tower of London under charges of corruption but fortunately, for the world, he was not there long.

Chapter 9 - An Evolution of Death - Enlightenment and Romance
[1500 - 1850 CE]

"In his works, Bacon stated 'the explanation of which things, and of the true relation between the nature of things and the nature of the mind, is as the strewing and decoration of the bridal chamber of the mind and the universe, the divine goodness assisting, out of which marriage let us hope (and be this the prayer of the bridal song) there may spring helps to man, and a line and race of inventions that may in some degree subdue and overcome the necessities and miseries of humanity' meaning he hoped that through the understanding of mechanics using the Scientific Method, society will create more mechanical inventions that will to an extent solve the problems of Man. This changed the course of science in history, from an experimental state, as it was found in medieval ages, to an experimental and inventive state – that would have eventually led to the mechanical inventions that made possible the Industrial Revolutions of the following centuries."[249]

Life had remained so little changed compared to what was in store. The first half of the period covered in this chapter is marked by changes at the intellectual and cultural level. These changes move into the world of religion, and then as they further evolved, into inventions and industry, and soon there were few whose lives were not changed by what had become the first Industrial Revolution.

In the world of hand labor, humans worked far more directly for their food and survival. Scholars generally believe that it was the Industrial Revolution which led to the first major expansion of population, but also of the standard of living. Goods could be manufactured for a lower cost. There were more jobs, although factory work and coal mining, mainstays of the day, exacted huge tolls on the population as well. Even as the Scientific Method promoted the study of anatomy through dissection, cities were growing crowded, people knew their neighbors less, and urban pollution was on the increase.

"The anxiety these expedients articulate also served to make undertaking a profitable business. During the same period in which the bodysnatcher flourished, so also did the undertaker. The desire for security in the grave went hand in hand with the growth in the commercial provision of funerary services. During the course of the eighteenth and early nineteenth centuries, the same period in which bodysnatching became a separate profession, undertakers had begun to set up shop in urban areas and to purvey their services in the creation of funerals to suit the pockets and aspirations of the growing middle class."[250]

- **Romanticism**

"Romanticism (also the Romantic era or the Romantic period) was an artistic, literary, and intellectual movement that originated in Europe toward the end of the 18th century and in most areas was at its peak in the approximate period from 1800 to 1850. Partly a reaction to the Industrial Revolution, it was also a revolt against the aristocratic social and political norms of the Age of Enlightenment and a reaction against the scientific rationalization of nature. It was embodied most strongly in the visual arts, music, and literature, but had a major impact on historiography, education and the natural sciences. Its effect on politics was considerable and complex; while for much of the peak Romantic period it was associated with liberalism and radicalism, its long-term effect on the growth of nationalism was probably more significant."[251]

Imagining what had happened, if you allow me a simplistic overview, is that Western culture which was once rich with beautiful music, architecture, and ritual, often richly embroidered with a fabric of the mystical, had done quite well, thank you, as the average person sought refuge from a dreary life first in the beauty and majesty of the pyramids and henges, later in the beautifully crafted temples which reached their height during the Classical Times.

During the Middle Times, cathedrals were often larger than castles, built by the skilled tradespeople but also by the workers. Although they

Chapter 9 -An Evolution of Death - Enlightenment and Romance
[1500 - 1850 CE]

were indicative of the wealth accumulated by the European (Catholic) Church, even a village might have as its most prominent building with the tallest tower, the church. No matter how difficult life, the church building and its teachings were a refuge. Although many might grouse over the wealth of the Church, still there was comfort to be found by embracing the spiritual while surrounded by beauty and art. Those whose lives were dreary and always without education could look at the religious art in the windows and on the walls and see what they could not read.

Following the Middle Times, the Renaissance began to set loose the threads of change which began to unravel the settled fabric of life, often tightly woven against a fear of plague or of condemnation to hell. By the time the Industrial Revolution was underway, Protestant services were, compared with the Roman Catholics, sometimes spartan. Life was in increasingly crowded cities and the skies overhead were increasingly dark with pollution.

Near the end of the 18th century, we now find a reaction to move back toward the beauty of the natural world, often embroidered around the edges with the mystical. In the latter third of the 18th century, artists were turning increasingly to landscapes which gave them the freedom to paint ethereal light.

In music the Romantic movement was originally thought of as encompassing late Mozart and Beethoven, although the later 19th century musicians such as Wagner, Chopin, and Brahms are now what we think of.

> "The movement validated intense emotion as an authentic source of aesthetic experience, placing new emphasis on such emotions as apprehension, horror and terror, and awe— especially that which is experienced in confronting the sublimity of untamed nature and its picturesque qualities: both new aesthetic categories. It elevated folk art and ancient custom to a noble status, made spontaneity a desirable characteristic (as in the musical impromptu), and argued for a natural epistemology of human activities, as conditioned by nature in the form of language and customary usage.

Chapter 9 - An Evolution of Death - Enlightenment and Romance
[1500 - 1850 CE]

Romanticism reached beyond the rational and Classicist ideal models to raise a revived medievalism and elements of art and narrative perceived to be authentically medieval in an attempt to escape the confines of population growth, urban sprawl, and industrialism. Romanticism embraced the exotic, the unfamiliar, and the distant in modes more authentic than Rococo chinoiserie, harnessing the power of the imagination to envision and to escape."[252]

Thus has the stage been set for the Modern Times.

● Monuments and Markers

The Good Death in Seventeenth-Century England

"In seventeenth-century England, whatever their hopes, people did not expect healers and medicines to cure them. ... In addition, seventeenth-century medicine-taking, illnesses, births, and deaths were very social, in contrast to the privacy required by twentieth-century conventions."[253]

"The ideal death took place at home. It should not be sudden. In addition, the final illness should not be so painful that the person dying became totally distracted from his or her duties. In addition, lengthy or not, illnesses, both of the self and of loved ones, served as practice fields for the death which must, in any case, come some time. Seventeenth-century contributors to the *ars moriendi* literary tradition followed both their Catholic and their Protestant forebears in advocating stoicism in the face of death and, indeed, in celebrating the glories of the good death. The works directed toward educating laymen in the proper method of dying are too numerous to be adequately detailed or described here..."[254]

"When illness came and the believer took to his or her bed, care of the soul was of the highest priority. In most cases,

Chapter 9 - An Evolution of Death - Enlightenment and Romance
[1500 - 1850 CE]

the minister should be summoned."[255]

"... a consensus of opinion concerning desirable and undesirable deaths existed in seventeenth-century England. Good death was pious and prepared. Bad death was unregenerate and, with the possible exception of suicide, unprepared. ... That the good death existed both as an ideal and a reality in seventeenth-century England there can be no doubt."[256]

Death without fear

"Death without fear, thought Dr. John Ferriar, should resemble 'falling asleep.' ... We see sickness and medicine before the coming, say, of anaesthetics, as being excruciatingly painful... But relative to earlier times, the eighteenth-century was an anaesthetized age, precisely because of the startling surge in the use of powerful narcotics, drawing above all upon alcohol and opium and its derivatives, laudanum and paregoric; a habit sanctioned by regular doctors, and encouraged amongst the people at large by a free market in the sale of drugs."[257]

"Abundant evidence, however, points to increasingly heavy consumption of opium before the nineteenth-century, used as an analgesic, a sedative, a febrifuge, and as a specific against gastro-intestinal problems. Opiates were widely recommended, almost as a panacea, as medical magic, by eminent physicians of the second half of the eighteenth century."[258]

Adonais: An Elegy on the Death of John Keats
By Percy Bysshe Shelley
[the first three of 55 stanzas]

I

I weep for Adonais—he is dead!
Oh, weep for Adonais! though our tears

Chapter 9 - An Evolution of Death - Enlightenment and Romance
[1500 - 1850 CE]

Thaw not the frost which binds so dear a head!
And thou, sad Hour, selected from all years
To mourn our loss, rouse thy obscure compeers,
And teach them thine own sorrow, say: "With me
Died Adonais; till the Future dares
Forget the Past, his fate and fame shall be
An echo and a light unto eternity!"

II
Where wert thou, mighty Mother, when he lay,
When thy Son lay, pierc'd by the shaft which flies
In darkness? where was lorn Urania
When Adonais died? With veiled eyes,
'Mid listening Echoes, in her Paradise
She sate, while one, with soft enamour'd breath,
Rekindled all the fading melodies,
With which, like flowers that mock the corse beneath,
He had adorn'd and hid the coming bulk of Death.

III
Oh, weep for Adonais—he is dead!
Wake, melancholy Mother, wake and weep!
Yet wherefore? Quench within their burning bed
Thy fiery tears, and let thy loud heart keep
Like his, a mute and uncomplaining sleep;
For he is gone, where all things wise and fair
Descend—oh, dream not that the amorous Deep
Will yet restore him to the vital air;
Death feeds on his mute voice, and laughs at our despair

Chapter 9 - An Evolution of Death - Enlightenment and Romance
[1500 - 1850 CE]

"Throughout the Middle Ages, and during the Renaissance that followed, Europe still retained enough of the Mystery teachings concerning death to understand the paramount importance of knowing how to die; and many treatises, hereinafter referred to, on the Art of Dying were then current there."[259]

Notes for Chapter Nine

[235] Houlbrooke, Ralph, ed., *Death, Ritual, and Bereavement*, Routledge in association with the Social History Society of the United Kingdom, London, New York © 1989, page 27

[236] The exact date is not known although we do know of the Mainz press in 1457. Your author was born in 1945. I must believe that Gutenberg and a few others were already thinking toward this development.

[237] http://en.wikipedia.org/wiki/Henry_VIII

[238] Houlbrooke, Ralph, ed., *Death, Ritual, and Bereavement*, Routledge in association with the Social History Society of the United Kingdom, London, New York © 1989, pages 26-27

[239] http://en.wikipedia.org/wiki/Renaissance 27 October 2013 ce

[240] http://en.wikipedia.org/wiki/Humanism 6 September 2014 ce

[241] http://en.wikipedia.org/wiki/The_Renaissance#Religion 6 Sept. 2014 ce

[242] http://en.wikipedia.org/wiki/History_of_science_in_the_Renaissance 12 October 2014 ce

[243] http://en.wikipedia.org/wiki/History_of_science_in_the_Renaissance 12 October 2014 ce

[244] "Why Was Death So Big In Victorian Britain" by Ruth Richardson in *Death, Ritual, and Bereavement*, Routledge in association with the Social History Society of the United Kingdom, London, New York © 1989, page 110

Chapter 9 - An Evolution of Death - Enlightenment and Romance
[1500 - 1850 CE]

---

[245] "Why Was Death So Big In Victorian Britain" by Ruth Richardson in *Death, Ritual, and Bereavement*, Routledge in association with the Social History Society of the United Kingdom, London, New York © 1989, pages 107-9

[246] http://en.wikipedia.org/wiki/Age_of_Enlightenment#Time_span 27 October 2013 ce

[247] Houlbrooke, Ralph, ed., *Death, Ritual, and Bereavement*, Routledge in association with the Social History Society of the United Kingdom, London, New York © 1989, pages 26-27

[248] Houlbrooke, Ralph, ed., *Death, Ritual, and Bereavement*, Routledge in association with the Social History Society of the United Kingdom, London, New York © 1989, page 28

[249] http://en.wikipedia.org/wiki/Francis_Bacon October 29, 2014 ce

[250] "Why Was Death So Big In Victorian Britain" by Ruth Richardson in *Death, Ritual, and Bereavement*, Routledge in association with the Social History Society of the United Kingdom, London, New York © 1989, pages 110-111

[251] http://en.wikipedia.org/wiki/Romanticism

[252] http://en.wikipedia.org/wiki/Romanticism

[253] "The Good Death in Seventeenth-Century England" by Lucinda McCray Beir in *Death, Ritual, and Bereavement*, Routledge in association with the Social History Society of the United Kingdom, London, New York © 1989, page 44

[254] "The Good Death in Seventeenth-Century England" by Lucinda McCray Beir in *Death, Ritual, and Bereavement*, Routledge in association with the Social History Society of the United Kingdom, London, New York © 1989, page 47

[255] "The Good Death in Seventeenth-Century England" by Lucinda McCray Beir in *Death, Ritual, and Bereavement*, Routledge in association with the Social History Society of the United Kingdom, London, New York © 1989, page 49

[256] "The Good Death in Seventeenth-Century England" by Lucinda McCray Beir in *Death, Ritual, and Bereavement*, Routledge in association with the Social History Society of the United Kingdom, London, New York © 1989, page 61

Chapter 9 -An Evolution of Death - Enlightenment and Romance
[1500 - 1850 CE]

---

[257] "Death and The Doctors in Georgian England" by Roy Porter in *Death, Ritual, and Bereavement*, Routledge in association with the Social History Society of the United Kingdom, London, New York © 1989, page 91

[258] "Death and The Doctors in Georgian England" by Roy Porter in *Death, Ritual, and Bereavement*, Routledge in association with the Social History Society of the United Kingdom, London, New York © 1989, page 92

[259] *The Tibetan Book of the Dead*, compiled and edited by W.Y. Evans-Wentz Oxford University Press © 1960; preface to the second edition, W.Y. Evans-Wentz, page xiv

Chapter 10 - An Evolution of Death

The Victorian and Modern Eras Begin [1840 - 2000 CE]

- The background story
- The industrialization of funerals
- Professionalism and the Funeral Industry
- Changing Christian Values
- The Cemetery: Gardens of the Dead
- Changing Social Values
- Monuments and Markers

● The background story

Although we, today, are dazzled by how dramatically life has changed due to the ongoing technological revolution, I have often thought that we don't have a clue. The timing of my grandparents births and my growing view of the world around me led me to frequently muse about the amount of change they experienced in their lifetimes. My maternal grandparents, with whom I was very close, were born in the 1890s.

What began as the steam and coal-powered Industrial Revolution a century earlier, never stopped. The astounding inventions of the beginning of this modern era (as I am calling it for the purposes of this book) allowed for the rise of the working class, of more and more people having income and access to education. News began traveling fast. Electricity speeded up the first Industrial Revolution and now we were adding technology. Goods could be moved fast and farther. During just a short period, imagine how these new creations changed the world beyond belief.

- The telephone was patented by Alexander Graham Bell in 1876.
- The Edison phonograph was invented in 1877... still one without electricity.
- The automobile was patented by Benz in 1879 in Europe but not

until 1895 in the United States.
- The incandescent light bulb was patented by Edison in 1879 and in Britain by Swan in 1880.
- The first successful central electricity was Edison's Swan Lake Station in New York which started up in 1882.
- Diesel patented the first diesel engine in 1892.
- The first radio receiver was built by Alexander Stepanovich Popov in 1895.
- The Wright brothers made the first flight with an air vehicle heavier than a human. This took place in 1903.[260]

By the time of my Grandmother's death in 1963, there had been two massive world wars fought on a bloody scale unimaginable without all of this technology. Bombs dropped from flying machines... Radar, nuclear submarines... But even more... Communication. The world of the 20th century was, I believe, the greatest departure for humans from the way they had been living previously.

By the time my Grandfather passed away in 1980, I had already been working with computers, which were now moving into home use as well. His life spanned Victorian clothing styles to the mini-skirt and frankly, I don't think he thought either were appropriate for women.

Not just simple propellor airplanes, but jets... Large jets. And then the atomic age with destruction on a scale so vast that, just as was hoped for at the end of World War I, people wished to never again see such slaughter. I was born in 1945, less than a month following the bombing of Hiroshima. This was a new scale for death caused by humans. However, although I am writing of death, I dare not step upon my soapboxes regarding the violence humans wreak upon other humans. The Industrial Revolution and subsequent technology revolutions have allowed the most amazing good and wonders, but also the most terrifying and massive threats both through war and through our damage to the environment.

My grandparents were born at a time when indoor plumbing was uncommon, when there were no homes with electricity, when food preservation was a challenge. Travel was by horse or, for the fortunate, by coal-fueled steam locomotive.

By the time they died, reading a newspaper in the early morning or evening was taken for granted. Instant communication by telephone with people living thousands of miles away (even on another continent) was taken for granted. Every village, every city, was ablaze with electricity, enough that it was increasingly difficult to see the star-filled night as they had known it.

These changes were not limited to the United States, obviously, and I now wish to turn temporarily to England for another perspective.

The background in England

On May 24th, 1819, a baby was born in England. Alexandrina Victoria came to be a woman, becoming Queen of England in June 1837, whose extraordinary reign of 63 years and seven months encompasses what may have been the most dramatic shift into our modern world. By the time of her death (January 22, 1901) new inventions and processes had put change in motion which was unparalleled. There were other changes as well which emerge from this era.

Victoria's reign saw the British Empire reach so far that the sun never set upon it, as the saying goes. Less visible, perhaps, were other changes which led to a period of spiritual renewal. The far reaches of the British Empire along with increased capability for publishing brought astounding books into the hands of readers.

The Egyptian Book of the Dead (as we know it) began to emerge with the Lepsius translation, the first complete version of the book, in 1842. By the end of the century the more familiar version by Budge appeared.

Overall, however, Queen Victoria's era "was a period of industrial, cultural, political, scientific, and military change within the United Kingdom, and was marked by a great expansion of the British Empire."[261]

The second Industrial Revolution refers to the latter period from 1840 and 1870[262] which now included the growing use of steam railways and water transport with steam-powered engines. These were important to carry the huge shift in factory output from the growing scale of manufacturing powered by steam. What allowed development in Europe to move forward became sidetracked in the United States with the need to redirect these new sources of power toward the horrendous civil war which broke out.

The American Civil War

On April 12th, 1861, armed Confederate forces fired shots at Fort Sumter, a strategically important fort in South Carolina which was held by Union troops. The war was fought for four years, almost to the day, when Lee surrendered on April 9th, 1865.

> "The American Civil War was one of the earliest true industrial wars. Railroads, the telegraph, steamships, and mass-produced weapons were employed extensively. The mobilization of civilian factories, mines, shipyards, banks, transportation and food supplies all foreshadowed World War I. It remains the deadliest war in American history, resulting in the deaths of an estimated 750,000 soldiers and an undetermined number of civilian casualties."[263]

In the United States there is a level of death which laid waste to the male work force at a scope reminiscent of the plague years in Europe. This was not some contagious disease, however, in which a pathogen took out vast amounts of the population. The United States Census Bureau lists a population of 31,443,000 in 1860 just before the Civil War broke out. By comparison the population estimate for 2014 is ten times that at 319,920,000.[264] An equivalent number of casualties today would be 7.5 million lives. Soldiers transported by steam power on ships and trains to the war zone became vast numbers of dead. Families wanted the bodies returned. As mentioned in Chapter 5, the Civil War led to a far greater acceptance of embalming, if only due to necessity.

> "Not only did the Civil War increase the use of embalming as a method for transporting the dead, of which there were many, but it created a large relocation of the population. In addition, the shifting economic, political and religious climates further influenced undertakers."[265]

• The industrialization of funerals

Life in the small town of Colby, Wisconsin, was not much different than life 20-50 years earlier. Colby was such a small, rural town that, in my early childhood, it was a half hour removed from what we considered a 'city' - the larger town or small city of Marshfield, Wisconsin. An even larger city would have been Wausau, about thirty miles east and, with 30,000 people was large enough that many did not go there, ever. Life in Colby was inevitably a few decades behind areas with a more urban lifestyle. Until age ten our telephone was a large, wood model attached to the wall. To call you turned the crank. I still remember my parents' phone signal: one long and two shorts. Thanks to a basement cistern we could hand-pump water in the kitchen, but the toilet held a large bucket that my brother and I had to hand-carry out into the fields and dump.

Far removed from the Civil War, it was not much mentioned. World War II took many away. Some came back to their family farms. Some went to the cities. Many came back for burial.

In the latter-19th century, if someone died in Colby, Wisconsin, the following scenario was very likely the reality. The hearse would have been horse-drawn, taking the coffin from the home to the cemetery, possibly by way of one of the churches for a funeral.

In the mid-20th century when a family member died, sometimes in hospital or in an accident but more often at home, the funeral director (still called the 'undertaker' by the older generation) was called. He handled nearly everything. The family went to his place of business to select as fine a casket as could be afforded - and not uncommonly more than they could afford. The body was shown in the funeral parlor, with its dim lighting, serene atmosphere, flowers all about the casket and near where the deceased was lying in state, made up to look far better than she or he had at death, and embalmed so as to look real, as if sleeping.

How can I best convey the attitude toward death in the first half of the nineteenth century?

Chapter 10 - An Evolution of Death - The Victorian and Modern Eras [1840 - 2000 ce]

"Death was integrated, through a series of rituals and symbols, into the life of the community. At the center of this network of practices and significations was the corpse, an irreducible object that evoked feelings of dread, fear, and resignation, as well as reverence, respect, and hope. ... From the place where death occurred, usually on a bed in the home, to the final destination of the body ... the treatment of the corpse generally depended on certain pre-established rituals in northern, Protestant communities at the end of the eighteenth century. And yet, during the course of the nineteenth century, the rigid structures that determined how to dispose of the physical remains began to waver, and new meanings, rituals, and technologies began to be imposed on that site where signs of death made their most impressive mark - the corpse."[266]

Three-quarters of a century later, when I was in upper elementary school, I attended St. Mary's Catholic School in Colby and was an altar boy. I assisted the Priest with many funerals, riding in procession behind a modern hearse, usually a Cadillac, as we drove from the church (an occasional funeral service would leave from the funeral home, once called a funeral 'parlor') and went directly to the cemetery.

Prior to the industrialization of the funeral profession,

"in the small towns and rural areas where most Americans lived, a death in the family set a train of tradition into motion. A member of the family or a neighbor began to prepare the body for burial. He - or she, for often these last rites were performed by women - placed a board between two chairs, draped it with a sheet, laid the body upon it, and washed the corpse. Sometimes the features of the corpse had to be prepared for presentation. To close the mouth, people used a forked stick between the breast bone and chin, fastened with a string around the neck. To close the eyes, they placed a coin on the eyelids. Then they dressed the body for burial, either in a winding sheet or a shroud. In warm weather, they put a large block of ice in a tub beneath the board, with smaller chunks about the body.

"While these preparations proceeded, another neighbor went to notify the cabinetmaker or furniture dealer, who provided a coffin from his small stock or made one to order. In the early nineteenth century, the coffin was simply a six-sided box with a hinged lid. After 1850, the coffin might be lined with cloth to counter the severity of the rough wood."[267]

"In either case, on the day of the funeral the undertaker carted the coffin to the house in a spring wagon. There, he placed the body in the coffin for the funeral, which usually proceeded according to a religious formula under the direction of a minister."[268]

The undertaker of this era had learned his trade by experience, improving the skills he had learned.

"Over the course of the nineteenth century, families called undertakers to perform more and more of the services of the funeral. Instead of notifying a neighbor or a friend, survivors asked the undertaker to the house to prepare the body. Beginning as a carpenter providing rough boxes, the undertaker moved to the position of cabinetmaker, furnishing ready-made polished coffins for four to ten dollars. Then he became a furniture dealer, with a small stock of ready-made coffins and some trimmings. Eventually he added a special box to his wagon to make a hearse and went out as an undertaker on service calls... After the Civil War, however, the average undertaker found himself caught in currents of change that flowed from several sources."[269]

The tools of the trade as well as the items for retail sale were improving.

"In 1876 [the Stein Manufacturing Co. of Rochester, New York] sponsored a lavish display of caskets at the Philadelphia Centennial Exposition, in order to stimulate consumer demand for its product. In that same year, the Stein Co. financed the publication of *The Casket*, the second trade journal for funeral service ... Through the columns of *The Casket*, undertakers encountered new styles of funeral goods which encouraged them to offer new forms of funeral service. ... the availability of caskets with silk-lined interiors undoubtedly encouraged efforts to make the corpse look as good as its container. And the manufacturers of embalming fluids promoted a product to help undertakers achieve such results."[270]

Earlier, "the term 'casket' had also referred to the human body itself, and denoted the body as a mere receptacle for the precious soul." As Farrell sees it, "The use of the word 'casket' to describe a container for the body suggests a reevaluation of the relationship of the body to the soul. Precious in its own right, the body now began to superseded the soul in funeral service."[271] Increasingly the casket became something which was also designed to delay the decay of the body. I simply cannot imagine exhuming a casket which is 200 years old with a 200 year-old corpse in it. Even if I were able to believe that one could be resurrected with one's body, any deity able to make that happen might be generous and provide me with a newer, improved model!

"In the 1880s methods of arterial injection were introduced, and for the first time effective cosmetic restoration became generally available; the funeral industry grew rapidly as a consequence."[272]

Only a year since the Colonies fought the British to become independent and yet the processes of managing the bodies of those who died were parallel, although it took two wars to hasten Colonial America and the early United States along. In that earlier time a young man who showed some skill, an above average ability to learn and enough of a work ethic would be apprenticed to the local carpenter. Although today we think of the carpenter as someone who is in the construction trade, before the industrial revolution it was a carpenter who was ideally also suited for cabinetry, for making furniture, who

Chapter 10 - An Evolution of Death - The Victorian and Modern Eras [1840 - 2000 ce]

brought lumber back to life as a work primarily utilitarian but also able to show the grain and texture of the wood yet reflect the shifting beliefs of his environs.

Certainly there would be *some* who made their own coffins, but more and more communal life allowed for the individual to make the transition from agrarian to urban life, from a life in which the adults had to work together to do everything from constructing their homes and barns to guaranteeing there was enough food for livestock and for family.

"In colonial times, the undertaker was a part-time specialist only, his main skills were those of the carpenter. In addition to making coffins, he assisted in the laying out of the corpse."[273] There were other changes taking place on both sides of the Atlantic as well. The pressures of growing urban areas made it increasingly difficult for a church to hold enough land to provide burial space to hold all of the past generations and those dying at present, and to ensure people with a sense of security that there would be enough space for their children and their grandchildren as well. Cemeteries were increasingly located where there was space at that buffer zone between the urban village or city and the land needed for the agrarian, who provided the food.

Who better, then, to move the coffin but the undertaker. He made the coffin and laid out the body. As an aside I would also note that I do refer to this profession in the masculine. While I would like to believe that a woman could gain access into this profession, and that she would be accepted, I have seen no references to it happening and I believe it would have been news worthy.

"At the conclusion of the [Civil War] the assassination of Lincoln brought further attention to the new techniques. The funeral cortege, with Lincoln's body on display, traveled from Washington across the Northeast and Midwest to Springfield, Illinois."[274] Despite the horror and tragedy of losing Lincoln, this was a national experience demonstrating the changes in a public manner perhaps never before done.

"Embalming allowed the period between death and burial to be extended, giving time for the deceased to journey home or for relatives

Chapter 10 - An Evolution of Death - The Victorian and Modern Eras [1840 - 2000 ce]

to assemble. After restorative techniques were introduced, attention was focused upon the display of the corpse and a more sumptuous setting was provided for it."[275] What was once a wake held in the family home is now growing into gatherings held where the body was... and the undertaker's commercial space became known by that nice, domestic name of 'parlor.'

The onset of the 19th century brought state licensing to many parts of the U.S. Ostensibly this was done to safeguard the consumer. As more people moved into urban areas where there were jobs, they were now earning more money and could hire various services, increasingly essential as the standard of living rose but income was in money rather than in produce and food. In some areas there were news-making events as the criminal element realized that this was a growing industry and there was money to be made.

The inventions which arrived in the latter 19th century changed the 20th in ways unimaginable and, often, incomprehensible to those living when the Victorian and Modern Eras arrived. The furniture-maker's basement became a welcoming showroom. The horse and cart became the hearse. The image familiar to most in the U.S. of an earlier time was typically a Cadillac, now engineered with a lower frame that made moving the casket on and off with far greater ease. The telephone allowed arrangements to be made with the family no longer having drive back and forth and forth and back.

The family could stay at home and tend to their needs and be available for friends and family who wished to provide consolation in private. Increasing scientific developments in embalming and cremation along with new products and techniques created the image of a loved one looking healthy, at peace, and sleeping. More and more Americans removed themselves from death and the dead as a reality.

Soon, as the electrical grid proliferated, the parlor from someone's home was now a parlor setting with ambient lighting and music and comfortable seating. The family and friends had more than enough space to mingle and talk. It was all staged with great care. Seeing the professional's certification and state license created security for the family.

Those who were more successful certainly welcomed that licensing. Licensing would do for the funeral profession what it had done for some other commodities and services. Those who were successful would also be those who were most influential in the establishing of a licensed profession.

By lining the newer, more attractive caskets with silk and by displaying an embalmed body, people were able to feel much better about those who had died. In truth, however, the funeral 'industry' grew and was also exploring ways in which to sell more expensive wares as well as to to achieve a type of scientific cachet, through embalming. NFDA members pushed for the more scientific status and they were also able to have far more services (at higher prices) available to grieving family members.

- **Professionalism and the Funeral Industry**

Growing up in Colby, Wisconsin, a town of 900 people in the 1950s, provided me with an opportunity to experience life as it had been. When I later lived in Minneapolis, just 140 miles west, upon being asked where I was from I used to reply in humor, "150 miles and fifty years east of here." When I studied Farrell's book, even when he writes about the late 19th century, that was my life!! Undertaking was "often the adjunct of a furniture business." In our town the caskets were in the basement of the furniture store. In fact, as late as the early 1980s I was seeing a man who lived in Dodge Center (at that time not much larger than Colby) who was a licensed mortician and owned a combination furniture store/funeral parlor. Even the word parlor is a reflection of that late 19th century shift from the body being placed in the front 'parlor' of the family home to the care of a professional.

Leaving the Romantic Period and entering what I am calling the Modern Era, the profession which became central to tending the death of the body underwent a great amount of change. Many professions in the United States upgraded themselves in order to hold a stronger role in society, to command a greater share of the money the working population was spending on services, but also to create a higher quality of education and techniques provided by their peers.

Chapter 10 - An Evolution of Death - The Victorian and Modern Eras [1840 - 2000 ce]

There was a significant change taking place in society. More and more we were becoming a culture which no longer worked directly to produce our own food and goods, or in which we worked and then exchanged goods and services with those living in our community or neighborhood. Goods produced in one region could easily be shipped to another. The emergence of a working class which had time away from their employment, of people turning more and more toward others for many of their services, led to more change. In addition, as more people could read and word of mouth was now almost secondary to the printed word, news delivered to your door each day meant that social expectations changed.

The American Medical Association was incorporated in 1897, having had fifty years to evolve a clear sense of where they wanted things to go. Similar changes were afoot in the industry regarding the burial of the dead.

Modern funeral practices are the product of the burial industry far more than any changes in religious practices. Not wishing to diminish the sincerity of many good practitioners, it should be noted that the driving forces behind the burial industry and many modern professions are no different. As a Master Herbalist who has been practicing for forty years, I have watched professional organizations and credential-seeking organizations arise in my own profession. The following quotation could well apply to the modern herbalist as well, although most of my peers would be deeply uncomfortable with the word *power*.

"Undertakers ... wanted the same status as doctors or clerics, and the power over people which such status implied."[276] In the context here, I believe the word *power* would represent such things as holding a role with enough *power* that they are among the first to whom a family would turn. Would an herbalist or a Wiccan Priestess not want the same? Or for the alternative healing professions, from massage to acupuncture to botanical medicine, one of the issues is having access to being paid by the patient's insurance, which would greatly expand their paid client base. This is also power.

And power is money. It is easy to level criticism at the funeral industry. "As the critics have shown, funeral directors have not failed to exploit their position in order to make a profit ... funeral directors regularly play upon the emotional state of their customers in order to get them to purchase a more expensive coffin than they had intended."[277]

Before I allow you to get too wound up here, in my research Hunting & Metcalf also present some objective perspectives. The cost of flowers is not a direct part of the funeral industry but part of the floral industry whose advertising loves to coerce the consumer into aiding the sales of flowers at Valentine's and Mother's Day into a huge financial windfall. Then, there are the flowers for weddings. And the money spent on weddings is a far greater amount but typically the voices are quiet about the wedding cost than they are about funerals.

"Considering the economic explanation as a whole, there is no doubt that the existence of a tightly organized group of specialists who control every phase of the disposal of corpses is the most significant single feature of American funerals. It explains why funerals cost what they do, and why nonspecialists, such as kin and clergy, appear only in passive roles."[278]

"In 1880 the average American undertaker could expect to supply almost two hundred funerals; in 1920, he could anticipate only fifty-seven. Because they proved unable to reverse the law of marginal utility, funeral directors were forced to realize a greater profit per funeral in order to maintain a constant income. economic pressures joined technical expertise, professional aspirations, and changing cultural tastes to transform the American funeral between 1880 and 1920."[279]

One of the most significant events for burial services in the United States was the emergence of the NFDA. Formed a little more than 140 years ago, today the NFDA is an international organization which provides professional support and education and standards for its members. What was once simply a large number of independent local craftsmen who evolved into a large market for the casket manufacturers took control of their own destiny, a move which had an influence far larger than the average citizen could imagine.

"The creation of the National Funeral Directors' Association (NFDA) in 1882 signaled the self-consciousness of this group, and a willingness to work for significant modifications in funeral ceremonies. Changes in funeral service practices accompanied the professional shift from undertakers to funeral directors. These changes were in four areas: 1) the care of the body, 2) the container for the body, 3) the places of the funeral, 4) funeral procedures."[280]

"Between death and the cemetery lay the field of funeral service - the preparation of the body for burial, and the formal rite of passage of the funeral ceremony. The institution of funeral service changed markedly between 1850 and 1920, both in personnel and practice. In personnel, funeral directors began to replace family members, ministers, and friends as managers of funerals. In funeral service as in cemetery and life insurance institutions, an informed, interested group of people played a primary role in social change."[281]

What were those social changes? It was not all that long ago that upon the death of a loved one or family member, the initial laying out of the body was done in the home, often by a family member. As the population in the U.S. gradually had more income for services of all types, those with greater skill grew into more identifiable roles within the community. The home-constructed wooden coffin usually looked home-constructed, even rough. In that era the head of the family (or even the other spouse in a farm or home-business model) was expected to be able to wield hand tools for simple construction, if not more, and for repairs. As families had more income, the local furniture maker had a growing market making better quality and more durable furniture. Shifting values meant honoring one's deceased as well as showing neighbors, coworkers, and relatives that you cared enough to provide decent burial and the best coffin you could afford. Who better to make a good and attractive wood coffin?

The ability to embalm a body, protecting it against fast decay was knowledge which began to set the undertaker apart. The NFDA lobbied for a licensed profession, for standards, for the public to go only to someone with professional recommendations. The undertakers in turn learned new skills, but also business techniques. In a relatively short period of time the profession went from a furniture store with coffins out of the way, to a comfortable and comforting environment in which the family did not have to do much other than grieve and interact with those who came to pay their respects.

Undertakers emphasized, over time, the science of it all. Embalming would no longer be a trade learned through a type of apprenticeship, but it would become mortuary science. The NFDA also provided marketing and business skills and collectively worked to have laws passed which elevated their standards but also kept the political power in the hands of the NFDA.

They became funeral directors and tried to set themselves apart from the older nomenclature of undertakers. This was not a simple change, either.

> "At the first National Funeral Directors' Association convention, a debate ensued over the appellation of the organization, and the term 'funeral director' was chosen in an attempt to elevate the occupation in an age of progress. Just as the word 'cemetery' represented a new conception of burial place, so the new term 'funeral director' symbolized a new sense of professional identity."[282]

> "To induce people to patronize funeral homes, funeral directors tried 'to make our places of business as cheerful and pleasant as possible.' They removed coffins and caskets from their show windows, and replaced them with flowers or potted palms. They divided the reception room from the show rooms, eliminating evidences of death from the first encounter with the client. And, when possible, they furnished the funeral parlor in the full fashion of the day.

> "The result was 'well-fashioned, cheerful establishments where you will find well-appointed offices where business can

be privately transacted [and] luxurious funeral parlors where funeral services can be quietly conducted.' The cheerful luxury of these fine homes invited public patronage, even as it paralleled styles in cemetery and casket design, directing attention away from death and bereavement and toward the trappings of death."[283]

"By banishing the parlor from the home to the funeral parlor, families also banished the associations of death that lingered in the [home] parlor after a funeral."[284] With the exception of the growing cost, it was a winning solution for all.

The issues which shaped all of these changes are so complex I can but touch upon them lightly.

"An American funeral in 1920 included a life-like body resting in a sightly and comfortable casket. Usually both body and casket rested in the family home, but increasingly the funeral began at the funeral director's establishment. In their book on *The History of American Funeral Directing*, Rohert Habenstein and William Lamers describe the rise of the funeral home as 'a consolidation of three functional areas, the clinic, the home, and the chapel, into a single operational unit.'"[285]

- **Changing Christian Values**

The manner in which we tend to our dead is reflective of the nature of our religion. Science and technology were changing, social values were changing, the economic layout of the Western world was changing and, as we ought expect, there were changes taking place in the primary religions of the day as well.

Christianity, as we begin studying the Victorian and modern times, could be described as *Liberal Christianity*. Before you begin to draw conclusions or respond with disbelief, I would address the meaning of that phrase. In the previous chapter I wrote about the *Age of Enlightenment*. In many ways the Enlightenment was pragmatic. I have

Chapter 10 - An Evolution of Death - The Victorian and Modern Eras [1840 - 2000 ce]

not lived through that period (at least in this incarnation), nor have I studied it extensively, but I get a sense of "just the facts, ma'am." The evolution of science encouraged people to examine factually and then explore the subject with thought, inquiry, and discourse. As time progressed, the Enlightenment grew into what was called Liberal Christianity.

Farrell describes this process far better than I am able:

"The Enlightenment introduced cosmological conceptions which repudiated 'the Puritan cosmology' and affected American intellectual development throughout the nineteenth century. Between 1700 and 1800, but especially in the final forty years of the eighteenth century, Enlightenment thought spread among the educated classes of the Eastern seaboard, presenting an alternative to the ideas of the Reformed Tradition. In this new Enlightenment formulation, God relinquished the foreground of the cosmological canvas to nature, but retained a place in the background and the past."[286]

According to Farrell, "Religious liberalism combined elements of Romanticism and scientific naturalism in a cosmology which developed in America largely between 1859 and 1940. The liberal movement spanned almost all Protestant denominations ... [reflecting] the attitude and values of a new urban middle class."[287]

This was the type of Christianity which dominated the United States when I was young. I introduce this personal perspective because it was not until I was doing research for this book and, in my attempt to fill in some missing information, encountered James Farrell's book. Farrell writes about the shift in Christianity from Enlightenment to Liberal as he discusses how it was reflected in changed attitudes toward death and dying and some shifts in the actual practices.

Later, into the 20th century, Christianity underwent another change with the rise of fundamentalism. In the early 20th century the Pentecostalist movement gained in popularity. The predominant Christian paradigms of my childhood represent a very different Christianity than what we have today. A thoughtful look at Christianity over the centuries leads to the obvious: it is a very flexible religion and

Chapter 10 - An Evolution of Death - The Victorian and Modern Eras [1840 - 2000 ce]

oftentimes so different from an earlier era that I cannot imagine Jesus being at all comfortable in one of the modern mega-churches with high-salaried officials and parking lots filled with the cars of those who live well and who believe the poor deserve poverty.

But let me act a little more 'enlightened.'

"Enlightened people did not dwell on death as had their Puritan ancestors. ... they emphasized the idea of death as a natural occurrence, an essential part of the economy of nature."[288] How had the Puritans dealt with death? Not so happily. "The corpse was a horrible sight that signified both human sin and the flight of the soul."[289] Even worse, the body became food for worms and one was immediately judged by God, as if dying was not already trauma enough.

At the beginning of this era the older, Puritan view was not holding up. There were numerous other perspectives entering the landscape. The United States was struggling over many issues, not just slavery. One example would be Henry Ward Beecher, brother of the abolitionist author Harriet Beecher Stowe and the eighth of thirteen children. His father, Lyman, was a Presbyterian preacher who was considered by many "America's most famous preacher."[290] The Presbyterians were divided over the theological issues surrounding the concept of original sin and also divided over the issue of slavery. Henry Beecher was very successful as a preacher, one of the "most popular speakers in the country" according to the same article.

Taking a far more open view than even his father, Beecher encouraged people to set aside the old customs of mourning, encouraging people to set aside black clothing and become joyous. Beecher "viewed death primarily as a portal to heaven, because that view softened the evangelical emphasis on divine judgement. ... Before going to sleep at night, they should picture heaven in their minds, looming near and beckoning. 'That we are so near death,' he said, 'is too good to be believed.'"[291]

Beecher was also a strong abolitionist, and known well enough that President Lincoln, in 1863, called upon Beecher to tour Europe and speak on behalf of the cause against slavery and to rally support for the Union. Following the war, Beecher used his political capital to

Chapter 10 - An Evolution of Death - The Victorian and Modern Eras [1840 - 2000 ce]

advocate treating the south with compassion, lobbying for restoration. He spoke out in favor of railroad workers, he worked hard to support the Chinese who had been emigrating, and he became a prominent figure for the right of women to vote.

Christianity struggled with the emerging understanding of the sciences. Beecher clearly saw the future and embraced it.

> "Liberal Christians responded to the currents of scientific naturalism and the higher Biblical criticism that threatened to make religious orthodoxy intellectually insignificant. They drew on transcendental idealism and pietist immediatism to create an optimistic interpretation of religious experience. They tried to define the place of evolution in God's plan, and the place of death in evolution. In the process, they revised earlier religious interpretations of the afterlife by showing that both death and evolution led naturally to an exalted immortality."[292]

There were other views as well. A popular view was that of "Millennialism, a religious sensibility popularized before the Civil War [which] fused beliefs about the imminent destruction of the world, a new age of social harmony, and the return of Jesus Christ." The apocalyptic view was "centered primarily on the prophesies of William Miller."[293]

Truly, the variations of Christianity were all over the theological map. But when the issue of cremation would be raised as viable, that was very difficult to reconcile with most of those variations of that faith. "Early opponents of cremation claimed that 'neither the present generation nor the next will be prepared to go back to this old barbaric system, because it is against our religious feeling, and as Christ was laid in his grave, the Church will not change this sacred ceremony,"[294] although no one seemed to comment on Jesus having walked away from Earth burial! Even stronger "was a traditional belief in the resurrection of the body."[295]

Add to this the view of many Protestant churches that the more traditional views of death were holdovers from that old adversary which was firmly stuck in the Middle Ages - the Catholic Church.

With such a lack of consistency and unity among the primary religion of the people, what did remain constant were the services being offered with the support of the NFDA.

"With modifications in all the accouterments of the funeral, changes in the funeral service itself were virtually inevitable. In fashioning the modern funeral, funeral directors redefined the roles of all major participants - ministers, families, and funeral directors themselves. In directing the dying of death, funeral directors tried to create a funeral service that minimized the suffering of survivors. In the process, they also minimized the importance or death and grief.

"Between 1880 and 1920 American funeral services became shorter, as the solemn music and sermon of the old rite succumbed to the power of positive thinking."[296]

- **The Cemetery: Gardens of the Dead**

"The ideas of religious liberalism played an important part in the dying of death, especially as they affected the established forms of religious funeral practice. ... One of these institutions was the cemetery."[297]

From early on in life I found great comfort and solace exploring cemeteries. In addition to the cemetery of my parents' area in central Wisconsin, one of my favorites was Oakwood Cemetery in Rochester, Minnesota. Oakwood is a beautiful example. It dates to the Rochester Cemetery Association's founding in 1863 to have "a non-sectarian, nonprofit cemetery."[298] Located on higher terrain along the east side of the Zumbro River (which can flood with enthusiasm in the spring) it reflects the desire to provide a setting which is much like a garden in that it is well-kept, beautiful, with meandering drives and an abundance of nature.

"Between 1830 and 1855, the 'rural' or 'garden' cemetery predominated. During this period, the development of the cemetery

Chapter 10 - An Evolution of Death - The Victorian and Modern Eras [1840 - 2000 ce]

proceeded in tandem with the development of the profession of landscape architecture and the public parks movement."[299] I do not know whether the Olmsted brothers, who were very influential in the Rochester area as visiting landscape architects had any direct involvement in Oakwood, but their touch remained very strong in Rochester when I lived there in the early 1970s.

During the same (relative) period of time the public was increasingly reacting to the squalor of London and its pollution, described quite well by Charles Dickens. We humans had moved into the cities in increasing numbers but still lived as if we were our agrarian ancestors. We created trash, and we dumped it nearby. If it could be burnt for heat, so much the better. There were outhouses for toilets or worse, a chamber pot which could be emptied conveniently out of doors.

In London, cholera was rampant.

"During the early 19th century the River Thames was an open sewer, with disastrous consequences for public health in London, including cholera epidemics. These were caused by enterotoxin-producing strains of the bacterium *Vibrio cholerae*. Proposals to modernise the sewerage system had been made during 1856, but were neglected due to lack of funds. However, after the Great Stink of 1858, Parliament realised the urgency of the problem and resolved to create a modern sewerage system."[300]

The Dickensian conditions of London were exacerbated by the amounts of coal burned with the dark skies and dirty city legendary in fiction and fact. In the U.S. there were other issues. The cities were not nearly so large, so the squalor was not nearly so dramatic. "In the context of the growing urban centers in the North ... the placement of the dead ... related to a completely different set of dilemmas facing the young republic. [The Churches were changing and] even though the upkeep and management of these spaces fell into the hands of responsible municipal bodies and individual families, they seemed to be more of a public nuisance and distraction."[301]

Shifting social and religious paradigms in the U.S. were such that the idea of the rural cemetery grew in appeal. One stunning example in the U.S. is Mount Auburn, a stunning cemetery which I've seen only as photos. It was established in 1831, promoted as the first 'garden' or 'rural' cemetery in the country. At the time, even the use of the word *cemetery* was undergoing change, entering popular vocabulary. The word, derived from Greek, *koimētērion* meaning (loosely) a place where the dead may sleep. Mount Auburn was seen as a reaction against that harsh view of death. According to Wikipedia, Mount Auburn is credited "as the beginning of the American public parks and gardens movement. It set the style for other suburban American cemeteries ... [and] can be considered the link between Capability Brown's English landscape gardens and Frederick Law Olmsted's Central Park in New York (1850s)."[302]

"The picturesque landscaping of death in the nineteenth century was a reaction to the horrors of the appalling state of urban graveyards... The new cemeteries were to be as unlike the old graveyards as possible: landscaped, picturesque, and secure. Perimeter walls, solid gates and lodge-keeper's houses were crucial design elements in these enterprises..."[303]

"Two varieties of naturalism interacted in the nineteenth century to affect the treatment of death. The first, Romantic naturalism, influenced the development of rural, garden cemeteries. It opened the door for English landscape architecture to propose 'picturesque' styles that would differentiate male and female spheres of influence, the city and the suburb, the living and the dead. Romantic naturalism also highlighted the idea of death as decay, using death as a 'horrible' means to achieve the sublime. After the sublime passed from the center of aesthetic thought, disgust with decay shaped efforts to preserve human bodies."[304]

Those who set the concept in motion that the cemetery should be idyllic might have been pleased to see us riding our bicycles with our picnic food enjoying the beauty of the place.

Chapter 10 - An Evolution of Death - The Victorian and Modern Eras [1840 - 2000 ce]

It was into this approach to burial that I was born. Cemeteries were filled with markers and monuments. I particularly loved those large Victorian reminders of an era in which those with enough money would memorialize their importance or their loved one with marble or granite or stone. "Another common characteristic of Victorian grief, whether Christian or agnostic, was the establishment of a permanent memorial of some sort."[305] While I was never taken with Victorian styles in furniture or in clothing, there was something about the memorials they created for their loved ones that I found deeply moving.

But life moves on and tastes change. I still gravitate in taste to the older cemeteries. Yes, much of what was done was in order to impress and to claim one's place in social memory - often by how much money was spent. For me the monuments are mysteries, in that each has a story but only a few words are there to be read. It was not simply Victorian ostentatiousness for there is also innate desire to impress one's neighbors. Even that may be part of the natural setting. There are many species who try to build a better nest than their neighbor. How beautiful they must have been when new.

The maintenance of those large monuments and of family mausoleums increasingly fell upon hard times. Those families which did not suffer thinning ranks or die out began living further and further apart. The rampant growth of the human population once again put pressure on that valuable real estate. The cemeteries which were once outside the urban regions are now surrounded by the suburbs. In Britain, there are similar problems:

> "The great urban cemetery of the nineteenth century was designed for posterity. Just as its monuments, by and large, expressed optimism about the future life of the individual soul, so the cemetery itself was conceived and planned with a culturally and socially optimistic perspective upon the future. Trees would take years to grow; existing planting would need to be cultivated and further planting laid out; buildings and monuments would require long-term maintenance. Had the hopes of men like John Strang and J. C. Loudon been fulfilled and sustained, Victorian cemeteries by now would be great

Chapter 10 - An Evolution of Death - The Victorian and Modern Eras [1840 - 2000 ce]

planned landscapes, their monuments expressions of both piety and art, their planting fully mature. Instead, they have been damaged and depleted, frequently neglected or treated with indifference sometimes destroyed."[306]

The cemetery style which I enjoy the least is one which I thought of as relatively new, but to my surprise they are not. In this style the design is to favor those who do the maintenance, rather than the families and the manner in which they seek status or appearance to others. This style of cemetery is flat - like a lawn - with markers which are flat to the ground and so low that a riding mower can go right over the top. It is the convenience for the mower which left me thinking of them as new, but the style is attributed to one Adolf Strauch when he brought the first one into being in Cincinnati, Ohio. How long ago? 1855 when this Prussian-born landscape architect was only 33 years old.

Increasingly we see cemeteries creatively being able to serve more and more people by providing places for cremated remains ('cremains' in today's parlance). The columbarium wall allows for the cremains to be placed with a weatherproof plaque.

The most contemporary type of cemetery is, in a manner of speaking, the oldest, allowing for natural burial for those who simply wish to decompose.

Are the cemeteries with their intriguing monuments and wonderfully informative stone markers like so many statues, a thing of the past? Addressing the decline of the great, elaborate Victorian cemeteries in the U.K., Chris Brooks writes:

> "The origins of this decline are to be found in the fundamental processes of social, economic and cultural change that have shaped Britain in the twentieth century. Although the great Victorian cemeteries were interdenominational, they have been crucially affected by the post-Victorian shift in the significance of institutional religion. As early as the 1840s ... as urbanization and industrialization grew, Thomas Arnold saw the emergence of a large working-

class population neither High Church nor Low Church but No Church. ... The progressive secularization of education, social welfare, morality itself, has pushed organized religion far more on to the periphery of national life ... than it was a year ago. This process and its attendant shifts of priority within the churches themselves, has meant inevitably that cemeteries and the formalized commemoration of the dead no longer have the central imaginative and spiritual importance for us that they had for the Victorian."[307]

- **Changing Social Values**

I find the processes through which the views of burial and cemeteries were changed during this time to be much more of an evolution process than a revolution. The shifting tides of Christianity? From an objective, larger perspective time I hold the same view.

During the Industrial Revolution, the harnessing and domestication of electricity turned the world upside down. Manufacturing and social activity became a now 24 hours a day activity.

The printed word, once available by mass production only with water and steam is now produced on presses run with electricity. The electrical revolution means people can read the news in their homes, easily, after the sun has set, following a day's work. This development is quickly followed by the telephone and radio which deliver the news in an instant, which can communicate events live.

The arterial life of the nation was limited to the major rivers and to the railroads. With the technology for the automobile arriving and then mass production making it affordable for so many, and with travel by air beginning to fill the skies, the nature of the world changed. So, too, would the nature of war.

Our Western world which, for this book, is largely based upon countries which share the common language of English, was on the rebound. The British are reeling from the Napoleonic Wars, the wounds still fresh in their memory when this chapter begins.

"The wars resulted in the dissolution of the Holy Roman Empire and sowed the seeds of nascent nationalism in Germany and Italy that would lead to the two nations' respective consolidations later in the century. Meanwhile, the global Spanish Empire began to unravel as French occupation of Spain weakened Spain's hold over its colonies, providing an opening for nationalist revolutions in Spanish America. As a direct result of the Napoleonic wars, the British Empire became the foremost world power for the next century, thus beginning Pax Britannica."[308]

In the United States, the nation struggled with serious divisive issues, of which slavery was the strongest. Those differences tore the country in two and led to a massive death toll and a political resentment which can still be found today.

The British Empire may have been the last political empire to rule so much of the world. Britain ruled the seas, and when Russia was too aggressive, Britain and her former foe, France, joined forces and defeated Russia in the Crimean War which ended just five years before the U.S. Civil War broke out. All of this, from Britain's reach and access to global resources and wealth to the technologies put in motion for the Civil War in the U.S. all led to a tremendous surge in creativity and inventiveness. I first began listing the impressive list of patents all registered within a short period of time. They changed life for the coming century. And yet, with all of that wonderful potential?

War. War on a scale no one could have imagined, powered by the new technologies. That war was followed by the wild abandon of the Roaring Twenties. Next came the economic and, for many emotional, devastation of the Great Depression and then - whatever happened to the memories from that war which should have convinced people to never go to war again? The Second World War and this time leading to horrors that not even WWI could have brought to mind, from the Holocaust to Hiroshima.

In addition there were shifting economic values. During the nineteenth century:

Chapter 10 - An Evolution of Death - The Victorian and Modern Eras [1840 - 2000 ce]

"changes in domestic relations and urban housing flowed from capitalist control of workers. By wrenching work from its traditional household setting, capitalists conditioned a division between work and life that culminated in the privatization of the family. By paying low wages, they forced workers from individual homes into tenements. Both of these developments caused changes in domestic architecture that influenced funeral customs. The privatization of the family pushed the public funeral out of the home, even as tenements made such funerals impossible or inappropriate. Funeral directors capitalized on these developments by providing 'parlors' in their 'homes' for the funeral."[309]

Just as war was breaking out in Europe in 1914, Henry Ford, the industrialist known as the founder of Ford Motor Company, "announced in 1914 that he would pay his workers the then unheard-of wage of $5 a day." Ford later wrote that "it was smart business. When wages are low ... business and the economy are at risk. But when pay is high and steady ... business is more secure because workers earn enough to be good customers and eventually to be able to afford to buy Model Ts."[310]

Beginning with the Victorian Era, the United States was recovering from war and Britain went on a massive expansion of her domain. English (with its variations) is a dominant language today globally. World Wars I and II reshaped the political world as well. Neither of those wars was fought in the U.S. which emerged with the dominant economy and with prosperity, in part from the likes of Henry Ford who believed in financially secure employees. The "economic boom in the three decades after World War II delivered solid middle-class prosperity to a large majority of Americans. ... Three-fourths of America's 44 million families owned their own homes, and collectively they owned 56 million cars, 50 million television sets, and 143 million radios."[311]

In an ironic turn of fate, the period of history in this chapter sees the rise of the middle class in the United States to such a level of equity that future Supreme Court Justice Lewis Powell sent out a private memorandum in 1971 which turned the tide on the middle class and the

American Dream. As Smith stunningly documents in his *Who Stole the American Dream?*, "Lewis Powell's corporate manifesto hit a responsive chord."[312] Within a short number of years, corporate America began waging a massive siege to take control of the political infrastructure from the growing clout of the working class and return the business world to the heads of corporations. With an unprecedented level of support from lobbying by the Chamber of Commerce to the development of corporate think tanks, funding that could better support schools and health care for the working families was used to promote corporate interests over those of their workers. The balance of power was changed.

Entering the 21st century, home ownership has fallen and today the wage gap between corporate executives and the working class is described as the most extreme since the age of the robber barons of industry, bemoaned by James Farrell four paragraphs earlier.

The period of time I encompass with this chapter is characterized by revolutionary changes in technology which industrialized and electrified the world, wars which literally destroyed the older ways of doing things and which led to a faster industrialization than could otherwise have been imagined, and a period of prosperity for the average person in the dominant economy which shaped dreams for people everywhere.

The public became more middle class and people wanted to spend more to better reflect their growing middle class aspirations.

A "concern for the appearances of success carried over from a general concern for appearances and for the goods and services that symbolized the good life of the deceased. Coffins, for example, were superseded by decorative caskets. But the most literal example of saving face came in arterial embalming, which preserved the 'natural' appearance of the corpse. In all of these ways, people paid (literally) their last respects to the dead, and spared their own sensibility at the same time."[313]

Chapter 10 - An Evolution of Death - The Victorian and Modern Eras [1840 - 2000 ce]

We are a reactive species. Victorian styles of clothing, Victorian styles of graveside monuments, Victorian styles of architecture... All of them perhaps in design turning to elaborate construction, perhaps to conceal passion. The Victorian mindset may have sought to be *proper* but that should not automatically imply prudery. The British Empire was highly expansive and, as a result, had considerable wealth. Even the name, the *Commonwealth* is telling. Foreshadowing today's popular phrase for Las Vegas, what happened in India, stayed in India, what happened in Hong Kong, in the Cape, in British Guiana, and in the other areas? When you have enough money and power, you typically have your way with the locals.

The ending of the British Empire and the toll from two World Wars left even the elaborate Victorian cemeteries in peril.

"The Victorian era has been described as the 'golden age of grief.' During the mid decades of the nineteenth century funerary and mourning rituals reached heights of extravagance matched in few other societies or eras. As this orgy of materialistic and sentimental indulgence reached its apogee in the 1870's, a reforming movement emerged which challenged accepted practices and attitudes, confronting as it did so some of the central economic, aesthetic, and sentimental preoccupations of Victorian society. The advocates of cremation sought, unlike earlier burial and funeral reformers, not merely to improve sanitary practices, or to simplify funerary rituals, but rather, by manipulating the physical remains of the dead, to alter fundamentally attitudes towards death itself."[314]

Attitudes toward death and dying changed here in North America as well. It did not take long and the middle-class American was apt to set aside some of the older customs. Families had more money but less time and became dependent upon the services of others.

"If the minister in the new-fashioned funeral service generally played the role of consoling angel, the family and friends of the deceased played the passive part of comforted spectators. *The Embalmer's Monthly* declared that the undertaker 'should relieve the bereaved family of all responsibility ... of a burden they should, under no circumstances, carry in addition to the one already upon them.'"315

In today's world numerous laws have been passed, often on behalf of the funeral industry which has additional revenue streams but typically under the guise of protecting the public. Today, as I understand it from family experience, it is quite likely illegal to move a body from one state to another, unless it has been first embalmed.

"Between 1859 and 1920, Americans experimented with two novel treatments of the body in funeral service - embalming and cremation. By 1920, embalming had become a standard practice of Northern funerals, while cremation was still an infrequent option."316

Why did embalming become the preferred option for the body?

"The NFDA played a major role in this development by promoting rationales for arterial embalming. Sometimes funeral directors appealed to the religious belief of a liberal age, saying that as the casket of the soul or the temple of the Holy Spirit, the body deserved sacred respect. Sometimes they appealed to love, arguing that 'it is the natural attribute of affection to seek to avoid, in some degree, a painful separation, by preserving the remains of those they love and by whom they were beloved.' Sometimes they appealed to the progress of civilization. ... And finally, after 1883, funeral directors also embalmed bodies to preserve the living by disinfecting the dead."317

- **Monuments and Markers**
  In Tibet
  "At the termination of the funeral rites the *spyang-pu* or face-paper is ceremoniously burned in the flame of a butter-lamp, and the spirit of the deceased given a

final farewell...

"The ashes of the cremated *spyang-pu* are collected in a plate, and then, upon being mixed with clay, are made into miniature stupas... usually in molds leaving impressions either of symbolical ornamentation or of sacred letters. One is kept for the family altar in the room of the deceased, and the rest are deposited in a sheltered place at a cross-roads or on a hill-top, usually under a projecting ledge of rock, or in a cave if there happens to be a cave. ...

"Connected with the Tibetan funeral itself there is much interesting ritual..."[318]

"In Tibet itself all known religious methods of disposing of a corpse are in vogue; but, owing to lack of fuel for purposes of cremation, ordinarily the corpse, after having been carried to a hill-top or rocky eminence, is chopped to pieces and, much after the Parsee custom in Persia and Bombay, given to the birds and beasts of prey. If the corpse be that of a nobleman, whose family can well afford a funeral pyre, it may be cremated. In some remote districts earth burial is customary; and it is commonly employed everywhere when death has been caused by a very contagious and dangerous disease, like small-pox... Otherwise, Tibetans generally object to earth-burial, for they believe that when a corpse is interred the spirit of the deceased, upon seeing it, attempts to re-enter it..."[319]

Under lock and key

One of the unsavory and heart-wrenching desecrations of burial sites was directly stimulated by the growing advances in science and medicine. Just as medicine and surgery were more advanced than in the United States which was but an emerging economy, the need for human flesh and bones, for human organs for students of anatomy was a major concern in Europe. "The fear of bodysnatching was extremely pervasive... During the entire period from about 1700 and reaching a peak in the early nineteenth century - in parallel with the growth of private anatomy tuition - bodysnatching was both widespread and lucrative. The only legal source of corpses for dissection during the entire period was the gallows... Most of the corpses the resurrectionists supplied to anatomists were stolen from graves..."[320]

Just as the population was growing, the strengthening economy as well as the global domination by a few European countries led to medical schools with growing student numbers as well. All aspects of industry were growing with the new technologies and new sources of energy. To graduate doctors with a high calibre knowledge of anatomy and of surgery, dead bodies were needed.

The raiding of graveyards in Europe and also in the U.S. led to new patents and inventions for burial as well.

"Patents were taken out for special iron coffins with secure locks...."[321] Another advance was to fashion sturdy steel cages which could be locked. Called a *mortsafe* ('protect the dead') it looked like the dead were being not just buried but imprisoned... Not to keep the dead in but to keep the body robbers out.

It was a problem on this side of the ocean as well. None of my research indicates that it is in direct response as were the iron mortsafes, but it was near the same period of time when the Almond D. Fisk patented the cast iron coffin.[322] Not only did this provide greater security in keeping the dead where they had been placed, but they were said to be air tight which would also preserve the body.

Who stole the body?

"The respectable funeral before 1832 [The Anatomy Act became law in 1832, rendering bodysnatchers redundant] had served to signify that the body of the deceased was as safe as money could make it."[323]

"... that bodysnatching was an important factor in the growth and appeal of the respectable funeral: society-wide fear of grave-robbery stimulated both a rapid early growth of the undertaking business and the promotion of the great nineteenth-century cemeteries; *second*, that as the threat posed by grave-robbery receded, attention and expenditure focussed increasingly on funerary display; *third*, that legislative change was calculated to make death in poverty disgraceful, so that people lived in fear of a pauper's burial. ... The Victorian poor were prodded into expenditure on death insurance and funerals by the intensely painful knowledge that the misfortune of death in poverty could qualify them for at best a bed of quicklime, and at worst dismemberment. The Anatomy Act promoted 'prudence', and hence, the Victorian undertaker."[324]

"During the same period in which the bodysnatcher flourished, so also did the undertaker. The desire for security in the grave went hand in hand with the growth in the commercial provision of funerary services. During the course of the eighteenth and early nineteenth centuries, the same period in which bodysnatching became a separate profession, undertakers had begun to set up shop in urban areas and to purvey their services in the creation of funerals to suit the pockets and aspirations of the growing middle class."[325]

"From serving to signal the achievement of respectable *and* safe burial, the respectable funeral became an end in itself."[326]

Cremation has renewed appeal

"The early appeal of the funeral industry was fuelled by the endeavour to preserve the body's identity and integrity..."[327]

"The failure of improved burial practices to alleviate the disgust with decay shaped new responses to the troublesome confrontation with death. One response was that of embalming, a practice which, by the end of the [nineteenth] century, had gained almost universal acceptance in North America. The aim of embalming was to preserve the human corpse. The aim of the other response - cremation - was to destroy the corpse. Despite their different methods, both processes advocated human activity ... to dispel the aura of horror surrounding death."[328]

"Centuries of religious practice and local custom condemned cremation as a method of disposing of the human corpse when, in the 1770's, its reintroduction was first suggested by Italian scientists. Motivated primarily by scientific curiosity, these men produced, in the century following 1774, a huge body of literature dealing with the economic, sanitary, and religious aspects of the question. They were also responsible for the development of the first modern incinerary apparatus using irradiated heat rather than the naked flame."[329]

"Little serious consideration was given to the practical reintroduction of cremation... until the early nineteenth century, when the problem of burial in the crowded European capitals became so acute... the result of inadequate burial space... Graves ... were frequently reopened and further coffins added, often with up to twenty lying in a single grave. Graveyards were also trenched every few years, and the contents of graves consigned to bone houses and burning grounds. Under cover of darkness, bodies were regularly exhumed and burnt, and their coffins broken up and used for firewood... Drinking water was polluted by cemetery run-off, the soil was saturated with decaying organic matter, and the air, according to contemporary theories of disease causation, was filled with dangerous miasmas."[330]

"Cremation was, according to one writer, 'not only the healthiest and the cleanest, but the most poetical way of disposing of the dead.'[331] A deep vein or rural nostalgia runs through cremationist language recalling in many ways the enthusiasms of the rural cemetery movement earlier in the century.[332] The cremationist's Garden of Remembrance 'is beautiful and is bereft of those dismal depressing emblems of death and decay. It is a place suggestive of continued life and happiness, a spot where the ashes of those who have passed over repose unfettered, kissed by the sun, among the birds, the flowers and the trees. It provides a retreat where the living, in peace and quietness may pause to think, an abiding cenotaph, renewed by nature's hand.'[333]"[334]

"From serving to signal the achievement of respectable *and* safe burial, the respectable funeral became an end in itself."[335]

⁂

"An event that at one time would have been explained as 'an act of God' now precipitates lawsuits to determine who should be held financially responsible for its occurrence."[336]

Notes for Chapter Ten

[260] These dates were all found in various Wikipedia sites, November 23, 2012 ce

[261] http://en.wikipedia.org/wiki/Queen_Victoria 12 xi 2012 ce

[262] http://en.wikipedia.org/wiki/Industrial_Revolution 3 xi 2014 ce

[263] http://en.wikipedia.org/wiki/American_Civil_War 9 xi 2014 ce

[264] http://en.wikipedia.org/wiki/Demographics_of_the_United_States 9 xi 2014 ce

Chapter 10 - An Evolution of Death - The Victorian and Modern Eras [1840 - 2000 ce]

[265] Farrell, James J., *Inventing the American Way of Death, 1830-1920*, Temple University Press © 1989, page 148

[266] Laderman, Gary, *The Sacred Remains: American Attitudes Toward Death, 1799-1883*, Yale University Press © 1996, page 26

[267] Farrell, James J., *Inventing the American Way of Death, 1830-1920*, Temple University Press © 1989, page 147

[268] Farrell, James J., *Inventing the American Way of Death, 1830-1920*, Temple University Press © 1989, page 147

[269] Farrell, James J., *Inventing the American Way of Death, 1830-1920*, Temple University Press © 1989, page 148

[270] Farrell, James J., *Inventing the American Way of Death, 1830-1920*, Temple University Press © 1989, pages 148-149

[271] Farrell, James J., *Inventing the American Way of Death, 1830-1920*, Temple University Press © 1989, pages 171-172

[272] Huntington & Metcalf, *Celebrations of Death*, Cambridge University Press © 1979, page 190

[273] Huntington & Metcalf, *Celebrations of Death*, Cambridge University Press © 1979, page 190

[274] Huntington & Metcalf, *Celebrations of Death*, Cambridge University Press © 1979, page 190

[275] Huntington & Metcalf, *Celebrations of Death*, Cambridge University Press © 1979, page 191`

[276] Farrell, James J., *Inventing the American Way of Death, 1830-1920*, Temple University Press © 1989, pages 152-153

[277] Huntington & Metcalf, *Celebrations of Death*, Cambridge University Press © 1979, page 191

[278] Huntington & Metcalf, *Celebrations of Death*, Cambridge University Press © 1979, page 193

[279] Farrell, James J., *Inventing the American Way of Death, 1830-1920*, Temple University Press © 1989, page 156

[280] Farrell, James J., *Inventing the American Way of Death, 1830-1920*, Temple University Press © 1989, page 146

Chapter 10 - An Evolution of Death - The Victorian and Modern Eras [1840 - 2000 ce]

[281] Farrell, James J., *Inventing the American Way of Death, 1830-1920*, Temple University Press © 1989, page 146

[282] Farrell, James J., *Inventing the American Way of Death, 1830-1920*, Temple University Press © 1989, pages 154-155

[283] Farrell, James J., *Inventing the American Way of Death, 1830-1920*, Temple University Press © 1989, page 176

[284] Farrell, James J., *Inventing the American Way of Death, 1830-1920*, Temple University Press © 1989, pages 79-80

[285] Farrell, James J., *Inventing the American Way of Death, 1830-1920*, Temple University Press © 1989, pages 172-173

[286] Farrell, James J., *Inventing the American Way of Death, 1830-1920*, Temple University Press © 1989, page 23

[287] Farrell, James J., *Inventing the American Way of Death, 1830-1920*, Temple University Press © 1989, page 75

[288] Farrell, James J., *Inventing the American Way of Death, 1830-1920*, Temple University Press © 1989, pages 24-25

[289] Laderman, Gary, *The Sacred Remains: American Attitudes Toward Death, 1799-1883*, Yale University Press © 1996, page 52

[290] http://en.wikipedia.org/wiki/Henry_Ward_Beecher 19 November 2014 ce

[291] Farrell, James J., *Inventing the American Way of Death, 1830-1920*, Temple University Press © 1989, pages 79-80

[292] Farrell, James J., *Inventing the American Way of Death, 1830-1920*, Temple University Press © 1989, page 75

[293] Laderman, Gary, *The Sacred Remains: American Attitudes Toward Death, 1799-1883*, Yale University Press © 1996, page 52

[294] Farrell, James J., *Inventing the American Way of Death, 1830-1920*, Temple University Press © 1989, page 166

[295] Farrell, James J., *Inventing the American Way of Death, 1830-1920*, Temple University Press © 1989, page 166

[296] Farrell, James J., *Inventing the American Way of Death, 1830-1920*, Temple University Press © 1989, page 170

[297] Farrell, James J., *Inventing the American Way of Death, 1830-1920*, Temple University Press © 1989, page 99

Chapter 10 - An Evolution of Death - The Victorian and Modern Eras [1840 - 2000 ce]

[298] http://www.oakwoodcemeteries.com/ 19 November 2014 ce

[299] Farrell, James J., *Inventing the American Way of Death, 1830-1920*, Temple University Press © 1989, page 99

[300] http://en.wikipedia.org/wiki/London_sewerage_system 19 November 2014 ce.

[301] Laderman, Gary, *The Sacred Remains: American Attitudes Toward Death, 1799-1883*, Yale University Press © 1996, pages 68-69

[302] http://en.wikipedia.org/wiki/Mount_Auburn_Cemetery

[303] "Why Was Death So Big In Victorian Britain" by Ruth Richardson in *Death, Ritual, and Bereavement*, Routledge in association with the Social History Society of the United Kingdom, London, New York © 1989, page 113

[304] Farrell, James J., *Inventing the American Way of Death, 1830-1920*, Temple University Press © 1989, pages 7-8

[305] "Victorian Unbelief and Bereavement" by Martha McMackin Garland in *Death, Ritual, and Bereavement*, Routledge in association with the Social History Society of the United Kingdom, London, New York © 1989, page 153

[306] Brooks, Chris *Mortal Remains: The History and Present State of the Victorian and Edwardian Cemetery*, Wheaton (published in association with The Victorian Society, Exeter U.K. © 1989, page 77

[307] Brooks, Chris *Mortal Remains: The History and Present State of the Victorian and Edwardian Cemetery*, Wheaton (published in association with The Victorian Society, Exeter U.K. © 1989, page 77

[308] http://en.wikipedia.org/wiki/Napoleonic_Wars 19 November 2014 ce

[309] Farrell, James J., *Inventing the American Way of Death, 1830-1920*, Temple University Press © 1989, page 10

[310] Smith, Hedrick, *Who Stole the American Dream?*, Random House, © 2012, page 36

[311] Smith, Hedrick, *Who Stole the American Dream?*, Random House, © 2012, page 40

[312] Smith, Hedrick, *Who Stole the American Dream?*, Random House, © 2012, page 11

[313] Farrell, James J., *Inventing the American Way of Death, 1830-1920*, Temple University Press © 1989, page 10

Chapter 10 - An Evolution of Death - The Victorian and Modern Eras [1840 - 2000 ce]

---

[314] "Ashes to Ashes: Cremation and the Celebration of Death in Nineteenth-Century Britain" by Jennifer Leany in *Death, Ritual, and Bereavement*, Routledge in association with the Social History Society of the United Kingdom, London, New York © 1989, page 118

[315] Farrell, James J., *Inventing the American Way of Death, 1830-1920*, Temple University Press © 1989, page 179

[316] Farrell, James J., *Inventing the American Way of Death, 1830-1920*, Temple University Press © 1989, page 157

[317] Farrell, James J., *Inventing the American Way of Death, 1830-1920*, Temple University Press © 1989, page 159

[318] "Introduction: The Death Ceremonies," *The Tibetan Book of the Dead*, compiled and edited by W.Y. Evans-Wentz Oxford University Press © 1960; preface to the paperback edition, W.Y. Evans-Wentz, page 24

[319] "Introduction: The Death Ceremonies," *The Tibetan Book of the Dead*, compiled and edited by W.Y. Evans-Wentz Oxford University Press © 1960; preface to the paperback edition, W.Y. Evans-Wentz, pages 25-26

[320] "Why Was Death So Big In Victorian Britain" by Ruth Richardson in *Death, Ritual, and Bereavement*, Routledge in association with the Social History Society of the United Kingdom, London, New York © 1989, pages 107-9

[321] "Why Was Death So Big In Victorian Britain" by Ruth Richardson in *Death, Ritual, and Bereavement*, Routledge in association with the Social History Society of the United Kingdom, London, New York © 1989, page 110

[322] "The Fisk metallic burial case was designed and patented by Almond D. Fisk under US Patent No. 5920 on November 14, 1848." - http://en.wikipedia.org/wiki/Fisk_metallic_burial_case 13 xi 2014 ce

[323] "Why Was Death So Big In Victorian Britain" by Ruth Richardson in *Death, Ritual, and Bereavement*, Routledge in association with the Social History Society of the United Kingdom, London, New York © 1989, page 114

[324] "Why Was Death So Big In Victorian Britain" by Ruth Richardson in *Death, Ritual, and Bereavement*, Routledge in association with the Social History Society of the United Kingdom, London, New York © 1989, page 117

[325] "Why Was Death So Big In Victorian Britain" by Ruth Richardson in *Death, Ritual, and Bereavement*, Routledge in association with the Social History Society of the United Kingdom, London, New York © 1989, pages 110-111

Chapter 10 - An Evolution of Death - The Victorian and Modern Eras [1840 - 2000 ce]

[326] "Why Was Death So Big In Victorian Britain" by Ruth Richardson in *Death, Ritual, and Bereavement*, Routledge in association with the Social History Society of the United Kingdom, London, New York © 1989, page 115

[327] "Why Was Death So Big In Victorian Britain" by Ruth Richardson in *Death, Ritual, and Bereavement*, Routledge in association with the Social History Society of the United Kingdom, London, New York © 1989, page 111

[328] "Ashes to Ashes: Cremation and the Celebration of Death in Nineteenth-Century Britain" by Jennifer Leany in *Death, Ritual, and Bereavement*, Routledge in association with the Social History Society of the United Kingdom, London, New York © 1989, page 134

[329] "Ashes to Ashes: Cremation and the Celebration of Death in Nineteenth-Century Britain" by Jennifer Leany in *Death, Ritual, and Bereavement*, Routledge in association with the Social History Society of the United Kingdom, London, New York © 1989, pages 118-119

[330] "Ashes to Ashes: Cremation and the Celebration of Death in Nineteenth-Century Britain" by Jennifer Leany in *Death, Ritual, and Bereavement*, Routledge in association with the Social History Society of the United Kingdom, London, New York © 1989, page 119

[331] Quoted from the Cremation Society of England's *Cremation in Great Britain*, London, 1909

[332] Quoted from the Government Board of Health, *Report on a General Scheme for Extramural Sepulture*, London, 1850

[333] Quoted from Sir W. Arbuthnot Lane, 'Cremation from the public health view,' *Transactions of the Cremation Society*, XLIII, 1932

[334] "Ashes to Ashes: Cremation and the Celebration of Death in Nineteenth-Century Britain" by Jennifer Leany in *Death, Ritual, and Bereavement*, Routledge in association with the Social History Society of the United Kingdom, London, New York © 1989, page 122

[335] "Why Was Death So Big In Victorian Britain" by Ruth Richardson in *Death, Ritual, and Bereavement*, Routledge in association with the Social History Society of the United Kingdom, London, New York © 1989, page 115

[336] "Prologue: Principles of Thanatology" by Arthur C. Carr, *Principles of Thanatology*, ed. Kutscher, Carr and Kutscher, Columbia University Press © 1987, page 24

Chapter 11 - Heaven and Hell

Where does the soul go?

The Soul's survival

I wrote about the soul in Chapter IV - *What is the Soul?* I believe it a fair claim that a hands-down majority of humans throughout our recorded history believe that there is something of the individual which survives the death of the body. MacDonald writes that "belief in an after-life is inherent in man's nature and is practically as ancient as the early dawn of human consciousness."[337]

Again and again a pre-historic burial is unearthed indicating that the person was buried intentionally whether with specific postures, or tools and food included placed with the deceased in such a manner that the scientists find no other conclusion than these were for the next state of being for the deceased.

But if there is a soul or spirit or essence - the word is not so important as is the concept that there is something of energy or personality or being which is beyond physical (literally, *metaphysical*). And then it follows, if there is a soul which survives the body, *what happens to it*? Where does it go?

Some believe that it goes to a place called heaven - a word and concept far older than the Judeo-Christian paradigm of our western civilization. "The ritual soteriology that advances such a conception of heaven, specifically the notion that the ancestral rites win an eternal heaven, goes back to the oldest forms of ancestor worship."[338]

How old can this be? We find that these beliefs were found with the earliest recorded beliefs in the subcontinent:

> "The conception of an eternal heaven is found in the oldest text available to us, the *Ṛg Veda*; 'Where there is perpetual light, in which world the light is placed, place me in that imperishable, undecaying world, O Pavamāna. Flow for Indra, O Soma.'"[339]

But not just in the subcontinent, for "... the association of the after-life ... was an early belief of the Egyptians from which they never wholly escaped and which prompted them to rear eternal pyramids as homes for their royal dead. Among the ancient Chinese, too, the soul dwelt with the body."[340]

Whether the soul left the body for the light, or whether it would remain with the body, the belief that there was a spiritual essence which survived the body's death was fully established prior to the time when history was recorded. Twice since my Los Angeles years (the second surge of work on this book) we watched documentaries which were well-produced and which sought to show the origin of human civilization, of that species which emerged from evolution. I regret that I did not record the names of either film.

One documentary used the evolution of language, showing how the meanings of key words could be traced to show how civilizations could all be traced backward in history, mapped to the Fertile Crescent. The second, a few years later, used DNA and sought out pockets of families all over the globe. Even before this documentary, for years, *many* years, I had marveled at how similar various peoples looked. Carrying photos of the people the researchers found, those small numbers who had maintained the most original strains of DNA from the earliest human migrations, it didn't matter whether they were showing family photos to an isolated village in the Mongolian highlands or a mountain family in the Andes, or a first peoples tribal family in North America or... Over and over the family members would explain that the photo looked so much like... and name someone from *their* family. I have come to believe that our beliefs about the survival of the soul were already established when we began leaving the Fertile Crescent. Whether humans left because we were explorers, or because of the early techniques of water management which caused the fertility of the soil to fail, or whether we simply were growing in numbers and needed to move on out... Just as most of the oldest religious beliefs include a flood, I believe our beliefs were already established, most likely because our ancestors found they could not believe otherwise.

Only those cultures so brilliant in developing their own organic chemistries that the body, the temple for that soul, could be preserved for the ages. For the rest? That body was not a great place to stay!

"The body can be only a burden to the heaven-born spirit; life in the body is therefore a living death; and death is 'the door of freedom' for the soul."[341]

Crossing over: passage by water

Not only is the belief in a soul older than history, but so, too, do we find various beliefs by which the soul's *future* is connected to the life lived. Addison writes about the manner in which a man's worth is measured by his tribal culture based upon his ability to hunt food, to be brave in the face of danger. Although Addison only addresses that male culture, I must believe that women were also valued for their ability to produce food and to face childbirth, an event from which many of those brave warriors may have fled to the safety of the hunt.

"More varied and interesting than the tests which are based on a man's status or record in life are those that await him after death. These ordeals confront him on his journey to the after-world and often determine where he will go and how he will fare."[342]

"Less eccentric than these ordeals is the simple notion of a river or lake to be crossed, usually by ferry. Everyone knows of the Styx and the ferryman Charon. But the Fiji Islanders, too, have a rude ghostly ferryman who paddles a canoe, and the Ijaw of Southern Nigeria believe in an old woman who ferries the spirits across the river of death, and like the Greeks they bury with the corpse a fee for the passage. The Egyptian ferryman 'Facing-backwards' poled his boat across the river to the 'Fields of Earu...'"[343]

As if to reflect daily reality as they knew it, the dead could not escape their crimes. Death was not to be an escape from our sins, our mistreatment of others, or the hurtful ways of our lives. Even in death we are to be accountable. Let me turn to one of my favorite words:

Chapter 11 - Heaven and Hell: Where does the soul go?

Bardo. I so loved that word from Tibetan Buddhism and their 'Book of the Dead,' that I was compelled to use the word in my second major book, *A Wiccan Bardo*.

"What is the *Bardo*? It is the afterdeath journey of the soul on its way to its home in the higher spheres. Before the soul actually awakens Overthere, the pilgrim faces a mental journey. Call it a judgment if you will. The soul will find its abode - whether on a high plane or a low - depending on how it reacts to the initiation tests of the Bardo judgment journey. And its reaction usually reflects the pattern of the life just ended."[344]

That pattern is described as having to come face to face with all of the negative garbage of one's life to determine whether one has the courage to take major steps forward in spiritual growth or whether our past continues to be the prison for our dreams.

In many cultures it is not the ferryman, but the passage taken from one side to the other.

"By all odds the most familiar ordeal is the famous Bridge Test - a belief so common as to be found (without exhaustive research) among at least forty different tribes and peoples. The main idea is simple: at some point in the journey to the spirit world a river, pool, or chasm must be crossed by a narrow bridge. Those who can pass in safety reach their destination; the others are cast down to a tragic or unknown fate."[345]

"... the possession of courage is nearly equivalent to the possession of tribal rank and that a happy future for the brave is not exactly a reward, we have here, none the less, the crude beginning of a moral test to determine a man's fate."[346]

"Since bravery and prowess in battle are the prime characteristics of the tribal chief or warrior, it is only an extension of the idea of rank when courage is made the test for distinction in the next world. Such was the thought of the Mandans of South Dakota, who assigned to the brave the delightful villages of the gods, and of the Assiniboins who kept their paradise in the south for the brave and left to the cowardly a distant region of eternal ice and snow. In like manner, the Caribs believed that valiant fighters went to happy islands where there was good fruit and dancing and feasting and where their enemies served them as slaves..."[347]

"In the Orphic mysteries, too, a solemn trial awaited the soul at death. The details of that ceremony are familiar to readers of the Dialogues of Plato..."[348]

Having worked on this book off and on for so many years, and having delivered many presentations on death and dying it is interesting that almost inevitably I hear people assume that this judgement at death must be a Judeo-Christian device primarily to maintain control over people with fear. Would you rather be dragged before Yama?

"In Hinduism the terrible judge of the dead is the god Yama. His watchful messengers lay hold upon the soul of the deceased and drag him to the tribunal. ...at [Yama's] right hand the record-keeper Chitra-Gupta, in whose rolls are set down all the man's deeds, both good and evil."[349]

I have not read Plato's Dialogues. I attempted to read Plato years ago but was too young to really appreciate what I was reading. When I was in secondary school I excelled in geometry. There was something about the mathematics of Pythagoras which fascinated me, yet I had no clue at all that he was such an *interesting* scholar and that he established a mystery school near 530 BCE.

Pythagoras was not alone in his religious beliefs. The Eleusinian and Orphic influences shaped religion in ways the average person might never suspect.

"A revolution in attitudes to the afterlife began in the Greek-speaking world about the end of the 6th century BCE, in the teachings of Pythagoras and the Orphics and in the mystery cults, all of which involved ideas of reward and punishment after death. The philosopher Plato incorporated some of these myths about the afterlife into his dialogues and gave them currency in the philosophical world. Henceforth, the immortality of the soul would be regarded as a quintessentially Greek idea, but various mythic conceptions of the afterlife flourished in the Hellenistic age."[350]

It was from the classical pagan religions that Judaism embraced reward and punishment.

"Only in the Hellenistic period did belief in reward and punishment after death become accepted in Judaism. Usually, in Judaism, the afterlife required resurrection, in the sense that death was followed at first by an intermediate state. The earliest forms of resurrection involve a spiritual form of existence ... Often the spirit is raised up to join the stars or the heavenly host. In some cases, however, most notably in the Dead Sea Scrolls, the spirit proceeds directly to the place of reward or punishment."[351]

Passage to Yaru

"Perhaps the most popular of all the Egyptian other worlds, the one which is more frequently mentioned, and which reminds us of Tir-nan-Og, is referred to as the Field of Yaru, where the grain grows taller than any ever seen on the banks of the Nile, and the departed enjoyed plenty and security.

"The code of ethics which qualified for admittance to those happy elysian fields was lofty. The soul had to recite the ritual confession which gives a list of thirty offences of which he claimed to be innocent.

"Yaru was surrounded by water, and the waiting soul had to be helped across. Sometimes he was borne there on the pinions of the hawk, or ibis, or the Sun God took him over in his bark...

"After all is said and done, it was not so much moral purity but ceremonial punctiliousness which secured one a ready passage to Yaru."[352]

Death and the Underworld

As someone who accepts the evolution of our behavior and concepts as having evolved over a very long period of time, I find myself thinking about life in those pre-historic times. For most of human history, daily activities could not begin until the Sun rose in the east, ending the darkness. Daily activities, food gathering and hunting, even wandering any distance from one's residence, whether hut or tent or cave. It was wonderful when the Sun was up. You could *see* where you were heading and not worry about falling off the edge of a cliff, stepping into deep water, or not seeing the predator who saw you as a meal.

During the daylight there would be more warmth for those who lived further from the intertropical zone. The ability to harvest, gather, and hunt food was an activity needing the vitality of the Sun. The Sun was life.

Those who took their primary foods from the great waters would observe the Sun rise or set over the vast expanse of the sea. Those with water to the west watched the Sun lower himself, dropping down so quickly you could see Him disappear... The Egyptians of the fifth and sixth dynasties "believed in an elysium which was situated in the west, where the sun-god descended into his grave each night."[353]

And then... the quiet of the dark. It was gentle, peaceful... Wait, wait - what was that noise? Activity stopped at night. Creatures prowled, creatures flew, but we were unable to see them. Birds might fly overhead but it was a silhouette, a shadow against the sky, movement and sound that caused one's breath to pull in.

It was at night, during the dark, that we lay down to sleep, no longer moving, our minds set loose for the Dreaming.

And in the autumn, as the days shortened, the trees took their life from the leaves, and pulled it inside and then down into the roots beneath the soil where it would keep until spring when it would be reborn. Perhaps some of our ancestors in those days before history watched the bear hide away in a cave, or saw their food sources burrow away for the winter.

Chapter 11 - Heaven and Hell: Where does the soul go?

It is, however, one matter to sit here at the end of history which is but spun out from the loom of today into the past and imagine *why* a culture or religion would have a belief in the Underworld as a destination for the soul.

In the cosmology of Tibetan Buddhism all of the physical and metaphysical reality is centered around Mount Meru. Certainly it is more *conceptual* than real and provides an archetype for the manifestation of reality. I first encountered Mount Meru when negotiating the complex passages in the Evans-Wentz *Tibetan Book of the Dead*. The mandala-like symmetry of Mount Meru struck me as a metaphor for creation, an archetype of ritual itself. But what seemed so marvelous and appropriate was reading that it also extends downward an equal amount of its height.

I had not yet encountered the popular phrase adapted from the Hermetic texts we know: *As above, so below.*

> "The actual text of that maxim, as translated by Dennis W. Hauck from *The Emerald Tablet of Hermes Trismegistus*, is: 'That which is Below corresponds to that which is Above, and that which is Above corresponds to that which is Below, to accomplish the miracle of the One Thing.' Thus, whatever happens on any level of reality (physical, emotional, or mental) also happens on every other level."[354]

Although today there is a slightly different meaning to what many call *the Hermetic Principle*, there is that sense of reflection. We see it also in the Greek underworld. *Hades* is the name for the Underworld, the place named for the oldest son of Cronus and Rhea.

Although Hades is not the downward extension of Mount Olympus in terms of Greek cosmology, it is "considered the dark counterpart to the brightness of Mount Olympus."[355] It is as if the human soul believes that, if the radiant gods are found living on the highest peak, then the realm of the dead must be the counterpart.

> "Suggested by this thought that the sun spends half his time in the land beneath and that it is always day there when it

is night here is the fascinating idea that the underworld is a kind of looking-glass reversal of the world we know."[356]

"Deep caverns have naturally been suggested far and wide as likely entrances to the land of the shades."[357] "Even the modern Greek peasantry (despite the Christian Church) retain the ancient notion of an underworld where all the dead go, a twilight abode, cold, and 'thick with spiders' webs.' "[358]

It is tempting to accept that, for it *seems* like it would be true.

One of the most powerful experiences of my childhood were the occasional trips to a modest little cavern in Wisconsin. The cave itself is the longest in Wisconsin, but access for the public is in one location. It was a source of wonder for me and set in motion a love of caves which I continued to indulge with many cave tours over the years. We did descend into the cave with lighting. In the early 1950s the cave was lit with light bulbs every so often from a long cord that went deep into the cave. Rather than a place for the dead, it was more like the internal creative gentle force of Mother Earth. Even some of the cavern walls were almost womblike with the translucent moist film almost like human tissue. The darkness, itself, would not have been frightening. Were I *lost* in a cave and unable to see, being lost would be frightening, but the dark? It is in its own way also comforting.

Other terrestrial places where the literal Underworld intersects with our life on the Earth's surface would be fumaroles. I was introduced to *fumaroles* in Yellowstone National Park, where I have been on many years walking among the thermal areas. A Wikipedia article on fumaroles indicates there could be four thousand of them within the park. A fumarole is an opening, a vent, emitting gases and often sounds. Eerie sounds. If you wanted to believe that mythological creatures lived in the Underworld, what you hear from a fumarole might be convincing.

Why the Underworld? For our ancestors, when autumn moved into the killing frosts, most vegetative life seemed to disappear. Hibernating mammals, amphibians, all left the aboveworld. All went below, into their burrows and nests. The life force of the plant world moved down into the root world - the Underworld.

What I have not found and doubt that it can be found is the link between burying our dead in the earth and the belief in the Underworld. The beliefs and the practice of terrestrial burial predate recorded history. The concept of the Underworld seems so natural and is found in almost every culture. From Aralu of the Babylonians to Sheol of the Hebrews, it is so similar one might not even need a passport.

The Book of Him

"By far the most picturesque underworld is that of the Egyptians. For them it was the realm of Osiris, the god who had died and been restored to life and to whose protection the dead were committed. We learn of it in detail from 'The Book of Him Who is in the Underworld,' which was written on the walls of sepulchral chambers during the Eighteenth Dynasty (1580-1350 B.C.) and in later times."[359]

"In that dark region, through which a river ran, the great event was the daily progress of the sun-god Re in his bark. His voyage consumed the twelve hours when it was night on earth, and during each hour his radiance lit up the confines of one of the twelve divisions of the underworld. In each compartment, entered by a gate, were fields and houses, and along the banks of the stream dwelt all manner of fantastic spirits and demons in human and animal form. Slowly through their midst passed the state barge of Re on which sat the various divinities who were his vassals and the noted dead, fresh from the world above, who were privileged to be in his care. A few of these he leaves behind at each halting place, granting them rich fields to cultivate. In the sixth and seventh compartments dwelt the kings of Upper and Lower Egypt, but even with them there was darkness save for one hour a day."[360]

Destination: Heaven

"... A still higher flight of human thought is that which sends the departed to the sky or the sun or the stars. Because this theory calls for marked imaginative power it is not often found and always appears among races which have alternative

Chapter 11 - Heaven and Hell: Where does the soul go?

abodes for the dead. In other words, the sky land is almost never the region to which all the dead go but a special sphere for certain groups. The important question as to who goes where we must reserve..."[361]

According to Addison, this heaven that is so common a concept in today's world - today's *Christian* world - heaven typically is found in religions as a place for those special people who have lived their lives well. This is not to say that heaven is of Christian construction. Yama, the same deity who could be a fearful judge, lives in a radiant land. I hope he is a myth because he might not forgive the image I have of a divine bouncer who determines which of us merits access to the special club.

"In the earliest religious books of India, which began to take shape about three thousand years ago, the sky was the land of all departed souls who were favored by the gods. Yama, the first of mankind, dwelt there as lord of the dead. In his shining abode of light where 'all wishes are attained' dwelt 'the Fathers' surrounded by every joy of earthly life, including plenty of drink and women. In the succeeding age both sun and moon and stars were viewed as the destination of the pious dead, and one Upanishad explains that the moon expands during part of the month because of its growing load of souls."[362]

As a Wiccan Priest, I have had a love affair with the Moon since my childhood and one with the Sun only since my teens once I learned how to develop a healthy relationship with the Sun. But as a place where the 'pious' dead would go? That, for me, would be incentive to be a better person. It is not only the Hindu, however. "Nothing can compare in elaborate splendor with the celestial hereafter of the Pyramid Age in Egypt. Some twenty-five hundred years before Christ the belief prevailed that kings who died were taken to dwell with the sun-god Re in his region of heavenly light."[363]

"A notable parallel to this Egyptian picture appears in ancient Mexico, where warriors and nobles were supposed to live with the sun-god and follow him in his heavenly course from east to west."[364]

"The life of departed spirits in sun and moon and stars as depicted in the Greco-Roman thought of Stoics and Pythagoreans belongs on a level of culture more advanced... it is bound up with thoughts of the progress of the soul and of the soul's reward... Yet all the later heavens of higher religions, so far as their form goes, are only more refined versions of the happy sky land of simple and unsophisticated peoples."[365]

From the Sun and Moon, it is but a spiritual step away to now aim for the even greater lights. "The Eskimo of Behring Strait have a land of plenty in the sky where food and drink and light are in abundance and find their faith confirmed by the ghostly Northern Lights - the dance of the dead that occurs only when many have died."[366] There are tribes who place the 'Happy Hunting Grounds' high in the heavens, accessible by the Milky Way.

The concept of heading for the light is well-known in today's world. Whether the Sun or Moon, or the stars, there is something about one's soul and its relationship with the radiant light.

"The dying or deceased man is adjured to recognize the Clear light and thus liberate himself. If he does so, it is because he is himself ripe for the liberated state which is thus presented to him. If he does not (as is commonly the case), it is because the pull of worldly tendency (*Sangskara*) draws him away."[367]

"Although there are many paths to hell, the ways to heaven are few but plain. In all the earlier literature of Indian religion - the Vedas and the Brahmanas - the first requirement for eternal reward is to make use of the sacrifices which only the priests could offer to the gods... With the rise of Hinduism, however, which became the dominant religion more than a thousand years ago, the earlier emphasis on 'salvation by works' yielded in large measure to the belief in 'salvation by faith.' ...only through intense personal devotion to his chosen deity... And for the true philosopher ... neither works nor faith were the means to salvation. Salvation could come only through mystical knowledge, and it meant not a heaven of worldly delights but the final peace of union with that impersonal Absolute which is the one reality behind all change."[368]

"A person who is not disturbed by the incessant flow of desires - they enter like rivers into the ocean, which is ever being filled but is always still - can alone achieve peace, and not the man who strives to satisfy such desires.

"A person who has given up all desires for sense gratification, who lives free from desires, who has given up all sense of proprietorship and is devoid of false ego - he alone can attain real peace.

"That is the way of the spiritual and godly life, after attaining which a man is not bewildered. Being so situated, even at the hour of death, one can enter into the kingdom of God."[369] [Gita]

Or maybe just over the hill?
"The life that spirits are thought to lead when their world is on earth at a distance from the living may be a mere continuance of their old existence, but more often it is a life richer and happier than they have known before. The Mexican garden-land of Tlalocan hidden among the mountains, the lovely western valleys of the Haitians where the souls feed on delicious fruit, the 'happy hunting-grounds' of many other Indians, and those Egyptian 'Fields of Earu' (originally on earth) where men could hunt and drink and feast... all these are examples of fairer regions that await the departed."[370]

"In the tomb-paintings of the sixth and fifth centuries BC the prevailing theme may be said to be Elysium, with the dead imagined as enjoying, either as participants, or as spectators,

Chapter 11 - Heaven and Hell: Where does the soul go?

the jollities, sports, and pleasant pastimes of a well-to-do and cultured people - feasting, fishing and fowling, athletic games, horsemanship, dancing, and music, often portrayed in an idyllic setting of trees, plants, flitting birds, and dangling flower garlands."[371]

My grandparents used to joke about going 'over the hill' although I don't recall if that was a reference to dying or not. I was quite taken when doing my research to realize that there were people who believed that the soul remained on the earth, perhaps just relocated a little.

The following excerpt is from a Wikipedia article. In truth I was uncertain about the phrase as it seemed to me too much like Hollywood white folk creating words for the poor savages. However, I also found quite a few references from tribal elders affirming not just the concept but the people's language.

"The happy Hunting ground was the name given to the concept of the afterlife by several of the great plains Native American tribes, including the Oglala Lakota. It is an afterlife conceived of as a paradise in which hunting is plentiful and game unlimited. ... The Happy Hunting Ground resembled the living world, but with much better weather and animals such as rabbit, deer and buffalo that were both plentiful and easy to hunt."[372]

"You will have noticed that all the races we have dealt with - Egyptians, Babylonians, Greeks and Celts - were believers in two kinds of heaven, an underground heaven, and an island heaven. ... There is the class who love the sea and who would not be happy except on an island, or near the shore. ... There are also those who would be extremely miserable if they were doomed to live within sight of the sea. They could not thrive or be content unless their home was far inland, among hills or mountains."[373]

"To put it briefly, both god and man had something to do with inculcating a belief in immortality. God gave a revelation of the afterlife to almost every race, a revelation which suited that particular race's circumstances, light and progress in culture and knowledge."[374]

"In Celtic folklore we meet with a glorious variety of other worlds. No less than twelve are known to me and each one of these is different from the other. Their names are Tir-nan-Og; Tir Tairngire; Tir-fo-Thuinn; Rocabarraidh; Eilean-na-Fiacais; Eilean-na-Duibhre; Innis Subhach; Innis-nam-Ban; Tir-a-Chridhe-Bheo; Innis-nam-Fear-Fionn-Fiall; Innse-Geala-nan-Ra Soluis; and, Infrinn."[375]

"...the Celt is offered an elysium congenial to folks of widely different talents and temperaments. In all of them the human self or personality survives, but is transfigured and perpetuated."[376]

"The most perfect, the most reasonable word picture extant of the ancient Gael's conception of immortality... the legend of Tir-nan-Og where the good that has been shall be again. ...the beauteous green Isle of the Ever Young, lies in the west where the sun sets. At death the soul of the hero is ferried across the great sea in a white barge steered over the night waters by the will of fate. There they enjoy perpetual youth and happiness and receive healing balm for the wounds and music for the sorrows..."[377]

⁂

"The many interesting differences in the views of divers peoples are largely concerned with the question of whether the life below, compared with that above, is happier or unhappier."[378]

Notes for Chapter Eleven

[337] Rev. Norman MacDonald, *The After-Life in Celtic and Oriental Folklore*, pub. 1970 by the author in Cachan Locheport, page 5

Chapter 11 - Heaven and Hell: Where does the soul go?

[338] Sayers, Matthew R., *Feeding the Dead: Ancestor Worship in Ancient India*, Oxford University Press, New York NY © 2013, page 105

[339] Sayers, Matthew R., *Feeding the Dead: Ancestor Worship in Ancient India*, Oxford University Press, New York NY © 2013, page 104

[340] James Thayer Addison, *Life Beyond Death In the Beliefs of Mankind*, Houghton Mifflin Co., © 1932, pages 10-11

[341] James Thayer Addison, *Life Beyond Death In the Beliefs of Mankind*, Houghton Mifflin Co., © 1932, page 109

[342] James Thayer Addison, *Life Beyond Death In the Beliefs of Mankind*, Houghton Mifflin Co., © 1932, page 90

[343] James Thayer Addison, *Life Beyond Death In the Beliefs of Mankind*, Houghton Mifflin Co., © 1932, page 92

[344] Chaney, Earlyne, *The Mystery of Death & Dying: Initiation at the Moment of Death*, Samuel Weiser, Inc., York Beach, Maine © 1988, page 65

[345] James Thayer Addison, *Life Beyond Death In the Beliefs of Mankind*, Houghton Mifflin Co., © 1932, pages 92-93

[346] James Thayer Addison, *Life Beyond Death In the Beliefs of Mankind*, Houghton Mifflin Co., © 1932, page 88

[347] James Thayer Addison, *Life Beyond Death In the Beliefs of Mankind*, Houghton Mifflin Co., © 1932, pages 87-88

[348] James Thayer Addison, *Life Beyond Death In the Beliefs of Mankind*, Houghton Mifflin Co., © 1932, pages 168-169

[349] James Thayer Addison, *Life Beyond Death In the Beliefs of Mankind*, Houghton Mifflin Co., © 1932, page 168

[350] in *Religions of the Ancient World: A Guide*, Johnston, Sarah Iles (ed.), The Belknap Press of Harvard University Press, Cambridge and London, © 2004, page 470 *Introduction* by John J. Collins

[351] in *Religions of the Ancient World: A Guide*, Johnston, Sarah Iles (ed.), The Belknap Press of Harvard University Press, Cambridge and London, © 2004, pages 470-471 *Introduction* by John J. Collins

[352] Rev. Norman MacDonald, *The After-Life in Celtic and Oriental Folklore*, pub. 1970 by the author in Cachan Locheport, page 12

[353] Rev. Norman MacDonald, *The After-Life in Celtic and Oriental Folklore*, pub. 1970 by the author in Cachan Locheport, page 11

Chapter 11 - Heaven and Hell: Where does the soul go?

[354] http://en.wikipedia.org/wiki/Hermeticism#.22As_above.2C_so_below.22

[355] http://en.wikipedia.org/wiki/Greek_underworld

[356] James Thayer Addison, *Life Beyond Death In the Beliefs of Mankind*, Houghton Mifflin Co., © 1932, pages 62-63

[357] James Thayer Addison, *Life Beyond Death In the Beliefs of Mankind*, Houghton Mifflin Co., © 1932, page 62

[358] James Thayer Addison, *Life Beyond Death In the Beliefs of Mankind*, Houghton Mifflin Co., © 1932, pages 59-60

[359] James Thayer Addison, *Life Beyond Death In the Beliefs of Mankind*, Houghton Mifflin Co., © 1932, page 60

[360] James Thayer Addison, *Life Beyond Death In the Beliefs of Mankind*, Houghton Mifflin Co., © 1932, page 61

[361] James Thayer Addison, *Life Beyond Death In the Beliefs of Mankind*, Houghton Mifflin Co., © 1932, page 69

[362] James Thayer Addison, *Life Beyond Death In the Beliefs of Mankind*, Houghton Mifflin Co., © 1932, page 70

[363] James Thayer Addison, *Life Beyond Death In the Beliefs of Mankind*, Houghton Mifflin Co., © 1932, pages 70-71

[364] James Thayer Addison, *Life Beyond Death In the Beliefs of Mankind*, Houghton Mifflin Co., © 1932, page 71

[365] James Thayer Addison, *Life Beyond Death In the Beliefs of Mankind*, Houghton Mifflin Co., © 1932, page 71

[366] James Thayer Addison, *Life Beyond Death In the Beliefs of Mankind*, Houghton Mifflin Co., © 1932, page 70

[367] Foreword by Sir John Woodroffe, "The Science of Death" *The Tibetan Book of the Dead*, compiled and edited by W.Y. Evans-Wentz Oxford University Press © 1960, page lxxiv

[368] James Thayer Addison, *Life Beyond Death In the Beliefs of Mankind*, Houghton Mifflin Co., © 1932, pages 183-184

[369] *Bhagavad-Gītā As It Is*, A. C. Bhaktivedanta Swami Prabhupāda, The Bhaktivedanta Book Trust, Los Angeles, © 1981, page 49

[370] James Thayer Addison, *Life Beyond Death In the Beliefs of Mankind*, Houghton Mifflin Co., © 1932, page 67

Chapter 11 - Heaven and Hell: Where does the soul go?

[371] *Death and Burial in the Roman World*, J. M. C. Toynbee, The Johns Hopkins University Press, Baltimore © 1971, page 12

[372] http://en.wikipedia.org/wiki/Happy_hunting_ground 3 December 2014 ce

[373] Rev. Norman MacDonald, *The After-Life in Celtic and Oriental Folklore*, pub. 1970 by the author in Cachan Locheport, page 20

[374] Rev. Norman MacDonald, *The After-Life in Celtic and Oriental Folklore*, pub. 1970 by the author in Cachan Locheport, page 6

[375] Rev. Norman MacDonald, *The After-Life in Celtic and Oriental Folklore*, pub. 1970 by the author in Cachan Locheport, page 6

[376] Rev. Norman MacDonald, *The After-Life in Celtic and Oriental Folklore*, pub. 1970 by the author in Cachan Locheport, page 6

[377] Rev. Norman MacDonald, *The After-Life in Celtic and Oriental Folklore*, pub. 1970 by the author in Cachan Locheport, page 6

[378] James Thayer Addison, *Life Beyond Death In the Beliefs of Mankind*, Houghton Mifflin Co., © 1932, pages 55-56

Chapter 12 - The Past and the Future

Ancestors and Reincarnation

"It is much more astonishing that not everybody remembers his or her previous death... But, likewise, they do not remember their recent birth - and yet they do not doubt that they were recently born. They forget that active memory is only a small part of our normal consciousness, and that our subconscious memory registers and preserves every past impression and experience which our waking mind fails to recall. ...

"If, through some trick of nature, the gates of an individual's subconsciousness were suddenly to spring open, the unprepared mind would be overwhelmed and crushed. Therefore, the gates of the subconscious are guarded, by all initiates, and hidden behind the veil of mysteries and symbols."[379]

If at first you don't succeed, try try again...

"It may be argued that nobody can talk about death with authority who has not died; and since nobody, apparently, has ever returned from death, how anybody know what death is, or what happens after it?

"The Tibetan will answer: 'There is not *one* person, indeed, not *one* living being, that has *not* returned from death. In fact, we all have died many deaths, before we came into this incarnation. And what we call birth is merely the reverse side of death, like one of the two sides of a coin, or like a door which we call *entrance* from the outside and *exit*, from inside a room.'"[380]

Chapter 12 - The Past and the Future: Ancestors and Reincarnation

It was quite interesting to become a serious student of both contemporary and classical mysticism and then have various popular figures emerge in so public a way as to change the dialogue. An example of this would have been the publication of Shirley MacLaine's autobiography in 1983, *Out on a Limb*. Although the belief in reincarnation dates back to prehistory and may be accepted by more people than do not believe in it, MacLaine's book, due to her fame as an award-winning actress, had almost everyone talking about reincarnation, whether to poke fun at an easy target or to come out of the closet.

As I was working on *this* chapter my partner, Rev. Gerry, stopped me from talking as he was listening to a story on public radio. I sat down at my desk and listened. It was a story on Nicky Vreeland who is a Buddhist monk and the abbot of one of the Dalai Lama's monasteries. And there was this: "The Dalai Lama's attendant once took me by the arm and said to me, 'You know, when our robes get worn out we get rid of them and we have new ones made. It's the same with the body. When we die, the body has ceased to exist and we reincarnate and continue our lives."[381]

I tried very hard when I was young to believe in the Catholic paradigm for what happens when the body dies. Having numerous out-of-body experiences, near death experiences, and other mystical experiences, I could never quite feel at one with the Christian view of heaven and hell and then, some of the Christian beliefs about the body and spirit after death? That was not me.

I have no idea how old I was when I first encountered the *concept* of reincarnation. I don't recall ever *not* believing in it but certainly a child in rural Wisconsin would not have known about the word. Who was that blessed soul or that source which first gently dropped that word into life? Whomever it may have been, I give thanks.

As someone with innate mystical abilities, I began to sense the difference between those manifestations of reality which arose from having 'been there before,' as with a precognitive dream. As years passed I clearly knew there a difference between the déjà vu from my dreams, and something deeper, more profound. I began to understand it

Chapter 12 - The Past and the Future: Ancestors and Reincarnation

all better in November of 1973 when I found myself in London. There were many things about London which had previously felt so familiar. I spent years reading English literature. There were moments of recognition, or perhaps of comfort or familiarity here and there watching something filmed in London. Those moments, however, do not suggest that I might have lived in London previously. They only suggest that I might have something of the Anglophile in me.

And then, there I was. It was so profound an experience, only a week, that I returned the following spring and spent three weeks there. I had the same experience. I could walk *anywhere*. I knew my way around the older areas. From the Tower to Albert Hall and much further, I simply knew my way. I knew the streets and there were places I knew the architecture, but anything newer than World War I was not familiar. I did not sense the life I had, but I knew how to live there and the manner of life in those earlier times was what I longed for. What can I say? Surely I had lived at least once in London. There was no other explanation.

"The word 'reincarnation' derives from Latin, literally meaning, 'entering the flesh again.' The Greek equivalent metempsychosis (μετεμψύχωσις) roughly corresponds to the common English phrase 'transmigration of the soul' and also usually connotes reincarnation after death, as either human, animal, though emphasising the continuity of the soul, not the flesh. The term has been used by modern philosophers such as Kurt Gödel and has entered the English language. Another Greek term sometimes used synonymously is palingenesis, 'being born again.'

"There is no word corresponding exactly to the English terms 'rebirth,' 'metempsychosis,' 'transmigration' or 'reincarnation' in the traditional languages of Pāli and Sanskrit. The entire universal process that gives rise to the cycle of death and rebirth, governed by karma, is referred to as Samsara while the state one is born into, the individual process of being born or coming into the world in any way, is referred to simply as 'birth' (jāti). Devas (gods) may also die and live

Chapter 12 - The Past and the Future: Ancestors and Reincarnation

again. Here the term 'reincarnation' is not strictly applicable, yet Hindu gods are said to have reincarnated (see Avatar): Lord Vishnu is known for his ten incarnations, the Dashavatars. Celtic religion seems to have had reincarnating gods also. Many Christians regard Jesus as a divine incarnation. Some Christians and Muslims believe he and some prophets may incarnate again. Most Christians, however, believe that Jesus will come again in the Second Coming at the end of the world, although this is not a reincarnation. Some ghulat Shi'a Muslim sects also regard their founders as in some special sense divine incarnations (hulul)."[382]

Not long after my second trip to London, I had a choice to make. The relationship I had with London was so ... *suited* to me. I had housing waiting for me and a position working for a to-the-trade antique dealer with a wonderful shop in the Portobello Market area. The thought of living in London was more than a dream coming true.

And then, reality began to happen. It was the Upper Mississippi River Valley. I could leave family and friends behind but somehow the thought of no longer having easy access to what was my own sacred river? I made the difficult decision to cancel my plans to relocate to London and I stayed living in Minnesota.

Within two years I had found the couple who were to be my instructors and guides as I converted to the Wiccan religion and underwent years of training to become a Priest.

It was an extensive education including many aspects of religion and of metaphysical disciplines. Among those skills were those needed to conduct regression therapy. I applied myself with great diligence and began working with students of mine and clients who knew of my work. What I learned about the potential of reincarnation as reality was so enriched. I feel so much gratitude for the many hundreds who came to me for past life regression work.

"The origins of the notion of reincarnation are obscure. Discussion of the subject appears in the philosophical traditions of India (including the Indus Valley). The Greek

Pre-Socratics discussed reincarnation, and the Celtic Druids are also reported to have taught a doctrine of reincarnation.

"The ideas associated with reincarnation may have arisen independently in different regions, or they might have spread as a result of cultural contact. Proponents of cultural transmission have looked for links between Iron Age Celtic, Greek and Vedic philosophy and religion, some even suggesting that belief in reincarnation was present in Proto-Indo-European religion. In ancient European, Iranian and Indian agricultural cultures, the life cycles of birth, death, and rebirth were recognized as a replica of natural agricultural cycles."[383]

When I began my years of intensive work into past and other lives, we thought of time as being linear. A number of earlier cultures thought of time as cyclic, more akin to the Wheel of the Year, whereas the Judeo-Christian model is that time is linear. Ah, but today? We know that what we think of as time varies considerably throughout the Universe. It is not a constant. What I was finding through my work also led me to expand my own definitions. I quickly began referring not to *past life regressions* but to *past and other life regressions.*

My belief in reincarnation combined with what I had experienced with my clients left me convinced that there was no reason at all to believe that the series of lives like beads on the thread of reincarnation would be in the same historical order as we expect from our linear perspective. I came to believe that someone living in the 1990s CE but who had a deep fascination with the Renaissance, who lived and breathed that era could certainly have her 'next' incarnation in that earlier (by linear measurement) time.

"In a universe of oneness, death is impossible.

"The richness of connectivity renders personal extinction impossible, because personal extinction is possible only in a universe of personal isolation. We do not live in such a universe.

"The modern tradition of equating death with an ensuing nothingness can be abandoned, for there is no reason to believe that human death severs the quality of oneness in the universe. If we participate in this universal quality before our death, our survival after death is demanded. The oneness principle endures, and we with it."[384]

"In Jainism, the soul and matter are considered eternal, not created and perpetual. There is a constant interplay between the two, resulting in bewildering cosmic manifestations in material, psychic and emotional spheres around us. This led to the theories of transmigration and rebirth. Changes but not total annihilation of spirit and matter is the basic postulate of Jain philosophy. The life as we know now, after death therefore moves on to another form of life based on the merits and demerits it accumulated in its current life. The path to becoming a supreme soul is to practice non-violence and be truthful."[385]

From my previous life experience of being sentenced to death by hanging I began to theorize - and *believe* - that the experience of dying itself might often create one of the residual memories of a previous incarnation. Is *memory* the correct word? Not at all. I would describe it more as a type of imprint or a record, some clearly with a greater imprint left behind, some with greater detail.

With those clients I believed able to grasp how profound and life-changing such an experience could be, I began by explaining the nature of death, and that event of dying likely having left the strongest imprint or memory, I suggested that, if at all possible, they allow me to guide them through the death of that body and experience a glimpse of the *liberation* some of the great mystical religions speak of.

"During the Renaissance translations of Plato, the Hermetica and other works fostered new European interest in reincarnation. Marsilio Ficino argued that Plato's references to reincarnation were intended allegorically, Shakespeare made fun but Giordano Bruno was burned at the stake by authorities after being found guilty of heresy by the Roman Inquisition for his teachings. But the Greek philosophical works remained available and, particularly in north Europe, were discussed by groups such as the Cambridge Platonists.

"By the 19th century the philosophers Schopenhauer and Nietzsche could access the Indian scriptures for discussion of the doctrine of reincarnation, which recommended itself to the American Transcendentalists Henry David Thoreau, Walt Whitman and Ralph Waldo Emerson and was adapted by Francis Bowen into Christian Metempsychosis.

"By the early 20th century, interest in reincarnation had been introduced into the nascent discipline of psychology, largely due to the influence of William James, who raised aspects of the philosophy of mind, comparative religion, the psychology of religious experience and the nature of empiricism. James was influential in the founding of the American Society for Psychical Research (ASPR) in New York City in 1885, three years after the British Society for Psychical Research (SPR) was inaugurated in London, leading to systematic, critical investigation of paranormal phenomena.

"At this time popular awareness of the idea of reincarnation was boosted by the Theosophical Society's dissemination of systematised and universalised Indian concepts and also by the influence of magical societies like The Golden Dawn. Notable personalities like Annie Besant, W. B. Yeats and Dion Fortune made the subject almost as familiar an element of the popular culture of the west as of the east."[386]

The reservoir of insight I gained through the many hands-on (not literally!) sessions with clients reshaped my own beliefs.

I began to believe that the exploration and study of one's past and/or other lives was certainly interesting, but that it had less value than one might expect. Where we had *been* (in a manner of speaking) might provide insight into matters of behavior or psychoses which were found carried over from life to life but awareness of them did not provide as much solution as popular culture might lead us to believe.

More and more I became convinced that it was not where we had been, but where we were going which mattered. My understanding of what we referred to as past lives had come to emphasize one's next life as being far more central to the overall issues regarding the meaning of life and of death.

I wished to place the emphasis of my work as a Priest to an emphasis upon one's death as an opportunity to open the doors of growth and learning. I also felt strongly that, unlike my spiritual ancestors living in the Tibetan Plateau, I did not wish to escape the wheel of rebirth. My greatest goal would be to develop the skill set necessary to enable my ability to return and to locate my spiritual path and continue this journey which I have been taking with many variations throughout my lives.

"During recent decades, many people in the West have developed an interest in reincarnation. Feature films, such as *The Reincarnation of Peter Proud, Dead Again, Kundun, Fluke, What Dreams May Come, The Mummy and Birth*, and *Chances Are*, contemporary books by authors such as Carol Bowman and Vicki Mackenzie, as well as popular songs, deal with reincarnation.

"Recent studies have indicated that some Westerners accept the idea of reincarnation including certain contemporary Christians, modern Neopagans, followers of Spiritism, Theosophists and students of esoteric philosophies such as Kabbalah, and Gnostic and Esoteric Christianity as well as of Indian religions. Demographic survey data from 1999–2002 shows a significant minority of people from Europe and America, where there is reasonable freedom of thought and access to ideas but no outstanding recent reincarnationist tradition, believe we had a life before we were born, will survive death and be born again physically. The mean for the Nordic countries is 22%. The belief in reincarnation is particularly high in the Baltic countries, with Lithuania having the highest figure for the whole of Europe, 44%. The lowest figure is in East Germany, 12%. In Russia,

Chapter 12 - The Past and the Future: Ancestors and Reincarnation

about one-third believes in reincarnation. The effect of communist anti-religious ideas on the beliefs of the populations of Eastern Europe seems to have been rather slight, if any, except apparently in East Germany. Overall, 22% of respondents in Western Europe believe in reincarnation. According to a 2005 Gallup poll 20 percent of U.S. adults believe in reincarnation. Recent surveys by the Barna Group, a Christian research nonprofit organization, have found that a quarter of U.S. Christians, including 10 percent of all born-again Christians, embrace the idea.

"Skeptic Carl Sagan asked the Dalai Lama what he would do if a fundamental tenet of his religion (reincarnation) were definitively disproved by science. The Dalai Lama answered, 'If science can disprove reincarnation, Tibetan Buddhism would abandon reincarnation... but it's going to be mighty hard to disprove reincarnation.'"[387]

My fascination with Tibet has not waned. Its very location allowed its indigenous traditions of Bön to become interwoven with the the later Buddhism, a beautiful amalgamation of Mahayana and Vajrayana which came from the Sanskrit Buddhist traditions to the south.

Despite our romanticized views of life in the Tibetan Plateau, with the stunning city of Lhasa, or the scenic views of the plateau, "'the Roof of the World' and is the world's highest and largest plateau, with an area of 2,500,000 square kilometres (970,000 sq mi) (about five times the size of Metropolitan France)."[388]

A high-altitude area of the world, surrounded by some of the highest, most challenging mountains of the world, life is very difficult. What rainfall there is, which can be as little as just under 4" per year to as much as 12" per year, *falls as hail*. In the United States that would range in rainfall from Las Vegas (4.2") to Los Angeles (12.8"). Compare that to Seattle (37.7") to New York City (at 49.9"). Add to this extreme temperatures and life is very much a sharp edged sword. Only the Priesthood has those within it who would willingly choose to return to continue their work.

"Buddhist traditions vary in precise views on rebirth. The Tibetan schools hold to the notion of a bardo (intermediate state) that can last up to forty-nine days. An accomplished or realized practitioner (by maintaining conscious awareness during the death process) can choose to return to samsara. They believe many lamas choose to be born again and again as humans and are called tulkus or incarnate lamas. The Sarvastivada school believed that between death and rebirth there is a sort of limbo in which beings do not yet reap the consequences of their previous actions but may still influence their rebirth. The death process and this intermediate state were believed to offer a uniquely favourable opportunity for spiritual awakening. Theravada Buddhism generally denies there is an intermediate state—though some early Buddhist texts seem to support the idea-- but asserts that rebirth is immediate.

"Within Japanese Zen, reincarnation is accepted by some, but wholly rejected by others. A distinction can be drawn between 'folk Zen,' as in the Zen practiced by devotional lay people, and 'philosophical Zen.' Folk Zen generally accepts the various supernatural elements of Buddhism such as rebirth. Philosophical Zen, however, places such emphasis on the present moment that rebirth may be considered irrelevant because, even if it does exist, it can never be consciously experienced. Specifically, in Zen the past and future are considered to be merely ideas which are held in the present. Because as living beings rebirth can only be viewed as something which may have happened in the past or that might happen in the future, we must essentially reject the present moment, or Dharma, in order to even consider it. For this reason, rebirth is often either rejected or considered unknowable in Zen and therefore a distraction. Dōgen Zenji, the founder of Japanese Sōtō Zen, writes the following regarding reincarnation:"[389]

"According to that non-Buddhist view, there is one spiritual intelligence existing within our bodies. When this body dies, however, the spirit casts off the skin and is reborn. If we learn this view as the Buddha's Dharma we are even more foolish than a person who grasps a tile or pebble thinking it to be a golden treasure."

— Dōgen Zenji, Shōbōgenzō

Notes for Chapter 12

[379] Introductory Foreword by Lāma Anagarika Govinda, *The Tibetan Book of the Dead*, compiled and edited by W.Y. Evans-Wentz Oxford University Press © 1960, page liii

[380] Introductory Foreword by Lāma Anagarika Govinda, *The Tibetan Book of the Dead*, compiled and edited by W.Y. Evans-Wentz Oxford University Press © 1960, page liii

[381] http://www.npr.org/2014/12/06/368518722/from-chic-manhattanite-to-monk-with-a-camera 6 December 2014 ce

[382] http://en.wikipedia.org/wiki/Reincarnation - 6 December 2014 ce

[383] http://en.wikipedia.org/wiki/Reincarnation - 6 December 2014 ce

[384] Dr. Larry Dossey, *Space Time and Medicine*, Shambhala © 1982 as printed in the memorial service program for Claude Zetty, held at Trinity College, Texas May 4, 1991

[385] http://en.wikipedia.org/wiki/Reincarnation - 6 December 2014 ce

[386] http://en.wikipedia.org/wiki/Reincarnation - 6 December 2014 ce

[387] http://en.wikipedia.org/wiki/Reincarnation - 6 December 2014 ce

[388] http://en.wikipedia.org/wiki/Tibetan_Plateau - 9 December 2014 ce

[389] http://en.wikipedia.org/wiki/Reincarnation - 6 December 2014 ce

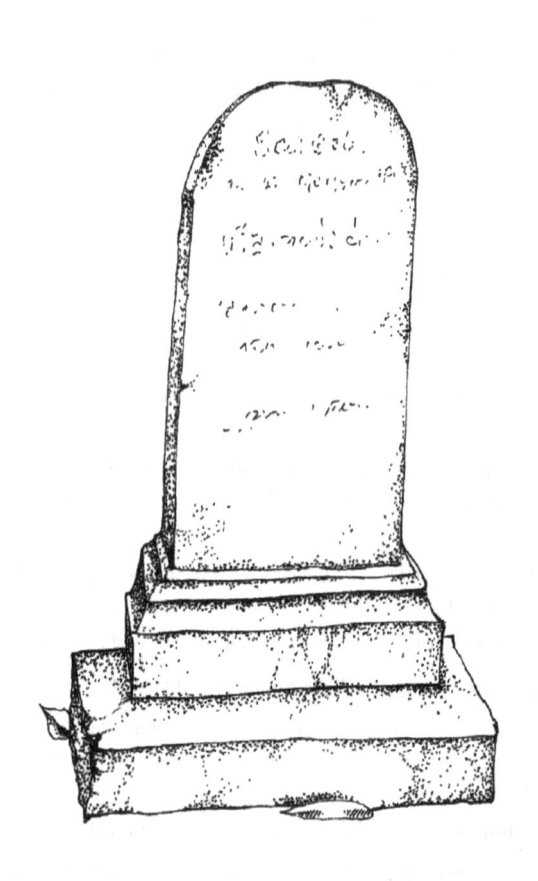

Chapter 13 - Eating with the Dead

Gone but not Forgotten

From the time our babies are born into this incarnate world until they reach death, we feed them. And for many, from death until the soul reaches rebirth, we continue to feed them. Providing food for our loved ones whether they are incarnate and living or passed over into the Otherworld is instinctive to many cultures and many people.

During the course of our lives, sharing food with one another is so integral to our experience of familial bonds, of welcoming an acquaintance or stranger into our lives at a deeper level, of sharing and observing celebrations and rites of passage, that it should not seem at all unusual that we might wish to also share a meal with those no longer incarnate. Despite a tendency among today's modern cultures to avoid thinking about death, to set aside the old practices of Right Dying, of having one's older generations pass away at home, those deaths remain with us. No one who has lost a loved one with whom they shared living space can sit down to a meal and not be aware of the absence. It is not a simple matter to simply rearrange meal habits as if the the deceased had simply never been there.

Ancient burial sites so often show that foods were buried with the body as well. I think of the numerous times throughout my life when, having spent days or weeks together, having shared conversation and meals and worked together... And at departure? Everyone who is leaving is sent off with more food. So, too, many of us would send a loved one off to the next life with food. "The custom of making offerings to the dead at the time of burial finds its origin in no religious motive, but in the instinct to give the dead what belongs to him."[390]

Death is so much a part of our lives that in some languages the conceptualization of orgasm is that of a 'little death' or letting go: a major release of life forces. In even more cultures it is common for a meal to be proffered as an invitation (or expectation) for sex.

Chapter 13 - Eating with the Dead: Gone but not Forgotten

Given that food is so connected with intimacy and bonding, it should not be at all odd that a meal is often a means of sustaining a loving bond after the passing of a loved one. I have often heard of people continuing to set the loved one's place at the table, or including their place setting at a special, family holiday. I opened this book remembering those picnics my sister and I had with classmate, out in the rural farmland cemetery.

"If the souls of the dead are near at hand and still feel the wants they felt in life, it is natural not only to provide for them, but to keep on providing for them."[391] I have no idea whose idea it was but several times my sister Jeanne and I along with two friends of ours rode our bicycles out to the Colby Cemetery for a picnic. It was scenic, on a rise about 50 feet higher than the farmland surrounding it which meant it had a view - something not easily found in that flat, slightly undulating farmland. To us, young ones on the verge of our teens, a picnic overlooking the bucolic farmland among the dead seemed like a lovely and appropriate place for a picnic. I was, after all, different and already a little beyond the norm for that village. But up there on that rise, surrounded by the ... the heritage of our village and surrounding farms, it seemed like a familial, loving location and a wonderful place for a picnic. Frankly, if we were not so puritanical in the United States, if we were not so removed from not only death, but from birth and from the full cycles of life, we might also think that conceiving the next generation in the presence of the spirits of one's ancestors would bring blessings and reward, but that is for a different discussion.

As I left the relative cultural isolation of the village and eventually ended up in a truly urban metropolis, I learned so much. I was thrilled to learn about the customs from south of the U.S. border. "Among the many peoples who practise in some form the cult of ancestors a familiar custom is the annual Festival of the Dead."[392] This was a far more sensible approach to All Hallows Eve than I had ever imagined possible.

Although most Euro-Americans think of the Mexican Dia de los Muertos as largely of Spanish origin, it is a custom which clearly predates the Spanish invasion of what was called the New World (*new* only to the Spanish invaders).

"The Miztecs of ancient Mexico believed that the souls of the newly departed came back once a year in November to revisit their old friends. On the eve of this day they would deck their houses in festival style to welcome the spirits, set out choice food and drink on the table, and go out with torches in hand to welcome the ghosts and invite them to enter."[393]

Nor is this belief limited to one culture. "The Urabon-ye - the Japanese All Souls' Day - is celebrated during four days in the last half of August... the souls of the departed are believed to revisit their old homes, and all the rites are designed to give them a reverent and affectionate welcome."[394] Indeed, according to John J. Collins in *Death, the Afterlife and Other Last Things*, "From earliest times, people laid out food and drink for dead relatives and performed rituals on their behalf. In many places, people shared communal meals with the dead. These practices were meant to ensure the well-being of the deceased and also to appease the spirits of the dead and to protect the living from their displeasure."[395]

Today within The Rowan Tree Church, we have our Feast for the Dead but for weeks we collect food. For our Feast of the Dead, as I announced when I set this custom into our Tradition, we collect food for and feed the living, donating a large amount of food to a local food bank.

Oh, the poor pigs

Jocelyn Mary Catherine Toynbee, part of the illustrious family of historians, produced as part of her life's work a wonderfully detailed monograph on the death and burial customs of the ancient Romans. *Death and Burial in the Roman World* is one of the sources I greatly value, although her propensity for detail can be daunting. And yet, I wish there was far more information about the ritual of suffitio in her text.

"Various statutory regulations had to be complied with on all occasions of death and burial. Only when a pig had been sacrificed was a grave legally a grave. There were also a number of other acts to be performed by the family. On returning from the funeral the relatives had to undergo the suffitio, a rite of purification by fire and water. On the same day there began a period of cleansing ceremonies held at the deceased's house; and again on the same day a funerary feast, the silicernium, was eaten at the grave in honour of the dead. There was also the cena novendialis eaten at the grave on the ninth day after the funeral, at the end of the period of full mourning, when a libation to the Manes was poured upon the actual burial."[396]

Suffitio translates loosely as a cleansing with incense or perfume. And I know so little. Oh, to have had autumn afternoons to sit about with Ms. Toynbee to learn some of what must be far more than what made it into the text of her book.

Conduits to the underworld

"Early Roman ideas as to where the Manes dwelt, after the body had received due burial, are not explicitly recorded. It is, however, likely that they were thought of as being underground, at or near their burial place, where they could be given nourishment. From later periods there is, indeed, abundant evidence of an urge to keep the dead 'alive' by offerings made to them of food and drink, oil, and even blood and by their share in the funerary meals partaken of at the tomb by the survivors... For this purpose holes were pierced and pipes provided so that the offerings and portions allotted to the dead could penetrate to the burials... There the departed were believed to rest in the kindly bosom of maternal Earth, to whom they had descended. Hence the representations of Terra Mater in sepulchral art. Hence the reiterated prayer of the epitaphs 's(it) t(ibi) t(erra) l(levis).'[397] Hence, too, the notion of immortality as union with the Earth-Goddess - 'cinis sum cinis terra est terra dea est ergo ego mortua non sum;'[398] and the imagery of bones or ashes giving birth to flowers: 'hic iacet Optatus pietatis nobilis infans/cui precor ut cineres sint ia sintque rosae, /terraque quae mater nunc est sibi sit levis oro/

namque gravis nulkli vita fuit pueri' ('Here lies Optatus, a child noble and dutiful. I pray that his ashes may become violets and roses and that the Earth, who is his mother now, rest lightly on him, who in life weighed heavily on no man'). There would seem to be no reason to hold that such thoughts deny individual survival or involve 'renunciation of personality,' absorbed into the pure life-essence of earth. Rather they imply the continuance of the dead's identity."[399]

And elsewhere?

"The Spaniards sometimes offer bread and wine at the tombs of those they love on the anniversary of their decease, and the Bulgarians hold a feast in the cemeteries on Palm Sunday, leaving what remains for the spirits to eat during the night. On the Eve of All Souls' Day, when poor souls from purgatory are released for the night, the peasants of the Tyrol place candles on the graves, keep a fire burning on the hearth, and leave milk and cakes on the table all night for the ghosts to eat."[400]

"Celebrated hundreds of years ago by Native American tribes, the Feast of the Dead was a Native American burial ritual practiced to celebrate life and to socialize with other tribe members. Traditionally celebrated by the Iroquois, Huron, Algonquin and Ottawa, the Feast of the Dead was held every 10-12 years, depending on when a tribe moved on from the village. Each time the tribe moved, a Feast of the Dead celebration was held to bury corpses and release family members into the afterlife. Instead of leaving the dead behind, these Native American tribes moved the corpses to a central location because they believe that it allowed the spirits to move into the next life."[401]

"As the name implies, jhator is considered an act of generosity: the deceased and his/her surviving relatives are providing food to sustain living beings. Generosity and compassion for all beings are important virtues or paramita in

Buddhism. Although some observers have suggested that jhator is also meant to unite the deceased person with the sky or sacred realm, this does not seem consistent with most of the knowledgeable commentary and eyewitness reports, which indicate that Tibetans believe that at this point life has completely left the body and the body contains nothing more than simple flesh."[402]

"It has, indeed, been an ancient belief all over the Celtic world that the dead return en masse to join the living on the day which they knew as Samhain and which we call All Saints'. So both in Scotland and Ireland there long survived the custom of setting chairs and table for the dead and leaving fire and food for their use."[403]

Here in North America many, if not most, of us have heard of the Day of the Dead celebrated in Mexico and other Spanish-American countries. Cross-cultural interaction and emigration have brought the United States further into being truly American, embracing (not always willingly) the cultures which have their roots in Spain, not in England.

Honoring one's ancestors with food, however, is far more universal. Rituals surrounding the honoring of one's ancestors with food are found in some of the oldest literature of the Asian subcontinent, the Rig Veda [Ṛg Veda]. The oldest known Hindu scriptures, they provide insight into a highly developed culture and region which had beautiful, elaborate rituals with which to provide food for the dead.

In this ritual, the piṇḍapiotryajña, a monthly offering (sacrifice) of a rice ball to one's ancestors, the ancestors are perceived to be divinities. Following the death of a family member, they may be elevated to the status of Ancestor which is not so distinguishable from divinity. Although I risk having the following taken out of context, the correct 'context' would need me to cite dozens of pages from Sayers' text. *Feeding the Dead* is a deeply moving book, as is this ceremony which may be as old as 3500 years.

Chapter 13 - Eating with the Dead: Gone but not Forgotten

"The piṇḍapiotṛyajña is performed once a month in the afternoon of the new moon... The priests follow the same paradigm, making alterations to accommodate the divinity of this rite, the Ancestors. The Sacrificer sits behind the householder's fire (gārhapatya), facing the south wearing his sacrificial cord over his right shoulder (prācīnāvītin). He prepares the ritual space as in the model ritual..."[404]

The rice is winnowed and husked by the Sacrificer's wife one time (not three times as is done in the model ritual). The rice is cooked "over the southern fire, stirring counter clock-wise" and an offering of clarified butter is stirred into the ridge along with mantras and an offering to the deities Agni and Soma.

"After drawing the lines with the wooden sword, the Sacrificer lays down a firebrand at the south end of the lines to ward off demons, who can tamper with the food... He makes the Ancestors wash themselves, as he would a guest about to eat; he takes a water pitcher and pours out the water." His father is addressed by name, and asked to wash himself, next his grandfather and then his great-grandfather. "He cuts the sacrificial grass with one stroke and spreads the grass along the line with their tops oriented toward the south." The rice balls are placed upon the grass and he tells his father, grandfather and great-grandfather in turn that "this is for you," again calling each by name. "Enjoining them to enjoy the food with another mantra, he turns his back to allow them to eat."[405]

Ah, and then there is this, "the other solemn rite of ancestor worship [which] occurs during the Sākamedha. The pitṛyajña is performed in the autumn on the full ion of Kārttika (October-November) or Mārgaśīrṣa (November-December). ... The ritual begins on the new moon, so the moon is waning, that is, 'dying,' and the Ancestors are dead." Sayers mentions that "autumn is the waning of the year, therefore, the tradition may have associated the decline into winter with the Ancestors."[406] He also refers to Hermann Oldenberg who, in wrote about Vedic ceremonies in the late 19th century, that this may be a remnant "of an Indo-European winter all souls feast." Sayers

Chapter 13 - Eating with the Dead: Gone but not Forgotten

is unwilling to commit himself to that historical connection but it fascinates me as it will many of those reading this book.

Cakes, a ritual drink made of milk, and fried grain are offered to "the six types of Ancestors on pieces of pottery." As the ritual progresses, at one point in this beautiful and moving choreography:

> "He mixes portions taken from the cakes, milk-drink, and fried grain to make the rice-balls offered to the Ancestors. While circumambulating the altar in a counter-clockwise direction, either the Adhvaryu or the Sacrificer sprinkles water on it for the Ancestors to wash, then places the three rice balls on three of the corners of the altar also in a counter-clockwise direction: first the father's on the northwest, then the grandfather's on the southwest, and the great-grandfather's on the southeast. All the ritual actors move to the north of the ritual space, leaving the Ancestors to eat."[407]

The Ghost Festival

"The Ghost Festival, also known as the Hungry Ghost Festival in modern day, Zhong Yuan Jie or Yu Lan Jie (traditional Chinese: 盂蘭節) is a traditional Buddhist and Taoist festival held in Asian countries. In the Chinese calendar (a lunisolar calendar), the Ghost Festival is on the 15th night of the seventh month (14th in southern China). ...

"On the fifteenth day the realms of Heaven and Hell and the realm of the living are open and both Taoists and Buddhists would perform rituals to transmute and absolve the sufferings of the deceased. Intrinsic to the Ghost Month is veneration of the dead, where traditionally the filial piety of descendants extends to their ancestors even after their deaths. Activities during the month ... include preparing ritualistic food offerings, burning incense, and burning joss paper, a papier-mâché form of material items such as clothes, gold and other fine goods for the visiting spirits of the ancestors. Elaborate meals (often vegetarian meals) would be served with empty seats for each of the deceased in the family

Chapter 13 - Eating with the Dead: Gone but not Forgotten

treating the deceased as if they are still living. Ancestor worship is what distinguishes Qingming Festival from Ghost Festival because the latter includes paying respects to all deceased, including the same and younger generations, while the former only includes older generations. ...

"These ghosts are believed to be ancestors of those who forgot to pay tribute to them after they died, or those who were never given a proper ritual send-off. They have long needle-thin necks because they have not been fed by their family, or as a punishment so that they are unable to swallow. Family members offer prayers to their deceased relatives, offer food and drink and burn hell bank notes and other forms of joss paper. Joss paper items are believed to have value in the afterlife, considered to be very similar in some aspects to the material world. People burn paper houses, cars, servants and televisions to please the ghosts. Families also pay tribute to other unknown wandering ghosts so that these homeless souls do not intrude on their lives and bring misfortune. A large feast is held for the ghosts on the fourteenth day of the seventh month, when people bring samples of food and places them on an offering table to please the ghosts and ward off bad luck."[408]

⊂⊃

"I conjure thee: of the Earth, a gift of Her bounty; Grains which grow 'neath Her light and ripen in His glory... Oh Cakes, that thou nourish the temples of our souls. Let us share in love and feast in joy.

"I conjure thee: of the Earth, a gift of Her bounty; herbs of the Mother, Honey of the bees, Nectar of the Gods... Oh Cup of Life, that in sharing we create the bonds of joy."[409]

Chapter 13 - Eating with the Dead: Gone but not Forgotten

Notes for Chapter 13

[390] James Thayer Addison, *Life Beyond Death In the Beliefs of Mankind*, Houghton Mifflin Co., © 1932, page 16

[391] James Thayer Addison, *Life Beyond Death In the Beliefs of Mankind*, Houghton Mifflin Co., © 1932, page 23

[392] James Thayer Addison, *Life Beyond Death In the Beliefs of Mankind*, Houghton Mifflin Co., © 1932, page 32

[393] James Thayer Addison, *Life Beyond Death In the Beliefs of Mankind*, Houghton Mifflin Co., © 1932, page 32

[394] James Thayer Addison, *Life Beyond Death In the Beliefs of Mankind*, Houghton Mifflin Co., © 1932, page 35

[395] in *Religions of the Ancient World: A Guide*, Johnston, Sarah Iles (ed.), The Belknap Press of Harvard University Press, Cambridge and London, © 2004, page 470 *Introduction* by John J. Collins

[396] *Death and Burial in the Roman World*, J. M. C. Toynbee, The Johns Hopkins University Press, Baltimore © 1971, page 51

[397] As near as I can translate on my own, it has to do with a rapid union with the Earth. When I put that phrase into my search engine the only source I found was an archaeologist's work with a tomb ... with that epitaph ... and in a Latin language I did not recognize.

[398] Toynbee's translation, provided in an endnote: "I am ash, ash is earth, earth is a goddess, therefore I am not dead."

[399] *Death and Burial in the Roman World*, J. M. C. Toynbee, The Johns Hopkins University Press, Baltimore © 1971, page 37

[400] James Thayer Addison, *Life Beyond Death In the Beliefs of Mankind*, Houghton Mifflin Co., © 1932, page 36

[401] http://voices.yahoo.com/native-american-burial-ritual-feast-dead-7299864.html

[402] http://en.wikipedia.org/wiki/Sky_burial 27 xi 2008 ce

Chapter 13 - Eating with the Dead: Gone but not Forgotten

[403] James Thayer Addison, *Life Beyond Death In the Beliefs of Mankind*, Houghton Mifflin Co., © 1932, page 37

[404] Sayers, Matthew R., *Feeding the Dead: Ancestor Worship in Ancient India*, Oxford University Press, New York NY © 2013, page 43

[405] Sayers, Matthew R., *Feeding the Dead: Ancestor Worship in Ancient India*, Oxford University Press, New York NY © 2013, page 43

[406] Sayers, Matthew R., *Feeding the Dead: Ancestor Worship in Ancient India*, Oxford University Press, New York NY © 2013, page 44

[407] Sayers, Matthew R., *Feeding the Dead: Ancestor Worship in Ancient India*, Oxford University Press, New York NY © 2013, pages 44-45

[408] http://en.wikipedia.org/wiki/Ghost_Festival

[409] from *The Ritual of Lothloriën* by the author. These are used to bless the cakes and the drink which are shared as communion.

Chapter 14 - How do I view death as a Wiccan Priest?

There's nothing wrong with being compost

For one who has taken his birth, death is certain; and for one who is dead, birth is certain. Therefore, in the unavoidable discharge of your duty, you should not lament."[410]

Why is it that it's taken me over twenty seven years' work on this manuscript and I am not yet done? [Unfortunately, this does mean a few of my memories are told in this book more than once.] Death fascinates me. I do not recall ever having a *fear* of death. I certainly knew that there were some modes of dying for which I had absolutely no desire. Even today I think of death in a fire as abhorrent. If I learn of a death by fire I inevitably feel a deeper compassion and send fervent hopes into the Universe that that individual or those people were not awake and conscious. That intense pain combined with the knowledge that it would bring death seems particularly terrifying.

I am not afraid of dying. Early on when I began walking this path (even a few years before I was aware enough to notice the 'street' signs), I was given the privilege of having my fears tested. In January, 1974, I came home from work at 1:00 am to find my apartment occupied by a stranger. My friend, Jim, was there. He sometimes sofa-surfed and had been temporarily staying in my apartment and was scared as all get-go.

Armed and dangerous

One of my coworkers, Alicia[411], a lovely woman my age, had spent some time working as a teacher in the Pine Ridge Indian Reservation, South Dakota. Pine Ridge was one of the poorest areas in the United

Chapter 14 - How do I view death as a Wiccan Priest?

States. Reservation life combined with internal dissent between those who were growing increasingly dissatisfied and those who were more traditional. Not only was it an area of great unrest, but many of the Oglala Lakota began following the American Indian Movement, ready to stand up and fight for their rights.

Alicia had become deeply involved with Frank, a man plagued with alcohol addiction and always ready to fight. His intense possessiveness caused Alicia to flee the reservation when his drinking and obsession with her (as well as seeing her as part of the establishment's problems), took their relationship into abuse.

Frank was in federal custody for murder, according to both Alicia and Frank. Feeling safe with him in prison, she began responding to his requests for correspondence. This only fueled his passion, and he broke out of prison and made his way to Rochester, Minnesota. Alicia had given Frank only a post office box so he did not know where she was, but he was able to track me down, knowing that I was a friend and coworker.

Armed and drinking, Frank went from a melancholy drunk obsessed with finding Alicia to his AIM militant anger. As he drank his way through all of the beer and alcohol I had, I became the target for his anger and focal point for all the sins of the white invaders who had taken away their land.

Already convicted of murder, he had nothing to lose.

I was there in my home striving to be a more spiritual and equitable person. I was fully sympathetic and compassionate regarding the treatment of the First Peoples, herded into squalor, all of their land and resources taken away. Angry? You bet. I would have been. Had I been Lakota, trapped in that squalor, I could have turned violent. There I was, drinking a little of my beer while Frank grew more and more angry. He would hold the gun at my head, ready to pull the trigger if I sounded too much like the white bureaucracy.

I could sense how having power left him fearless and reckless. Those who have lost everything and have no power can in turn become ruthless themselves when suddenly holding power in their hands. Somehow Frank loved the idea of killing me for the white man's sins. He also suspected - rightly - that I knew where he could find Alicia

Chapter 14 - How do I view death as a Wiccan Priest?

despite my pretense of not knowing.

And then, I realized that either he was going to or not. I'd had it. I said, "Frank, either you're going to kill me or not. If you do, then it doesn't matter, but if you don't, I have to work tomorrow and I'm tired." I told him I was going to bed and went upstairs to my bedroom.

I knew, then, that what I'd said was sincere. There was no more direct way to say it. Then the worst. Frank saw my act as trusting him and came up, sitting on the edge of my bed, babbling on and on, his anger gone, about how I clearly had trusted him. Damn. I still wasn't getting any sleep.

Two hours later the FBI arrived. Frank was now docile and they took him away. And I began rereading my copy of the Evans-Wentz.*Tibetan Book of the Dead*.

> "As *The Tibetan Book of the Dead* teaches, the dying should face death not only calmly and clear-mindedly and heroically, but with an intellect rightly trained and rightly directed, mentally transcending, if need be, bodily suffering and infirmities, as they would be able to do had they practised efficiently during their active lifetime the Art of Living, and, when about to die, the Art of Dying."[412]

Interestingly - and it only now occurs to me - it was close to a year later when I met my teachers and came to understand that the religious lifestyle I craved as a child and the path I looked for as a Profound Agnostic (my 'adult' religion) would be taking me into becoming the founder of a Wiccan Tradition and of a Wiccan Church.

There were not so many of us, back then, compared with today's Wiccan and neopagan populations. Most of us knew each other, and one couple that I so enjoyed were Bob and Christina. Bob was taller than I, something of a rock musician in appearance. For some reason today I am thinking him Jethro Tull-like. And Chris? She was not very tall, just the sweetest but also brilliant woman. She was an inch below the legal size for adult human stature and, in those days, was technically defined as a midget. Nobody cared. It was part of their charm.

Chapter 14 - How do I view death as a Wiccan Priest?

And then... she died. Suddenly and unexpectedly. The genetic problems associated with her size brought her down. And Bob? Bob was devastated. They had been so in love and he was completely bereft.

Attending her funeral, I was somewhat aghast. All of her identity as a Wiccan Priestess, as well-loved leader of a coven, was stripped away as her family buried her as if she had never strayed from their fundamentalist Christian church, and Bob was too grief-stricken to do anything but continue weeping.

Christina would have been furious. And probably was, but not with Bob.

"The Victorian celebration of death represented a society-wide desire to honour the dead, and a large measure of agreement upon what forms that honour could, and indeed should, take."[413]

And I went home and began writing what would become the Ritual for the Dead for the Wiccan Church I had founded. I realized that none of us seemed to be prepared to handle death, and yet as we were part of a religious movement considered both a Mystery and a Fertility Religion, death was a part of life.

I was so passionate about the importance of our embracing death and bringing that dialogue into our religion, that I began writing a book on death and dying. Less than two years after completing the Ritual for the Dead of Lothloriën, I was diagnosed with HIV in March of 1988.

I tried, but it was just too odd to be writing a book on death and dying, when that was my life and I was considered likely to die within a handful of years. Was I afraid of death then? No, it just seemed markedly inconvenient. The work I was doing, devoting my life to the church which grew around my Priesthood, was far more important. I set the book aside. Ensuring the survival of my Wiccan Tradition was paramount.

Three years later, I arrived in Los Angeles having been detoured in Dallas. My plans were, before heading back to Minneapolis, to take a few years with the students I had in southern California. One of them was a delightful young woman working on her graduate degree in folklore and mythology. She made arrangements with the faculty in charge, and suddenly I had a new world of academic research into death and dying. You can thank UCLA for at least half of the primary books I turned to when writing this one.

I accomplished a lot of research, leading to pages and pages and pages of quoted passages with page numbers.

I moved into serious author mode, which led to a number of my books in print as well as my moving north to Rose Hill where my partner had earlier purchased land and a little house. Moving here in June of 1994, there was work to do. The church to administer, students to teach, publishing deadlines, bookkeeping and so much more, and in the spare time, we dug. We saved all the soil and composted the weed-ridden sod.

For more than twelve years, almost all spare time was spent digging. The books I did complete were written chapter by chapter as monthly columns in *The Hermit's Lantern* or *The Unicorn*. And my book on Death and Dying sat dormant.

"In *Elements of Social Organization*, Firth (1964:63) observes... that the funeral provides three elements to the living. The first element is the resolution of uncertainties in the behavior of the immediate kin. The funeral provides relatives with an opportunity to display their grief publicly and establishes a period of time for mourning. As such, it is a ritual of closure that also links our understanding of death at the psychological and societal level.

"The second element is the fulfillment of social consequence. This means that the ceremony helps to reinforce the appropriate attitudes of the members of society to each other. Although it focuses on the dead person, the funeral points out the value of the services of the living. Once again, societal and individual comprehensions of death are reflected in everyday ritualistic practices.

"The third element is the economic aspect. Firth explains that every funeral involves the expenditure of money, goods, and services. In this sense, the exchange process is important to the bereaved on a tangible social and economic level. Bereaved people may feel the need to make restitution to the deceased by purchasing such non-abstract items as funeral feasts, funeral merchandise, religious services, and so forth."[414]

"In *The Elementary Forms of Religious Life*, Durkheim (1915:435) points out that funeral rites are ceremonies that designate a state of 'uneasiness or sadness.' From this perspective, death produces personal anxieties, which are addressed by the funeral, a ceremony that is indicative of a society's overall comprehension of death. In this sense, then funeral rites mirror a society's interpretation of life and death."[415]

About two years after having the 45,000 square foot private botanical and ritual garden dug by hand (only old foolish men who love gardening would do that), a series of seemingly minor medical events took me to Evergreen Hospital for an preemptive appendectomy. The inflammation was mild but just enough that I went to the emergency room early in the morning just to see.

Just before I was put under, Dr. Marion Johnson asked me if any abnormalities about my kidneys had ever been mentioned. When I said no, she made me promise to have her suspected 'something' checked out. For three months I worked my way through progressively more detailed imaging. Whatever it was was something in reality and more imaging was needed. X-rays, then ultrasound, then CT scan, then MRI.

In August, 2008, I sat down with Dr. Tom Takayama, a brilliant surgeon. I would describe him as 'cutting edge,' but today he is one of those gifted surgeons who likes to cut as little as possible. We met with Dr. Takayama on August 6th. He set forth the possible course of events, pending the final imaging and testing. The following week he confirmed that yes, I did have malignant tumors, two of them on each kidney. And he simply stated the morning I was to be there for surgery.

I got everything together. We had only minor legal matters, having already been proactive, and off I went. My first major surgery was a

Chapter 14 - How do I view death as a Wiccan Priest?

success. That doctor is so fine! I was discharged from the hospital a week later, and home I went.

I was not yet ready for the bed and spent the night in my leather chair, a Scandinavian recliner. When Gerry left for work early in the morning around 4:00 am, I mentioned feeling possibly a little constipated.

Within perhaps half an hour, I was on the commode and life began slipping away. Something was wrong. I went into shock and knew that I had to have Gerry at home. With a new incision on my left sewn shut with sutures, a catheter and all manner of indications of major surgery, I could not arrive by ambulance without being able to communicate my immediate history.

I was unable to stay upright, so I crawled on all four limbs. It took me a long time, I think an hour, to retrieve the phone number from my wallet in the bedroom. I was losing blood internally at such a rate I was falling in and out of consciousness, and going from being so warm there were literally small puddles on the floor to chills so extreme I could not make even one forward step, the shaking was so violent.

A quick stop at the nearest emergency room and back across the lake to the University of Washington hospital. In the emergency room and further questions, and IVs...Suddenly Dr. Takayama was there, with a lot of medical staff. It was determined that my spleen must have pretty much exploded, and off I went for life-saving surgery. *Somehow* once again I had good timing. Good timing results from right living. Dr. Wright, the surgeon most able to save my life happened to be at the hospital early and was available. And my life was saved. Days in intensive care with tubes and monitors and (the absolute worst) a breathing tube.

And then, finally I was recovered enough for the *other* partial nephrectomy when Dr. Takayama removed the other two tumors from my right kidney.

My score card was looking quite good. Let's see. As a child I nearly drowned in the Black River when in a boat with my parents who were fishing. Death 0 - Me 1.

Chapter 14 - How do I view death as a Wiccan Priest?

In University, one night out for a midnight drive in the winter with Doug Wisby on a country road, when I had a fleeting image and told Doug that we needed to take action in an accident. A half minute later and the little car went sliding on some ice, rolled over and ended upside down half over the edge of a steep drop into a major, icy river. We had both followed my advice and emerged, unscathed.

Death 0 - Me 2.

The night with a drunken murderer? Death 0 - Me 3.

My HIV diagnosis? Death 0 - Me 4.

My three major surgeries in three months to become a cancer survivor (Death 0 - Me 5) who has had a splenectomy. Death 0 - Me 6.

My adult life is pretty good. My life is more than pretty good. I have emerged from a childhood so unhappy that I often wished that I could simply run off with death. I survived my early years having a genetic disposition toward depression plus being gay and Wiccan in an era when I didn't know what either was - other than everything I wanted to be. Did this mean I should end up in hell forever? Life-ending thoughts were almost never far from mind, but I made it.

As a professional astrologer I understood death. As an herbalist and horticulturalist? I accepted death. And in my own life, Death and I have often danced. Living with HIV for three decades, being arrogant and assuming I would somehow never die was not an option.

I live my life fully. I often work 80 to 90 hours a week which includes activities like gardening, teaching, writing books, and so much more. Death is a friend, and for a long time I've been very upfront about my own death being welcome when the time comes.

Living with these gardens that Rev. Gerry and I have planted and tend? We live in paradise, but it is all the result of our labor, our time, our money, and our love. For quite a few years I've said that when my time comes, I want to just go out into the gardens, lay down, and sink into the soil. Now *that* would be a fantasy death. I've gone around for many years, now, telling people that "there's nothing wrong with being compost."

I am aging and parts wear out. I have few complications from living with HIV other than having a greater appreciation of many things, including modern pharmaceuticals which I once called "my death-defying drugs."

One beautiful early summer day in 2011 I was working in the Yarrow Bed next to our Garden Barn.

Working vigorously, I was in bliss, as One with the Universe, tending Mother Earth, my hands in the soil like a child running baby fingers through the Mother's hair. It's so intimate.

I suddenly felt dizzy. I am so rarely dizzy in life (hold your jokes, please) that I went to stand up. I wondered if there might be an impending earthquake. During my years living in Los Angeles many people spoke about feeling a wave of dizziness or vertigo a minute or so ahead of the first shock. It was strong enough that when I tried to stand, the best option was to sit right down on my rear, and continue right on, tending the soil.

And then .... I woke up. I looked at the time, and it was perhaps 15 minute later, but I lay there, on my back, the soil soft, comforting and comfortable, the sun warm... It was true. When my time comes, laying on the soil? Sinking into it? I could not imagine a more delicious way to transition out of inhabiting this body.

It was time for Rev. Gerry to come home from work so I went up to the cottage and checked some of the prescriptions.

The years of increasing neuropathy from HIV combined with the neurological 'issues' from having had 34" of muscle and nerve endings severed during the three surgeries which needed to access the abdominal cavity? Sometimes it's like the lower and upper halves of my body have difficult communicating via the neural network. My neurologist, Dr. Weiss, had recently made changes in my medication. "May cause dizziness." Check. "May cause fainting." Check. With my years of telling people about wanting to lay down in the soil, I was so delighted. Now I had validation that it would be the best way to go.

Several months later on October 4th, I met with Dr. Weiss at the University of Washington. I was eager to tell him the funny story I had about the side effects from the medicine and how it fit my story. He was livid.

He informed me that those prescriptions couldn't do that. I parried, "but the studies..." and he was adamant. I thought he was excessive

Chapter 14 - How do I view death as a Wiccan Priest?

and overreactive, but I drove home wearing an ECG 24 hour monitor. I sent it back to the University, and we proceeded to relocate the Stone Circle. That's a long story, and the only relevant point here is that I personally moved over a ton of rock over the three days we worked.

We finished around 4:30 Monday afternoon, October 10th. At 6:00 pm Dr. Weiss called. He had a Cardiologist waiting and wanted me to drive over to the University... immediately. Well, I couldn't do that. I had a Tuesday morning appointment with a young couple for counseling. The husband was due to leave for Afghanistan, and I was the nearest Wiccan Priest they could find, even though it was 50 miles each way from the base to Rose Hill. It was then or never, and they *really* needed time with me.

When I suggested to Dr. Weiss, "How about Wednesday?" he was not amused.

"You could die," he said, for apparently I'd been snuggling with Death back in June when I lay happily in the Sun. "What would happen then?" he asked.

"If I die, we have a contingency plan," I answered, which is true. "But if I'm not dead, I'm a Priest and responsible first. "

Wednesday I walked into the ER at the University and came home many days later with a pacemaker. Death 0 - Me 7.

How do I view Death? Death is beautiful. Not all modes of death are at all desirable, and some would cause abject terror, but that's the pain, that's not Death.

⁂

"And the Wheel turns and the Wheel turns. And the Wheel turns again. And so it shall be as the Wheel turns us into infinity. For there are no endings which were not birthed in beginnings; and there are no beginnings which shall not lead each of us to the Gates of Death. And there is no reality in

Chapter 14 - How do I view death as a Wiccan Priest?

which the Gates of Death do not lead to the Cauldron of Rebirth."[416]

Notes for Chapter 14

[410] *Ghagavad-Gita As It is*, A. C. Ghaktivedanta Swami Prabhupāda, The Bhaktivedanta Book Trust, Los Angeles © 1981

[411] I will use fictional names for these individuals as I relate this real life experience.

[412] *The Tibetan Book of the Dead*, compiled and edited by W.Y. Evans-Wentz Oxford University Press © 1960; preface to the second edition, W.Y. Evans-Wentz, pages xiv-xv

[413] "Why Was Death So Big In Victorian Britain?" by Ruth Richardson in *Death, Ritual, and Bereavement*, Routledge in association with the Social History Society of the United Kingdom, London, New York © 1989, page 115

[414] "Prologue: Principles of Thanatology" by Arthur C. Carr, *Principles of Thanatology*, ed. Kutscher, Carr and Kutscher, Columbia University Press © 1987, pages 13-14

[415] "Prologue: Principles of Thanatology" by Arthur C. Carr, *Principles of Thanatology*, ed. Kutscher, Carr and Kutscher, Columbia University Press © 1987, page 15

[416] From *The Holy Books of the Devas* by the author

Appendices

I - Entering the Wiccan Bardo

Reflection[417] [published in 1999 CE]

When I first wrote this chapter, I had been recently diagnosed with HIV. I was, at most, 40 and I had barely reached my spiritual maturity. As I work on revising this edition ten years have passed and, before this revision is complete, I will observe my eleventh anniversary. During this time I have conducted workshops in death and dying in many cities. The first was in Los Angeles at a Wiccan gathering. When I proposed the workshop to the organizers, it was rejected. I was told my topic was 'too morbid.' I submitted a new, vague proposal for a workshop 'dealing with ritual' and, when my appointed time began, went ahead and discussed the issues of death and dying. I believe strongly that we must face these issues. Those present were very pleased and I was asked to repeat the workshop a couple years later. For me any serious discussion of religion must include a discussion of death, for death is the key to the very soul of any religious philosophy. The nature of religion is to guide us in the manner of our lives so that the process of dying brings us to our goals.

In truth, there was a period during which I was uncertain whether it was my time to pass through the veil and seek Initiation into the Bardo through death. It took many months of deteriorating health and the collapse of what had appeared to be a promised life. But death was not mine and I set out upon a journey across the desert which unexpectedly brought me to the true fulfillment of my dreams. And this is one of the Mysteries of Life: there are those times we must experience a Death (in any one of Her splendid forms) in order to experience rebirth.

As a Tradition matures, it is unavoidable that those within it come to know the passing of loved ones. We are yet a young Tradition, barely more than two decades old, and we have not seen the passing of any prominent Members. We continue to prepare the astral temple and discuss and rehearse the Ritual for the Dead. The Charge of the Beloved was read at Trinity College in San Antonio, Texas, where I flew in for the memorial service of my dear friend and Church Member, Claude Zetty, back in 1991. The only Wiccan present, the words from our Ritual for the Dead moved people and brought them great comfort. Passages from the Ritual for the Dead have often been integrated into memorial services. Thus far The Ritual for the Dead has yet to be worked in its entirety while providing that final Initiation of a Beloved into the Bardo. Among the steps leading to this revision was my acquiring a larger and stronger computer system. As a consequence, one of my projects has been to take 25 years of natal charts from my work as an astrologer and enter them into computer files. The number of those who have passed over since I first wrote the Bardo *is humbling. I had not expected the actual number of people who have passed over into the Otherworld during such a brief decade. Although I remember friends and priests and priestesses and relatives and those who were woven deeply into my life, there were also many more than a hundred gay men who had been clients or those with whom I had worked as a priest. And there were the passing of some with whom I was bonded by both flesh and soul. Given the nature of the virus which is my companion, I cannot say that I anticipated that the work of my priesthood would today still be a seven-days-a-week vocation as we turn the wheel of civilization to the year 2000. When I wrote the first edition, it was my goal to see a group of individuals fully trained, able to conduct the Ritual for the Dead for my spirit. My body ready for compost, I would have gathered my magickal will, my memories and desires and taken the steps to the Temple of Loriën. As I waited among the familiar stones, my loved ones would gather upon our planet and begin guiding me through this powerful Initiation. Instead, I am writing a revision and our lives today are centered about the cycles of our gardens. We maintain the Memorial Grove, a small wooded garden where hang numerous bells and wind chimes which send their music among the Douglas firs and cedars and giant-leaved maples in memory of those who have passed over, and we live our days with joy for life and a love and respect for death and dying.*

Entering the Wiccan Bardo[418]

Death exists in the Universe with the same levels of joy and reality as does birth. For the soul which dies free from fear, death is a spreading of one's spiritual wings, the ability to merge into the Dreaming and find rest and recreation before again entering the womb. For those rare Christians who experience that which Buddhists call right dying, death is a gateway to the astral temple known as heaven, filled with the creations of the beloved's religion. Those who die with fear and guilt are more likely to enter other realms which are truly, in effect, astral temples created of the images of hell and of purgatory. No wonder that death, in so much of the world, is considered an evil thing.

Our Western culture clings to sensate reality as a balm against the fear of dying. Death is perceived as the culmination of all our worst fears. Medicine devotes untold costs to prolonging life. I prefer the way of the Inuit. Give me an iceberg upon which to sit and contemplate the Universe as the Crone's footsteps grow louder. I have no interest in numerous surgeries and gross amounts of chemicals with which to provide me final years spent barely conscious in a nursing home. Modern medicine encourages us to hang on at any cost. I would rather it promoted an understanding and acceptance of the realities and necessity of death in its appropriate time. But perhaps it is the work of the Priest/ess to teach us to be gracious when the time is placed before us.

Many death anxieties are born of terror instilled in a Christian culture. How many Christians might honestly face death believing that they are without sin? And what has Western culture taught those humans to expect? So many of those who practiced their religions faithfully remain terrified, expecting great suffering in a hell of their worst fears after their bodies have died. Can that truly be the gift of the same deity who is called All-Loving? And many others in those same religions continue to doubt that there is any existence beyond that of the body. No wonder there is fear of the unknowable when what our peoples are taught can only fill them with dread. We are not taught to move forward and embrace change. We are not told that a corollary to the deism, "God is everywhere," implies that our souls, our spirits, do not become extinct at the time of the body's demise.

There are cultures in which religion works to provide the means of escaping the ebb and flow of reincarnation. Life in those cultures is, typically, that of hardship, starvation, and deprivation; and it is beyond the human potential to wish to return again to such a hell. Yet those same cultures are often those in which the Priest/esshood is known for its ability to exert control over the rebirth process. Within those cultures there are many substantiated cases in which trained teachers consciously choose to reincarnate. There are even dramatic, from a Western perspective, examples, most notably the Tibetan traditions. Yet I seriously question whether escape from the wheel of death and rebirth is truly an option.

Personally, I have no desire to 'escape.' My love for this planet and for all who live upon Her is strong and unshakable. I have worked to develop this love and to make it non-selective, to include those who make me uncomfortable and those who live far outside my ethical and moral reality. There are mountains I have yet to see, oceans to swim in and tides to watch. There are cities I have yet to explore, holy places which call me. And before I can live throughout the world, I fully intend to reincarnate to my beloved Mothervalley. Perhaps I shall return again and again until I know all of the Mother's special places on this Earth and can take that knowledge with me into some black hole - Cauldron of the Goddess - to share with the Universe as it passes through the death and rebirth of a new reality.

Many of us believe that reincarnation is a desirable choice. We believe our work is unlikely to be done in one lifetime and no matter how painful the lessons which wait in the next life, one incarnation is insufficient to fulfill a Priest/esshood. I welcome my return. It will take me far more than one lifetime to evolve myself and attain my personal goals before I feel that my share in The Work is complete. Far more time is needed to finish weaving the threads of karma with those who share in my Circles and to snip other threads and take my parting from this Earth.

If death is a reality, ought we not transform it into a time of spiritual growth? There are role models for us in Asian religions and it is a challenge for modern Wiccans to create new role models for the future.

And I am of the Wicca. The thought of returning, according to the lore of Witchcraft, and of holding anew my athame, of reclaiming a Book of Shadows of Lothloriën in a disciplined, loving manner, is exciting. A common mind-game of humans is to sit and daydream about how we would do it differently if we had it to do over again. We do have it to do over again (in our next life) and I, for one, shall return. The strength of a Mystery Tradition exists in knowing that the teachers of future generations will be more wise than we. It is exciting to contemplate returning to the same Tradition, able to pursue Higher Ideals than I did this time, to quiet my Virgo self-criticism, which has known all along that an even better performance has been possible. I tell it, "Next life."

How does one pursue such an intent? By carefully working with the nature of desire and by selecting the images one holds sacred and constant within one's being, one moves along a Path to union with those images. It is this principle which reunites us with those we both love and hate, for their images are yoked to the emotional desire - both good and bad - which link us to those persons. But breaking away from the innate paths to use reincarnation as a spiritual discipline requires training and skill in the arts of visualization and control over one's mind and emotions. The process is enhanced when one lives with the knowledge of the realities of the Universe. Guilt over human failings is destructive. Better one should learn to make changes and continue moving forward with growth and an ever-increasing positive lifestyle. The achievement of goals in one's next incarnation requires keeping those goals constantly in focus and realizing that the work of the Higher Priest/esshood embraces far more than a single incarnation. Thus may one live more free of emotional constraints over the ups and downs of life, for when viewed from the mountain, they are of little significance.

Yet, one cannot become so enmeshed in spirituality that sight of the mundane, manifest reality becomes lost. As above, so below. In the same context as these laws, this life affects the next. If you continually work upon improvement and learn from your mistakes, your next life will be inevitably better. If you learn to work within all levels of manifest and non-manifest reality and keep yourself free from excess attachment to those realities, your next life holds greater wisdom than this. One of the most useful ways 'to keep pure your Highest Ideals' is to be mindful of your next incarnation. For those who work within a Tradition, the images and symbols of that religion ought be as ingrained as any desire. For the Priest/ess, religion is life, lived daily. I am reminded of a phrase I heard from my first Wiccan teacher. He said that, when asked why he was a Witch, his response was "because I can be nothing else."

This Ritual for the Dead should be conducted by an ordained Minister of The Tradition of Lothloriën of The Rowan Tree Church. The process of providing guidance for the Beloved's soul requires the skill and training of an adept. At this point in our Tradition's evolution, performed with far less frequency than The Ritual of Lothloriën and other ritual forms, The Ritual for the Dead remains one of the most important rites for those who work as Priest/esses of this Tradition.

Influenced by the Bardo Thödol of Tibet, the Ritual for the Dead may be conducted over a period of seven days, performed for any Rowan Tree Church member, whether or not that member has chosen to pursue the Initiatory Path. The ritual form has been established so that this rite is easily adapted for any person of any belief system, even if not affiliated with our Church. A Wiccan may, for example, choose to have this ritual performed for a family member, assisting that relative in moving into the Bardo realm. When performed as a single ritual, this form is of use for anyone who wishes spiritual assistance.

For Initiates of our Tradition and members of our Church, preparation for this rite includes not only the legal will, but also the compilation of what we call a 'Spiritual Will.' A Spiritual Will is essential in determining the disposition of one's ritual tools. For example, if one has taken a goblet and, through ritual, transformed it into a sacred chalice, it has been removed from the mundane world. The acquisition of magickal possessions implies a responsibility for all Priest/esses to determine the disposition of one's sacred tools.

In addition, this ritual form is designed to assist those who are pursuing the goal of Right Return, or attempting to carry spiritual training and disciplines into the next incarnation and, as is believed by the common lore of our Wiccan religion, being reunited with one's athame and those with whom we share the expressions of our religion. In the absence of a Spiritual Will, one's Mentor will proffer advice, but generally one's tools will be left to the whims of whichever family member has *the legal right* to deal with all the property of your estate, whether mundane or whether Magickal. The Sevenday Rite may also be performed for Priest/esses of Traditions other than that of Lothloriën, or for any person who elects to move into the next realm of being with the workings of The Ritual for the Dead.

This ritual will be scheduled when arrangements have been completed with either a funeral home or crematorium. In the absence of cremation, ashes from the First Day's fire may be substituted if so ordained in the Spiritual Will of the Beloved. The term 'Beloved' is used to refer to the deceased person, for it indicates emotional attachment yet enables us to begin the essential process of detachment which allows the deceased to move more easily into the Bardo realm, set free of this reality. Typically, the ritual will be performed so that the cremated remains enter the Temple on the Second Day of the Sevenday Rite.

The Ritual for the Dead, in its most complete form, takes place over a seven day period, with the burial of the Athame completing an additional 28 day lunar cycle. It is hoped that the power of this rite effectively separates the Beloved from attachment to the Earth plane and sets the spirit upon its journey into the future incarnation(s). That journey will ultimately complete a cycle when the Beloved returns again into this Priest/esshood. Life and Death are all Circles, and this rite is an Initiation into the future.

The printed brochure containing the information given to family and guests when we conduct the rite contains the following description of the ritual and of the beliefs which it expresses:

"*It is our belief that Death is a time of spiritual wonder, an opportunity to seek Union with the Divine. In this aspect, Death is like an Initiation into a state of religious being.*

"The state of being which follows the death of the body is similar to that of dreaming: the mind continues to experience, to imagine and to create; yet there is no substance, no Earth, for this is the astral (or place of the stars) world of being. It is for that reason that the process of dying is best accompanied by joy and a willingness to send the Beloved off with good wishes for a wonderful journey. This joy is for the coming Union with the Divine Being, the Beloved having gracefully let go of the past.

"The Rites you are going to experience are filled with the symbols of rituals drawn from many cultures, from the formidable heights of the Himalayas to customs of the Hopis; from the gentlest of Nature Religions to the imaginative imagery of a child.

"The Ritual will take place as a Circle, for a Circle is the oldest of symbols for the Divine, and within that sacred space will we send the Beloved's spirit into the new life which exists after the body's death.

"You will note that there are two Circles. The Inner Circle is composed of those who are functioning as clergy: the actual Minister and those working in assistance, either the four who represent the elements of Air, Fire, Water and Earth, or those who are the Dancers. These people will be working together to perform ritual theater which symbolically recreates, in a microcosm of manifest reality, our beloved planet. There will be various activities which take place between the Circles, for this represents between the worlds of God/dess and of humans.

"We believe that this Rite will assist the separation of the spirit from the mundane world, helping it to free itself of material and emotional attachments that hold it back from Union with the Divine. That journey into Union will ultimately complete a cycle, and the Beloved will again return. For even the seasons turn in Circles, as do all functions of being, of time, and even of death."

The Ritual for the Dead not only provides a specific spiritual space (a combination of the actual temple and the astral temple) which serves as the focus for the ritual work to assist the Beloved in transformation, but this particular Ritual is one of dance, for dance not only enhances the Initiation into the Bardo but it may also enhance the healing of emotions. Death should be embraced as an act of beauty.

Appendices : I - Entering the Wiccan Bardo

Notes for Appendix I

[417] The 'Reflection' was written in 1999 for the second edition of *A Wiccan Bardo*, as the '*Revisited*' aspect of the book.

[418] "Entering the Wiccan Bardo" was written perhaps in 1988 for the original edition of *A Wiccan Bardo*. This is the opening to Chapter 7.

II - A Commentary on The Ritual for the Dead[419]

It is a religious truth and belief within Lothloriën that Death is a time of spiritual wonder, an opportunity to seek Union with the Divine. In this aspect, Death is an Initiation into a state of religious being. It is for that reason that the process of dying is best accompanied by joy and a willingness to send the Beloved off with good wishes for a wonderful journey. Death ought not be approached with fear, but with awe and even a sense of delight. This joy is for the coming Union with the Divine Being, the Beloved having gracefully let go of the past. We believe that The Ritual for the Dead will assist in the separation of the spirit from attraction to the mundane world, helping it to free itself of emotional and material attachments which hold it back from Union with the Divine. That journey into Union will ultimately complete a cycle and the Beloved will again return. For even the seasons turn in Circles, as do all functions of being, of time, and even of death and birth.

The natural state of being which follows the death of the body is similar to that of dreaming: the mind continues to experience, to imagine and to create; yet there is no substance, no Earth for this is the astral (or 'star') world of being. Many cultures and religions have used ritual forms and well-defined images to provide the soul/spirit with control when in the Bardo. In Lothloriën our training provides us with a number of these forms. Our training to work with the four elements (in The First Ordeal) provides a very rudimentary collection of tools which will help the mind to stabilize itself having entered the immediate chaos of the Bardo.

Later, The Ritual of Lothloriën takes those mental tools much further, as does the work with the Temple of Loriën. It is for this reason your skill in learning to work The Ritual of Lothloriën in the astral is essential. Not only does this provide you with skill as a Mentor, as a High Priest/ess, but it also enables you to carry those skills with you when you will no more return to the body which is your present mundane temple.

Appendices : II - A Commentary on The Ritual for the Dead

The Ritual of the Dead is filled with the symbols of rituals common to many cultures, from the formidable heights of the Himalayas to customs of the Hopis; from the gentlest of Nature Religions to the imaginative imagery of a child. And yet, it is but an extension of The Ritual of Lothloriën. Now, as a High Priest/ess, you begin to study this ritual to a depth previously unknown. Not only will you learn how to use this ritual form to guide another to the Otherworld but you will develop an intimate knowledge of this rite to further your *own* Initiation at the hand of the Crone. Knowing this ritual well, carrying The Charge of the Beloved memorized within your heart, when the day comes, as it will, that The Ritual of the Dead will be performed for you, the bond between you and the Inner Circle will be strong and there will be many of Lothloriën to assist you in carrying your wisdom, your skills into the Bardo, there to take yourself to your own astral temple in such a manner that you can maintain the ability to visit the astral temples of Lothloriën through choice and to continue your work as a Priest/ess from the other side of the veil.

Preparations of a High Priest/ess

As written for Church Members and the public, "the Ritual will take place as a Circle, for a Circle is the oldest of symbols for the Divine, and within that sacred space will we send the Beloved's spirit into the new life which exists after the body's death. You will note that there are two Circles. The Inner Circle is composed of those who are functioning as clergy: the actual Minister and those working in assistance, either the four who represent the elements of Air, Fire, Water and Earth, or the Dancers. These people will be working together to perform ritual theatre which symbolically recreates our beloved planet and is a microcosm for manifest reality. There will be various activities which take place between the Circles, for this symbolically represents the present state of the soul's being; somewhat 'between the worlds' of God/dess and of humans. The Outer Circle is established with the seating for the friends, relatives and guests who are joining with us to wish the Beloved well on this journey into the Dreaming."

The Inner Circle is thus composed of the Priest/esshood and Bards of Lothloriën who are trained to link their skills with yours and help you achieve success in Right Dying and in making your transition to the Otherworld a successful Initiation. For a future generation, spending many years working the same ritual forms with other trained Initiates will create powerful abilities to meet again in astral temples.

The Ritual For The Dead, in its complete form, will take place over a seven day period, with the burial of the athame taking an additional 28 day lunar cycle. Circumstances will require a certain amount of flexibility but the importance of the two cycles should not be diminished. The primary factor in determining the Ritual of Parting and Farewell should be a balance between the ability of family and guests to attend and the service of cremation. It may be of importance to the family that the container of ashes be present at this Ritual. If so, it should be brought into the temple (or present prior to the beginning of the ritual) with all respect and care which will bring comfort to the family.

The Beloved has also chosen those who will dance, for dance is one of the most ancient forms of worship. As an expression of religion, it is an art, a form of communion with the Universe. Dancers may be chosen not only from The Rowan Tree but also from the personal life and relationships of the Beloved. Note that there are many different roles to be danced, and that dance is part of the role (usually, but not always) of the High Priest/ess. Although the Four Watchtowers *should* be Initiates of Lothloriën (this *is* an Initiation Ritual), the Dancers are not inherently connected to Lothloriën. In this case the Beloved was to have prepared anyone who had agreed (in the Spiritual Will) with the knowledge required to be a Dancer, but it is your role as High Priest/ess to ensure that the understanding of what to do (and when) is well-communicated and cued in a subtle manner.

Not only must you orchestrate and choreograph the ritual according to The Spiritual Will, but you must consult with the family and all ritual participants to ensure that each day of The Ritual is a work of art.

The Spiritual Will

Not only has a legal will been drawn up, but the Beloved has also drawn up a Spiritual Will, carefully choosing those persons who will function as clergy and ritual performers. You must devote time to the study of the Beloved's Spiritual Will. It would behoove you to consult those who have filed Spiritual Wills (with the College of Mentors) and to discuss the arrangements with them and to read and study those Wills on file.

The main text of the Rites will be performed by an ordained Minister of The Rowan Tree Church, assisted by Initiates of our Priest/esshood, Tradition of Lothloriën. Together they will represent the five classical elements, those of Air, Fire, Water, and Earth; with the High Priest/ess embodying that of Spirit.

Various ritual possessions of the Beloved are being brought into this rite. Some of them will be ritually prepared, placed in safe-keeping for the reincarnation of the spirit for we believe that the soul is immortal, representing the God/dess Within. Even as children were we taught that "God is everywhere." Many of us have come to think of 'God' as being both Mother and Father to us all. Even as Einstein's Theory of Relativity defines God/desshood and manifestation, so, too, do we believe that each spirit passes in and out of manifestation: glorious proof of the Universe's Divine Being. The ritual tools at the beginning of the ritual are (primarily, if at all possible) those of the Beloved. As you work the Ritual the Beloved's tools will be removed and yours will be brought into use. The preparation and maintenance of your own ritual tools is thus an integral part of your preparation and work as a High Priest/ess.

The Spiritual Will is essential in determining the disposition of one's ritual tools. For example, if one has taken a goblet and, through ritual, transformed it into a sacred chalice, that goblet has been removed from the mundane world. We believe that a Priest/ess has responsibility in determining the disposition of sacred possessions. In addition, this ritual is designed to assist those pursuing the goal of 'Right Return.' Right Return, in its Highest Ideal, is to carry spiritual training and disciplines into one's next incarnation. Wiccan theology states that we hold the potential for reunion with our religious possessions and with our kindred.

Appendices : II - A Commentary on The Ritual for the Dead

[In the absence of a Spiritual Will, one's Mentor or the Church Elder may proffer advice, but the actual right to determine the disposition of the Beloved's property belongs to whichever family member has the legal right.]

It is the Beloved who determines the 'guest list' for the seven days of the services. These rites are being performed according to the religious beliefs of the deceased. Space and time and beliefs permitting, all guests may be welcome to attend the subsequent days of these rites. Ask only that they do so in reverence and respect. The contacting of the guest list is not, inherently, part of your work but you should be prepared to do this work if necessary.

For Whom the Bell Tolls...

In its most complete form, this ritual takes seven days from beginning to completion. It is contained within the Book of Shadows of a Second Degree Initiate of our Tradition, as part of the workings of the Fourth Ordeal within the Pathworking. This Rite may be performed for any Church Member, for a person within a Member's family, or for any friend of The Rowan Tree Church. When performed in a singular (one-day) form, it may be of use for anyone wishing spiritual assistance. This ritual serves to work with the Beloved's (our name for the Deceased) energy, through the invocation of poetical imagery. In most services, only the first day, "The Ritual of Parting and Farewell" will be attended by all guests. Seven days of carefully performed ritual is too involved a discipline for many peoples. The final day is that when many of the possessions which were directly part of the Beloved's religious expression will be disposed of, carefully following the wishes of the Beloved as set forth in the Spiritual Will. These may include ritual robes, tarot decks, or jewelry worn only when expressing religion (for example). It is for this reason that our Beloved may have invited some of you to attend only the first and last days of the service.

What the guests will experience may not be the complete Ritual for the Dead, as it may have been the Beloved's expressed wish to have it adapted to her/his own beliefs. If the full ritual is to be worked, the ritual is scheduled as arrangements are made with a crematorium or funeral home. The Beloved's ashes are brought into the Temple on the second day of the Rite. It was the Beloved's choice to have one or more days of the service performed. Although created originally for The Rowan Tree Church's own clergy, it may be adapted in its function for any person.

Should cremation have been the choice for disposition, the ashes will either be taken to the Rowan Tree's cemetery and scattered or returned to the family. This will be following the seventh day of the service, when all is complete and the temple put to rest.

As an ordained Minister of the Rowan Tree Church, you should be prepared to discuss with the family further explanation of the symbols and forms used within the Ritual for the Dead. Recognize that our modes of religious expression may be unfamiliar to them.

The Spiritual Will
[Taken from the Church's publication]

The Spiritual Will should be established by any person desiring to have the Ritual For the Dead performed at her/his demise. It is the purpose of the will to have control over certain aspects of the ritual performance, and to determine the disposition of possessions and tools one has gathered during the past incarnation in order to better determine the nature of the next incarnation.

It is believed that the power of this rite effectively separates the Beloved from attachment to the Earth plane, and sets the spirit upon its journey into the future incarnation. That journey will ultimately compete a cycle when the Beloved returns again into her/his Path. Life and Death are all Circles, and this rite is an Initiation into the Future.

These rites may be performed for a Priest/ess whose interment will not take place here at the Rowan Tree, but whose interment is being conducted within the ways of her/his family. In such a situation, it is important that a person within the Beloved's family be responsible for the gathering and shipping of those ritual tools to The Rowan Tree for the performance of these rituals.

This ritual may also be performed for family of Rowan Tree Members. It may also be performed for those who work within the Grove, or who are Friends of the Rowan Tree. A Spiritual Will is still required, with the exception of a spouse/partner of a Rowan Tree Priest/ess; who may determine the disposition of all details.

Appendices : II - A Commentary on The Ritual for the Dead

This Rite may be amended into a single ritual, one of Farewell and Parting. For those who have not adopted the lifestyle of a Priest/ess of Lothloriën, these adaptions are permissible when done in agreement with the College of Priest/esses.

Please be mindful that The Rowan Tree has no desire to cause disease among your family, and it is possible to arrange a performance of the Ritual of Farewell and Parting so that it is pleasing, inspirational, and may be considered by those outside the Mysteries to be a memorial service performed in addition to the family's own religious rites.

In the absence of a Spiritual Will, one's Mentor will make the disposition of your Spiritual Estate. The Spiritual Will has the choice of determining who will perform the Ritual For the Dead. This person must be an ordained Minister of The Rowan Tree. The Ritual For the Dead is contained within the Book of Shadows of a Second Degree Initiate of our Tradition, as part of the studies and workings of the Fourth Ordeal.

The Spiritual Will also selects four persons, each of whom will represent one of the Four Elements; those of Air, Fire, Water, and of Earth. These Watchtowers should be Priest/esses of Lothloriën (First Degree Initiates or higher), but in special circumstances a role may be taken by a Novice.

In addition, there are Dancers who carry out various aspects of the Ritual. Primary among them is the Orb Dancer, who carries the Beloved's Crystal Ball throughout the Rituals. In the absence of a crystal ball (should the Beloved be of a different Path), a personal possession of that person may be chosen to represent the spirit of the Beloved, which would either be permanently given to the soil at the conclusion, or cared for and passed on to future generations.

In the complete presentation of seven rituals, the Orb Dancer will perform each day. For this reason, it would be appropriate to choose a Dancer who is capable of performing within the context of the Rowan Tree traditions, and who is comfortable in this Ritual Work.

Other Dancers include a Blade Dancer, who brings forth the magickal tools associated with the Element of Air, being set aside for the future incarnation; a Dancer of Staves who works with the Tools of Fire; a Dancer of Cups for the Tools of Water; and an Earth Dancer for the Tools of Earth. The final Dancer is s/he who will join with the officiating High Priest/ess at the Sixth Ritual; that of the Sacred Marriage.

Thus, there may be as few as five Performers, and as many as eleven. It is possible to designate by Will, one or more persons to represent the four elemental Dancers, but the Four Watchtowers need to be four persons capable of establishing ritual balance.

You may, if you wish, also select a Bard, and provide for songs, poems, or other materials to be used within the Sixth Day of the Ritual, when the four dances of the Ritual of the Sacred Marriage will be performed.

The Temple is set around an altar, which is that of the High Priest/ess, for the Ritual of Gestation will need your altar uninvolved in the performance of the Rites. The altar(s) are all set with your tools. As the ritual progresses through the Sevendays, these tools are sealed and replaced with those of the officiants. Thus, after your water chalice is sealed, the Dancer of Cups then brings into the temple the chalice of the High Priest/ess, and yours removed. By the completion of the Seventh Day, there are no possessions of yours remaining within the Inner Circle, save for your crystal ball and the sealed jewelry. All else has either been sealed and removed or passed on with the Magickal Estate. Following each day's ritual, all ritual implements will be properly cleansed and prepared for the following day.

The Inner Circle is composed of the Priest/esshood and Novitiate of the Rowan Tree, for it is they who will control and channel the Magick during the Rites. Between the Inner and Outer Circles is a wide path, within which much of the performance takes place.

The outer circle is for invited guests, family, and those who desire to attend your service. Chairs may be arranged, allowing for a North-East Portal, in order that those unaccustomed to ritual work may attend in comfort.

Your Preparation

In addition to the use of your ritual tools, incense, oil, and the like, you are asked to proved two items for the ritual. The first is a black candle, which you should dress with your own oil. this candle will be lit during each of the days of the Ritual. On the final day of the ritual, it will remain lit, burning itself out. This candle represents the Abyss, the Cauldron of Cerridwen, the night-aspect of the Universe, into which you are entering as spirit. This candle should be kept with the copy of your Spiritual Will filed with the Elder of the Rowan Tree.

You are also asked to prepare a small bunch of Hyssop, tied and dried by you, which will be used during the aspurging of the Circle.

The Sealing of Tools

Certain of one's spiritual possessions may be 'sealed' for the next incarnation. The nature of the seal would best be described as a sigil or symbol that one creates. It would be kept in a sealed envelope and placed with the tool during the Sevenday Rites. It is also common for the 'seal" to be the name of the tool, written upon a slip of paper, and placed within a sealed envelope with the tool. In some future time, when a Novice (Supplicant) or Initiate approaches a High Priest/ess believing s/he knows the seal of a tool, it would be the role of the Eldermentor to verify that knowledge and guaranteeing that the seal is never made known beyond the Eldermentor and the one who will now work with the tool during that incarnation. Any tool brought back into use in this manner must be sealed again with the same seal either at that person's death or if, for any reason, that person would leave The Mystery School. There can be no exceptions to this.

These tools will be kept by the Rowan Tree for your next incarnation, and only when upon correct identification will that tool be released for use in a later life. While it is not necessary to set aside any of your tools, it would further the Magick of your next life to have the ability to continue rather than start over. Tools which may be sealed include your:

Altar Stones/Crystals
Athame
Boline
Book of Shadows
Cauldron
Crystal Ball
Earthpot

East Censer
Pentacle
Ritual Necklace and Rings
South Firepot
Staff
Sword
Wand
Water Chalice
West Water Basin
Wine Chalice

Your cords, should you have received any through an Initiation are not sealed, as they represent your physical bonds to the Incarnation being left behind. Rather, they will be taken and buried, representing the gift to the Earth of the remains of your body.

Once a tool of yours is sealed, it will be removed from the Temple (with the exception of your crystal ball, athame, necklace and ritual rings), not again used in the Ritual For the Dead.

For those initiated into the Tradition of Lothloriën, it is possible to determine in your Spiritual Will that your cauldron be fired each year at the Hallowmas Ritual.

The Magickal Estate

Other tools which you have used in this life, which you do not desire to keep for your next incarnation, but which have been imbued with your essence are given as gifts. Priest/esses who have been Instruments in the forging of the Tradition of Lothloriën may choose to place one or more into the 'museum' held by the Mystery School, where they will continue your teaching. Others are dispersed, in order that there are no bonds to hold you to your past.

You are asked to select the person who will execute the Disposition of your Magickal Estate. Attached to your Spiritual Will should be a list that details the disposition of such tools. Which might include (in addition to any ritual tools not being sealed for the next incarnation):

altar cloths; altars (elemental); bells; candlesticks; charcoal tongs; containers; herbes; incense container; masks; measures; ritual bells;

ritual drums; ritual masks; robes; salt bowl; tarot decks; temple hangings

Be mindful that an object may be passed on to a person, with the request that it pass into the museum in that person's disposition, with a written attachment that passes it on with your athame to you in the next incarnation when you reclaim your tools.

Disposition of the Body

While this ritual is ideally suited for cremation, it is not essential. The Rowan Tree has provided for a crematorium capable of following our ritual procedures and the needs of our religious practices. Thus, they will be willing to include with your body such as you desire (some, for example, may wish their journals to be cremated with their bodies). Those who do not live in the Twin Cities area are able to make arrangements with this same service.

The Rowan Tree does not provide for burial of the body. The land we will purchase as a cemetery will be set aside as a Temple of the Earth, suitable only for the scattering or burial of ashes. If the land has not yet been purchased at the time of the Ritual, the ashes are to be kept safe within sacred space by the Eldermentor.

Those who choose to be buried with their families will note that it need not impede the ritual. The First Day is a Ritual of Parting, and there will be ash from that day which may be taken into the next six days of ritual. In addition, one might choose to have a measure of ash used within Lothloriën (and strewn about our land) and the remaining ash kept with family. In this case clear (and legal) arrangements must be made by the Beloved prior to death.

This ritual will be scheduled when arrangements have been completed with either a funeral home or crematorium. Ideally the ritual will be performed so that the cremated remains enter the Temple on the Second Day. If this rite is performed for a High Priest/ess of Lothloriën, the complete rite is essential.

Notes for Appendix II

[419] This commentary was written for and accompanies the complete published edition of our Ritual for the Dead, published by The Rowan Tree Church and is for our Members and clergy, ca 1994

III - Excerpts from The Ritual for the Dead of Lothloriën[420]

Preparing the Circle & Temple

☆ The Priest/ess lights the left altar candle:

> A new star shines in the night
> It is the joyful twinkle in the Father's eye,
> There to bring light to the darkness,
> To warm & make fertile worlds as yet unborn....
> A seed in the cauldron of the Universe.
> Shine brightly, our friend (lover, child, etc.),
> You are now the Sun,
>   and He shines now more brightly,
> For you are a candle in the Universe.
> You are truly God.

All: "Gone to rest in Father's nest,
Join the Ancients: You are blessed."

☆ The Priest/ess takes the wand & seals the Circle. As the wand is passed around the Inner Circle, the Priest/ess reads the following:

> You are the wand that seals the Circle.
> Completing your cycles,
> You now encompass us from without.
> You are the Universe which keeps us safe,
> And you are the power which flows
>   through the Circle...
> You are the wand that seals the Circle.

Appendices : III - Excerpts from The Ritual for the Dead of Lothloriën

Now freed of flesh & pain,
The dance you dance is that of Yin
& that of Yang,
      for you now walk in both worlds.
You are the Magick that works within the wand...

You are the wand that seals the Circle.
You have ended but one dance
& have many more before you,
For you walk the Path of the Wise.
Now journeying where Dreams are reality,
You are the power that becomes the Circle...

☆ The East lights the candle as the following is read:

Blessed Be the breeze that carries both
the butterfly and the sigh of death...

Should a bird light upon my windowsill,
might it be the soul of the Beloved,
come back for to share? Let me listen,
little bird, to the songs of the Mother
which spill from your heart,
Within is the voice of wisdom:
melodious Mysteries brought from
eternity into the present....
You have been set free,
Beloved _____,
and you wear your astral wings
like a rainbow:
reaching across the worlds...
The future is a garden,
and soon we shall sow the seeds
of Spring into your new life.

Appendices : III - Excerpts from The Ritual for the Dead of Lothloriën

> The old we shall take as ashes,
> and give them to the Mother
> where She dances 'round the Stones.
> They make the gardens fertile,
> for the past is enrichment
> for the future.
> The new we plant as hopes,
> as gifts of promise
> and of love unto the land of Lothloriën...
> And when you return,
> as you must,
> the seed will have grown into
> your Highest Ideals.
>
> Taking your athame again into your hand,
> you shall continue along this Path.
>
> Each butterfly we see might by your soul...

All: Blessed Be the butterflies...

☆   Each breeze that carries music
might be your smile...

All: Blessed Be the breeze...

> Even as the wind turns spring into summer,
> and chases autumn into the chilling deaths
> of winter, do you now pass through
> the Mysteries.
> You are the breeze which gives life
> to the fire...
> You are the bubbles of laughter in the brook...
> You are the song of the Dancing Earth...

Appendices : III - Excerpts from The Ritual for the Dead of Lothloriën

☆ The West lights the candle as the following is read:

> Blessed Be the rains that both
> water the crops and erode the fields...
>
> Should the waters swirl within
> the cup of my chalice,
> might it be the soul of our Beloved,
> back to sing the Goddess' song?
> Let me gaze with care
> into the depths for it will teach
> the Mysteries of the Cauldron,
> the depth of that love
> which transcends both life and death...
> You flow free, now,
> through the Universe,
> even as the waters of time.
> Dance with joy, now,
> in the rain-filled clouds
> and within the secrets of the oceans...
> Sail across the Universe,
> from shore to distant shore.
> As unfettered as the night,
> you ride the tides of heaven.
> Moving easily from the astral veils
> to the droplets of rain
> which bathe my gardens,
> you flow from world to world.
> Your life is the reality of dreams...
> Yet, you shall come anew,
> even as the clouds give forth tears
> to bathe Lothloriën's Sacred Stones...

Appendices : III - Excerpts from The Ritual for the Dead of Lothloriën

        And when you return,
        as you must,
        the waters will contain
        your Highest Ideals.
        Taking your chalice again in your hand,
        you shall continue along this Path.

        Each falling raindrop might be your kiss...

All: Blessed Be the rains...

☆   Each dancing river might carry your song...

All: Blessed Be the river...

        Even as the falling Summer rains
        are also Winter's snow,
        so, too, do they complete the cycles.
        Even as the soul comes forth
        into birth and returns through death,
        do we live the Mysteries.
        You are the Moon's reflection
        upon still waters...
        You are the droplets aspurged
        around the Circle...
        You are the tides of the cauldron...

The Charge of the Beloved

☆ I am the voice of the Beloved.
    Mine is the song of the Universe in motion...
    I am the sighing of the wind,
    the feathered sound of a bird's flight...

Appendices : III - Excerpts from The Ritual for the Dead of Lothloriën

Mine is the rhythm of all hearts;
those alive as you hear my words,
those passed before me into the Summerland;
and those who have yet to walk upon the Earth...

I am the voice of the Beloved.
My song is that of the starrèd night,
the cry of a baby wanting milk,
the dance of a hummingbird who takes nectar
       from the bloom...
I am the sound of a cloud gliding across the sky,
sailing toward the Mother...
I am the voice of thunder, giving birth to the sky-fires...
I am the sound of prayer, and the sound of dying.

I am the wail of a baby's first cry;
and my name is called when you make love,
for I am all words at all times
and
I Am Everything.

I am the voice of the Beloved.
If you listen to a flower break the soil at Spring,
you shall hear my song...
If you listen to the soaring of dandelion fluff in the breeze,
you shall hear my words...
I am the turning of the seasons and the passing
of Human Ages, for I am the sound of all life
and
I Am Everything...

I am the voice of the Beloved.
Call upon me with the names of the stars.
Know me as One with the Ancients,
but no longer may you call me by my old name,
for I am becoming One with The Universe...

Appendices : III - Excerpts from The Ritual for the Dead of Lothloriën

> I am a new star in the night...
> I am the gentle drop of rain upon your garden...
> I dance with the Lady,
> and I am the music found within His pipes...
>
> This is the Ritual of my Death.
> It is a Feast of Joy, for I leave my tools in your keeping,
> and, as Time makes its Circle, I shall be reborn...
>
> Ours is the Craft of Wicca.
> We shall dance in the temples
> Lothloriën has among the stars.
> We shall meet again, and dance again,
>   and love again, for such is the Law
> For now, let me take leave
> and hold me no longer, for I must be free...
>
> I am the voice of the Beloved.
> Find me within the Universe...
> Call upon me with as many names
> as there are stars in the sky...
>
> I am One,
> I am All...

☆ The High Priest/ess waits until all are calm, quiet, and again focused. The sword is held hilt to the temple floor as the following is said:

> Go now until the morrow.
> Take no sadness in your hearts,
> for our Beloved has gone
> with the joy of angels,

Appendices : III - Excerpts from The Ritual for the Dead of Lothloriën

with the flight of birds and
the beauty of life...
Let these rites be a time
of celebration and of love...
Hold no soul back with your longing...
Set our Beloved as free as the stars
which grace the night altars...

Go now.
This rite ends in peace...

Notes for Appendix III

[420] These are only a few of the passages from the complete ritual in order to provide you with insight into the Ritual for the Dead for the Tradition of Lothloriën created by the Author.

Bibliography & Sources

Addison, James Thayer, *Life Beyond Death In the Beliefs of Mankind*, Houghton Mifflin Co., © 1932
- James Thayer Addison (1887-1953) Thayer was well known as an Episcopalian author and educator, known for his books on other religions, notably non-Christian religions. Although Addison wrote a number of books on religions, I can find only the barest of information about him.

Allen IV, Dan Sumner, *The Mason Coffins: Metallic Burial Cases in the Central South*, paper prepared for the South Central Historical Archaeology Conference, September 20-22 2002, Jackson, Mississippi
- Staff archaeologist and President of Cumberland Research Group

Beyerl, Rev. Paul V., *A Wiccan Bardo, Revisited*, The Hermit's Grove, Kirkland, WA © 1999
- *A Hallowmas Eve Journey*, from the Book of Shadows of The Tradition of Lothloriën, Kirkland, WA © 2005
- *The Ritual for the Dead of Lothloriën*, from the Book of Shadows of The Tradition of Lothloriën, Kirkland, WA © 1986
- Rev. Paul V. Beyerl (1945-present) Author, educator, Wiccan Priest, Founder of the Wiccan Tradition known as The Tradition of Lothloriën.

Bhaktivedanta Swami Prabhupāda, A.C., *Bhagavad-Gītā As It Is*, The Bhaktivedanta Book Trust, Los Angeles, © 1981
- Hindu mystic born I'm Calcutta, 1896, died in 1977; Founder of the Hare Krishna movement

Brooks, Chris with Brent Elliott, Julian Litten, Eric Robinson, Richard Robinson, and Philip Temple, *Mortal Remains: The History and Present State of the Victorian and Edwardian Cemetery*, Wheaton Publishers Ltd, Devon, U.K. © 1989

Chaney, Earlyne, *The Mystery of Death & Dying: Initiation at the Moment of Death*, Samuel Weiser, Inc., York Beach, Maine © 1988
- Chaney. 1917-1997, prolific author in the field of spirituality. Founded Astara with her husband, Robert.

Daniell, Christopher, *Death and Burial in Medieval England: 1066-1550*, Routledge (Pub.), London and New York © 1997
- Daniell was an Associate of the Centre for Medieval Studies, University of York, when the book was published.

Evans-Wentz, W. Y., editor, compiler, author, *The Tibetan Book of The Dead*, Oxford University Press, © 1960, this reprint 1975
- Feb. 2 1878 - July 17 1965, American anthropologist who was a pioneer in the study of Tibetan Buddhism and was at the forefront of translating texts and bringing knowledge of Tibetan Buddhism to the Western world.

Farrell, James J., *Inventing the American Way of Death, 1830-1920*, Temple University Press, Philadelphia © 1980
- Professor of history and American studies at St. Olaf College, Minnesota. Died July 25, 2013

Gibran, Kahlil, *The Prophet*, Alfred A. Knopf, New York, 94th printing 1976 © 1923 by Kahlil Gibran
- Lebanese artist, poet and writer

Houlbrooke, Ralph, ed., *Death, Ritual, and Bereavement*, Routledge in association with the Social History Society of the United Kingdom, London, New York © 1989
- Professor, University of Reading, scholar, author, editor

Huntington, Richard & Peter Metcalf, *Celebrations of Death: The Anthropology of Mortuary Ritual*, Cambridge University Press, Cambridge © 1979
- Richjard Huntington, Harvard University
- Peter Metcalf, University of Virginia

Johnston, Sarah Iles (ed.), *Religions of the Ancient World: A Guide*, The Belknap Press of Harvard University Press, Cambridge and London, © 2004
- Professor, College of Humanities, Department of Greek and Latin

Kübler-Ross, Elisabeth, *On Death And Dying*, Collier Books, New York © 1969 by Elisabeth Kübler-Ross, paperback edition printed 1970
- Swiss American psychiatrist, pioneer in near-death studies

Kurtz, Katherine and **Deborah Turner**, *The Adept*, Penguin Putnam inc., New York, New York © 1991
- American authors

Kutscher, Austin H., Arthur C. Carr and Lillian G. Kutscher (editors), *Principles of Thanatology*, Columbia University Press, A Foundation of Thanatology Text, New York © 1987
- American authors

Laderman, Gary, *The Sacred Remains: American Attitudes Toward Death, 1799-1883*, Yale University Press, New Haven © 1996
- Department of Religion at Emory University

MacDonald, Rev. Norman, Corresponding Member of the Royal Gustavus Adolphus Academy, *The After-Life in Celtic and Oriental Folklore*, published by N. MacDonald 1970 in Chachan Locheport
- MacDonald is one of those mystery authors. Even with the internet I cannot come up with any dependable information about this scholar, not even the dates for his birth and (if he has passed) death. His style of writing implies him to have lived in the earlier half of the 20th century but I continue to be curious.

Mish, Frederick C. (ed. in chief), *Merriam-Webster's Collegiate Dictionary*, 11th edition, Merriam-Webster, Inc., Springfield, MA © 2005

Bibliography

- Editor-in-Chief Merriam Webster

Morse, Melvin M.D., *Closer To The Light*, Ivy Books, New York, © 1990
- American medical doctor with a special interest in near-death experience

O'Hara, Robert, *An Iron Age and Early Medieval Cemetery at Collierstown 1,Co. Meath:* Interpreting the changing character of a burial ground
- Director, Archer Heritage Planning

Sayers, Matthew R., *Feeding the Dead: Ancestor Worship in Ancient India*, Oxford University Press, New York NY © 2013
- Ass't. Professor of Religion at Lebanon Valley College, Annville PA

Smith, Hedrick, *Who Stole the American Dream?* Random House New York © 2012
- Pulitzer Prize-winning journalist and author

Toynbee, J. M. C., *Death and Burial in the Roman World*, The Johns Hopkins University Press, Baltimore © 1971
Jocelyn Mary Catherine Toynbee [1897-1985]
- Art historian and archaeologist of the classical era.

University of Chicago, *Ancient Group Believed Departed Souls Lived in Stone Monuments,* data released November, 2008 http://www.newswise.com/articles/view/546481/

Wikipedia, *The Free Encyclopedia*, online at http://en.wikipedia.org, research gathered 2008-2014. We are supporters and rely upon Wikipedia which strives for accuracy.

Rev. Paul Beyerl is the founder of The Rowan Tree Church (established in Minnesota in the 1970s) a fully-recognized Church now centered on Rose Hill in the Kirkland-Redmond area of Puget Sound. Rev. Paul is also the founder of The Tradition of Lothloriën and the head of The Mystery School, established in 1981 which provides education leading to Initiation and Ordination.

Beyerl has lived on Rose Hill since 1994 with his partner, Rev. Gerry, surrounded by a 45,000 private botanical and ritual garden. Beyerl is also known as an herbal educator, founder of The Hermit's Grove in 1993 with its Master Herbalist Program.

Beyerl is well-known for his many books (nearly a dozen works in print today).

The Rowan Tree Church http://www.therowantreechurch.org/
Rowan Tree open rituals and classes http://www.meetup.com/The-Rowan-Tree-Church/
The Hermit's Grove http://www.thehermitsgrove.org/
Hermit's Grove classes and events http://www.meetup.com/The-Hermits-Grove/

To contact the author:

Rev. Paul Beyerl
The Hermit's Grove
P O Box 0691
Kirkland, WA 98083

revpaul@therowantreechurch.org

[Address good until he reaches his expiration date.]